Lena Straßburger
Humor and Horror

Humor Research

Editors
Victor Raskin
Willibald Ruch

Volume 13

Lena Straßburger

Humor and Horror

Different Emotions, Similar Linguistic Processing Strategies

DE GRUYTER
MOUTON

ISBN 978-3-11-135797-3
e-ISBN (PDF) 978-3-11-076474-1
e-ISBN (EPUB) 978-3-11-076480-2
ISSN 1861-4116

Library of Congress Control Number: 2021951792

Bibliographic information published by the Deutsche Nationalbibliothek
The Deutsche Nationalbibliothek lists this publication in the Deutsche Nationalbibliografie; detailed bibliographic data are available on the Internet at http://dnb.dnb.de.

© 2023 Walter de Gruyter GmbH, Berlin/Boston
This volume is text- and page-identical with the hardback published in 2022.
Cover image: Christopher Schneider, Berlin
Typesetting: Integra Software Services Pvt. Ltd.
Printing and binding: CPI books GmbH, Leck

www.degruyter.com

Acknowledgments

First and foremost, I would like to thank Prof. Dr. Petra Schumacher who opened my eyes to an academic career and welcomed me to her team with enthusiasm. Through her knowledge, her groundbreaking advice and the exciting tasks, I was able to grow both professionally and personally. Her XLinC Lab made it possible to conduct my experiments. Prof. Dr. Martin Becker always gave me valuable advice, raised the right questions and made this book a pleasure to work on. I would like to thank Jun.-Prof. Dr. Roman Bartosch for being open to my psycholinguistic approach and for making sure that my first chapter did not become a horror. Furthermore, I would like to thank my colleagues Dr. Hanna Weiland-Breckle and Dr. Barbara Tomaszewicz-Özakın for their great commitment!

I would like to thank the graduate school a.r.t.e.s. for a full-time scholarship and many travel grants. I would also like to thank Dr. Jeffrey Power and Ying-Ying Chow for proof-reading my work!

I thank my parents for their unconditional love! But the biggest thank goes to my husband. He has always turned my moments of horror into humor. Thank you for being by my side.

Finally, I would like to thank the two editors-in-chief Willibald Ruch and Victor Raskin as well as Dr. Natalie Fecher and Kirstin Börgen for patiently accompanying my publication process in Mouton De Gruyter's Humor Research series.

The present work has been accepted by the Faculty of Arts and Humanities of the University of Cologne as a dissertation under the title "It's a matter of life and death – incongruity in humor and horror". It has been edited before publication.

Cologne, November 2021   Lena Straßburger

Contents

Acknowledgments —— V

List of figures —— IX

List of tables —— XI

List of abbreviations —— XIII

Introduction —— 1

1	**Horror: How to scream because of incongruity —— 4**	
1.1	Origins and iconography of horror in literature and film —— 5	
1.2	Horror theories: Why fear and disgust? —— 16	
1.2.1	Art-horror's emotions —— 16	
1.2.2	Psychoanalytic horror approaches —— 22	
1.2.3	Cognitive horror approaches —— 25	
1.3	Intermediate results —— 34	
2	**Humor: How to smile about incongruity —— 37**	
2.1	Humor theories: From antiquity to modern approaches —— 39	
2.2	Cognitive approaches: Incongruity and humor —— 50	
2.2.1	Script-based theories of humor —— 53	
2.2.1.1	Semantic Script Theory of Humor —— 54	
2.2.1.2	General Theory of Verbal Humor —— 58	
2.2.1.3	GTVH revis(it)ed: Pragmatics and context —— 62	
2.2.1.4	Space structuring model —— 68	
2.2.2	Graded informativeness, optimal innovation, and relevance —— 69	
2.3	Incongruity in humor and art-horror —— 72	
2.4	Intermediate results —— 80	
3	**Humor & horror: Processing incongruity —— 84**	
3.1	Measuring processing costs —— 85	
3.2	Comparing incongruity types experimentally —— 86	
3.3	Evidence for incongruity detection and resolution —— 89	
3.4	Evidence for emotions after incongruity —— 96	
3.5	Individual differences in incongruity processing —— 103	
3.6	Intermediate results —— 108	

4	**Humor & horror: An experimental comparison** —— 113
4.1	Stimuli norming: Questionnaire I and II —— 114
4.1.1	Questionnaire I —— 115
4.1.1.1	Methods —— 115
4.1.1.2	Results —— 119
4.1.1.3	Discussion —— 122
4.1.2	Questionnaire II —— 123
4.1.2.1	Methods —— 123
4.1.2.2	Results —— 125
4.1.2.3	Discussion —— 129
4.2	Reading times: Experiment I —— 130
4.2.1	Methods —— 132
4.2.2	Results —— 136
4.2.3	Discussion —— 138
4.3	Facial expressions: Experiment II —— 139
4.3.1	Methods —— 147
4.3.2	Results —— 149
4.3.3	Discussion —— 155
4.4	Neuro-electric activity: Experiment III —— 158
4.4.1	Methods —— 164
4.4.2	Results —— 169
4.4.3	Discussion —— 173

5	**Discussion & conclusion** —— 176
5.1	Summary of conceptual findings —— 176
5.2	Summary of experimental findings —— 179
5.3	Incongruity processing model of humor & horror (IPM) —— 187
5.4	Desiderata & outlook —— 191

References —— 195

Index —— 219

List of figures

Figure 1 Information-processing model of humor (adapted from Suls 1972: 85) —— **52**
Figure 2 Syntagmatic LM (adapted from Attardo, Hempelmann and Di Maio 2002: 18) —— **59**
Figure 3 Reasoning LM (adapted from Attardo, Hempelmann and Di Maio 2002: 19) —— **59**
Figure 4 GTVH's six Knowledge Resources in hierarchical order —— **61**
Figure 5 Expanded Knowledge Resources of the GTVH —— **64**
Figure 6 Humor implicatures on 7 levels (based on Canestrari 2012: 65–73) —— **65**
Figure 7 Continuum of contrariety depending on contrariety type and invariance of further feature (based on Canestrari and Bianchi 2013: 17–18) —— **67**
Figure 8 Correlation of incongruity type and humorous success (based on Canestrari and Bianchi 2013: 20) —— **67**
Figure 9 Expanded Knowledge Resources (equals Figure 5) —— **73**
Figure 10 Incongruity processing steps in art-horror and humor —— **76**
Figure 11 Rothbart's model of affective responses to incongruity (adapted from Rothbart 2017: 39) —— **79**
Figure 12 Three phases of the neural Circuit Model (NCM) (adapted from Chan, Chou, Chen, Yeh, Lavallee, Liang and Chang 2013: 175) —— **98**
Figure 13 Results of Questionnaire I regarding means per condition and question. Scariness, surprise, and funniness were rated on a 7-point Likert scale (1 = not at all; 7 = absolutely), error bars = sd —— **120**
Figure 14 Results of Questionnaire II for all 67 triplets. Means per condition and questions. Scariness, funniness and surprise were rated on a 7-point Likert scale (1 = not at all; 7 = absolutely), error bars = sd —— **126**
Figure 15 Results of Questionnaire II for the 36 triplets. Means per condition and questions. Scariness, funniness, and surprise were rated on a 7-point Likert scale (1 = not at all; 7 = absolutely), error bars = sd —— **127**
Figure 16 Schematic illustration of predictions of reading times (RT) for the three conditions art-horror, humor, and coherence —— **132**
Figure 17 Log residual reaction times for the six target segments over all conditions, error bars = sd —— **137**
Figure 18 Comparison of the muscular anatomy of the human face (left picture) and its notation in action units (AU), here AU 1, 2, 4, 6, and 7 (right picture). The encircled number indicates the ending point of a movement (Ekman, Friesen, and Hager 2002b: 15 —— **140**
Figure 19 Comparison of AU 12 (lip corner puller) as a schema of the oblique movement (left picture) and its facial expression (right picture) (Ekman et al. 2002b: 175,484). Side note: the facial expression on the right side also includes AU 25 (open mouth) —— **141**
Figure 20 Comparison of AU 6 (cheek raiser and lid compressor) as schema (left) and facial expression (middle). Combination of AU 6 and AU 12 (right) (Ekman et al. 2002b: 15,468,485) —— **142**

https://doi.org/10.1515/9783110764741-204

Figure 21 Comparison of AU 10 (upper lip raiser) and AU 9 (nose wrinkle) as schema (left picture) and facial expressions (middle: AU 10, right: AU 9) (Ekman et al. 2002b: 91,95). Side note: Middle picture also shows AU 25 (opened mouth) —— **143**

Figure 22 Comparison of AU 1 and 2 as schema (left) and facial expression (middle: AU 1, right: AU 2) (cf. Ekman et al. 2002b: 15,466) —— **144**

Figure 23 Facial expressions of AU 4 (brow lowerer, left) and its combination with AU 1 and AU 2 (right) (cf. Ekman et al. 2002b: 466, 472) —— **144**

Figure 24 Facial expressions of AU 5 (upper lid raiser, left) and its combination with AU 1 and AU 2 (right) (cf. Ekman et al 2002b: 467,472) —— **145**

Figure 25 Visual summary of predicted facial expressions. 1: happiness (AU 6,12). 2: disgust (AU 9), 3: disgust (AU 10), 4: fear (AU 1,2,4); 5: fear (AU 1,2 5) (Ekman et al. 2002b: 472–474,485) . Side note: In 3, AU 25 (open mouth) is activated additionally —— **145**

Figure 26 FACS results – mean frequency of action units (AU) per condition on and after the critical segment, and percentage of AU of 148 AU shown across conditions and locations —— **152**

Figure 27 Schema of recording procedure (adapted from Hung 2011: 46) —— **159**

Figure 28 Illustration of electrode cap (extended version) according to 10/20 system (adapted to recorded electrode positions from Luck 2014: 167) —— **167**

Figure 29 Electrophysiological results of the grand-averaged ERPs for 9 selected electrode sides for the conditions coherence, horror, humor, and incoherence —— **170**

Figure 30 Incongruity processing model for humor and art-horror (IPM) —— **188**

List of tables

Table 1	Humor families (Attardo 1994: 47) —— 46	
Table 2	Possible script combinations (Attardo 1994: 204) —— 57	
Table 3	Word frequency of critical segments (means and standard deviations (sd) per condition (cf. Universität Leipzig 2021) —— 116	
Table 4	Minimal triplet example for the three conditions art-horror, humor, and coherence —— 116	
Table 5	Pairwise comparisons of surprise; n.s. = not significant —— 121	
Table 6	Pairwise comparisons of exhilaration; n.s. = not significant) —— 121	
Table 7	Percentual comprehensibility values and Pearson's X^2 for the three answer possibilities of yes/no/I do not know —— 122	
Table 8	Word frequency of critical segments (means and standard deviation (sd) per condition (cf. Universität Leipzig 2021) —— 124	
Table 9	Percentual comprehensibility values and Pearson's X^2 for the three answer possibilities of yes/no/I do not know —— 126	
Table 10	Pairwise comparisons of surprise; n.s. = not significant —— 128	
Table 11	Pairwise comparisons of exhilaration; n.s. = not significant —— 128	
Table 12	Percentual comprehensibility values and Pearson's X^2 for the three answer possibilities of yes/no/I do not know —— 129	
Table 13	Example of minimal triplets of the SPR material in the three conditions art-horror, humor, and coherence —— 133	
Table 14	Association of emotions and facial movements (in Action Units) —— 141	
Table 15	FEE, STCI, STHI and Geloph<15> – Mean results of non-reacting participants compared to reacting participants and overall means over all conditions —— 152	
Table 16	FEE, STCI, STHI and Geloph<15> – Mean questionnaire results of non-reacting participants compared to reacting participants in the three conditions art-horror, humor, and coherence —— 153	
Table 17	Example of minimal quadruplets of the ERP material in the four conditions art-horror, humor, incoherence, and coherence —— 165	
Table 18	Means of critical segment per condition for word frequency (cf. Universität Leipzig 2021), word length and syllable length —— 165	
Table 19	Analysis of ROIs in first time window (300–450 ms) for main effects of midline electrodes and lateral electrodes per region of interest for six pairwise comparisons —— 171	
Table 20	Analysis of ROIs in second time window (600–700 ms) for main effects of midline electrodes and lateral electrodes per region of interest for six pairwise comparisons —— 172	
Table 21	Analysis of ROIs in third time window (950–1050 ms) for main effects of midline electrodes and lateral electrodes per region of interest for six pairwise comparisons —— 172	
Table 22	Interpretation of ERP results per condition and time window —— 184	

List of abbreviations

Amg	Amygdala (brain region)
AU	Action Unit in FACS
BOLD	Blood Oxygenation Level Dependent
CO	Context (Knowledge Ressource of SSTH/GTVH)
DI	Double Incongruity
EEG	Electroencephalogram
ERP	Event-Related Brain Potentials
FACS	Facial Action Coding System
FEE	Fragebogen zur Erfassung der Ekelempfindlichkeit (German Disgust Scale)
fMRI	Functional Magnetic Resonance Imaging
GP	Garden Path
GTVH	General Theory of Verbal Humor
ID	Individual Differences
IPM	Incongruity Processing Model of Humor and Art-horror
KR	Knowledge Ressource of SSTH/GTVH
LA	Language (Knowledge Ressource of SSTH/GTVH)
LAN	Left-Anterior Negativity (ERP component)
LLAN	Late Left-Anterior Negativity (ERP component)
LM	Logical Mechanisms
LPC	Late Positive Complex (ERP component)
LPP	Late Positive Potential (ERP component)
Meta-KR	Meta-Knowledge Ressource (Knowledge Ressource of SSTH/GTVH)
MFG	Medial Frontal Gyrus (brain region)
MTG	Middle Termporal Gyrus (brain region)
N400	Neuronal Negativity peaking around 400 ms post stimulus onset (ERP component)
NBF	Non-Bona-Fide Mode
NCM	Neural Circuit Model
NS	Narrative Strategy (Knowledge Ressource of SSTH/GTVH)
P600	Neuronal Positivity peaking around 600 ms post stimulus onset (ERP component)
PHG	Parahippocampal Gyrus (brain region)
RT	Reading Time
sd	Standard Deviation
SFG	Superior Frontal Gyrus (brain region)
SI	Situation (Knowledge Ressource of SSTH/GTVH)
SO	Script Opposition
SPR	Self-Paced Reading
SSTH	Semantic Script Theory of Humor
STCI	State-Trait-Cheerfulness-Inventory
STCI-S18	State Questionnaire of STCI with 18 questions
STCI-T30	Trait Questionnaire of STCI with 30 questions
TA	Target (Knowledge Ressource of SSTH/GTVH)
vmPFC	Ventromedial Prefrontal Gyrus (brain region)

Introduction

I'm a killer. I'm a clown.
    (Cooper and Bruce 1971)

Humor and horror provoke emotions that could not be more conflicting. While humor elicits exhilaration and laughter, horror triggers fear and disgust. According to this reasoning, the two phenomena seem to be in opposition to each other. However, this book shows that the underlying structures and the cognitive processing are, nevertheless, highly similar. The linguistic material that triggers humor or horror can both be traced back to incongruity, understood as a semantic violation through an unexpected combination of oppositional information via the same linguistic links. In the same way that an incongruent punchline in a joke needs resolution in order for the listener to understand it and be exhilarated, this book proposes that resolving incongruity can also be frightening.

Even though cognitive humor approaches have already shown conceptually and experimentally that incongruity plays an important role in the recognition and processing of humorous texts, psycholinguistic humor experiments to this day have not compared a humorous incongruity to a frightening incongruity condition systematically and directly. This missing comparison challenges known humor models that define incongruity and its cognitive resolution as distinctive humor criteria. They need to be refined to distinguish humor from horror processing. Especially from an art-horror perspective as employed in this book, the research gap becomes all the more apparent. Horror and its cognitive processing have not yet been examined experimentally from a psycholinguistic perspective.

The innovative idea of this work is to bridge the research fields through a transfer of incongruity findings and methodological merits, from humor to horror research. In humor research, incongruity detection, its resolution, and emotional elaboration have been associated with ways of cognitive processing that are more demanding and costly than those at play with coherent texts. This book deduces an analogous art-horror analysis to enable a deeper understanding of art-horror processing.

To comprehensively grasp linguistic similarities and differences between humor and art-horror, the following research questions are investigated:
1. Does art-horror evoke the same kind of incongruity as humor?
2. Does art-horror elicit additional processing costs compared to (in)coherent items?

3. How do the cognitive processing costs of art-horror differ from those of humorous, incongruent items, with respect to intensity and time-course of the observed costs?
4. Are these processing costs associated with the local incongruity of the stimulus? Can they be correlated with incongruity detection and resolution?
5. Do the recipients react emotionally after incongruity detection and resolution?

The following five chapters answer these research questions:

Chapter 1 defines horror as a literary and movie genre, *art-horror*, that utilizes semantic incongruities to evoke emotions of fear and disgust in recipients. Summarizing its typical figures, objects, and narrative strategies in a taxonomy of oppositions, it prepares the ground for an innovative, psycholinguistic exploration of the recipients' cognitive mechanisms required to process art-horror. In addition to the genre overview and the definition of art-horror and its emotions, this chapter discusses psychoanalytic and, especially, cognitive art-horror theories (cf. Carroll 1990; Grodal 2000). Finally, it highlights the research gap of an experimentally verified systematization of art-horror and its cognitive processing phases.

Chapter 2 addresses the question how it is possible that the two genres of art-horror and humor, which trigger such opposing emotions, show similar underlying cognitive mechanisms (cf. Rothbart 2017 [1976]). It identifies the phenomenon of incongruity and its resolution as the common denominator between art-horror and humor, allowing the two phenomena to be structurally compared despite their widely differing emotions. After an overview of the historical origins of humor's social, psychoanalytical, and cognitive theories, this chapter transfers conceptual findings from cognitive humor research (cf. Raskin 1985; Attardo, Hempelmann and Di Maio 2002; Canestrari 2010; Hempelmann and Attardo 2011; Tsakona 2013) to an analogous art-horror analysis. It lays the foundation for an experimental comparison of the cognitive costs in art-horror and humor.

Chapter 3 transfers the experimental insights on incongruity processing from humor research to art-horror. The experimental measurement of language comprehension and the identification of additional cognitive costs (cf. Bornkessel-Schlesewsky and Schumacher 2016) via reaction times or electrophysiological reactions is introduced. Experiments that address reaction times and neuronal correlates of incongruity processing in humor are then presented (cf. Coulson and Kutas 1998; Coulson and Kutas 2001; Coulson, Urbach and Kutas 2006; Chan, Chou, Chen, Yeh, Lavallee, Liang and Chang 2013; Feng, Chan and Chen 2014; Mayerhofer and Schacht 2015; Ferstl, Israel and Putzar 2017; Shibata, Terasawa, Osumi, Masui, Ito, Sato and Umeda 2017; Canal, Bischetti, Di Paola, Bertini, Ricci and Bambini 2019). Three humor processing phases comprising the detection of an incongruity, its resolution, and a subsequent emotional reaction are determined. This chapter deduces an analogous art-horror analysis, transferring findings and methodological merits from humor to art-horror research.

Chapter 4 broadens humor experiments by comparing humor, art-horror, coherence, and incoherence to attest that the incongruity in art-horror texts is cognitively processed, resolved, and elaborated in a manner analogous to humor processing. After an off-line norming of the stimuli through two questionnaires, the results of three experiments are reported. A *Self-Paced Reading* (SPR) experiment compares participants' cognitive processing of humor and horror by assuming that prolonged reading times reveal difficulties in reading and comprehending incongruities (cf. Just and Carpenter 1980; Jegerski 2014). The second experiment uses the *Facial Action Coding System* (FACS) to attest that the intended emotions associated with art-horror and humor are elicited and mirrored in participants' facial expressions (cf. Ekman, Friesen and Hager 2002a; Ekman, Friesen and Hager 2002b). Using the non-invasive and continuous method of *Event-Related Brain Potentials* (ERP) with a high temporal resolution (cf. Luck 2014), the final experiment[1] compares the time-locked and averaged neuro-electric brain activity that is required for the cognitive functions of detecting, resolving, and emotionally elaborating art-horror and humor.

Chapter 5 summarizes the conceptual and experimental findings and provides a synoptic incongruity processing model (IPM) that explains and predicts processing stages of humor and art-horror, verified by empirical data.

This book offers for the first time an innovative and detailed comparison of humor and art-horror processing by extrapolating incongruity as their common denominator, incorporating art-horror in a cognitive processing model, and refining cognitive humor models from a psycholinguistic perspective.

---

[1] The items of the SPR, FACS, and ERP studies are provided as supplementary material on De Gruyter's homepage (see https://www.degruyter.com/document/isbn/9783110764741/html).

1 Horror: How to scream because of incongruity

> The audience at Hollywood's Dolby Theater was spellbound
> when the disguised moderator opened the golden envelope.
> 'Row 1. Seat 9.' was written on the card. She pulled out the gun.[2]
> (adapted from Meimberg 2011: 34; transl. LS)

Creeps, fear, anxiety, disgust – the notion of *horror* is associated with the evocation of negative emotions. Since "horror is both an everyday occurrence – terrorism, the cannibal next door, torture – and a way of dramatizing our hidden fears and desires through fantasy that takes the everyday that few steps further" (Wisker 2005: 1), this chapter illuminates the phenomenon of horror in reference to Carroll's distinction between *natural* and *art-horror* (cf. Carroll 1990: 12). *Natural horror* describes real sources of dread and menace, and the emotions they trigger, whereas the concept of *art-horror* refers to the "cross-art, cross-media genre" (Carroll 1990: 12) and its effect on the recipient. Art-horror aims to simultaneously frighten and disgust the audience. It assumes a potential audience competence to decipher and experience the genre's intentions and is less about the actual performance of the audience during the screening of individual films (cf. Carroll 1990: 30f.).

First, Chapter 1.1 recounts the historical development of art-horror including its intentions, protagonists, topoi, and central themes through major works of literature and film. Although art-horror rather serves as an umbrella term for a huge variety of instantiations, this chapter shows that semantic incongruities and oppositions are a unifying element of (all) its subgenres: The characters, objects, and narrative strategies of the horror genre combine opposing categories, such as life/death or healthy/sick, evoking the emotions of fear and disgust. Investigating art-horror through an incongruity perspective offers a way to grasp its underlying mechanisms and finally understand how it is processed cognitively. Thus, the genre overview demonstrates to what extent art-horror negotiates incongruity and how these incongruities evoke the emotions of fear and disgust. This oriented chapter thereby prepares the innovative, psycholinguistic analysis of the current book.

Second, Chapter 1.2 discusses explanations of (the origins of) the emotional effects that horror literature and film have on recipients (namely fear and disgust, but also pleasure) by consulting psychoanalytic and cognitive theories.

---

[2] My own translations to English within a citation are marked through the abbreviation *transl. LS*.

The existing cognitive theories already suggest that incongruity plays a role in the evocation of art-horror emotions. However, they lack an experimentally verified systematization that also models cognitive processing phases. Thus, the research gap that this book seeks to close more precisely will be identified.

Third, displaying the intermediate results in Chapter 1.3 will help develop a working definition to be used in subsequent chapters and for the experimental design.

1.1 Origins and iconography of horror in literature and film

Most commonly, research on horror centers on, or at least explicitly engages with, the literary and cultural techniques used to evoke the emotional responses always at play in the horrific. Such forms of response have defined the horror genre since its inception and are now a well-documented field of research in literary studies. In extant research, the notion of *horror* usually describes a film and literature genre and its effects on the recipients. According to Leeder (2018), genres are conventions about content, formal and narrative features, and further aspects that reveal a text or film collection's typicality (cf. Leeder 2018: 92). Within a genre, some representatives assemble numerous typical features and become central to the genre. Others only include some of the characteristic features and, thereby, range at the genre's periphery (cf. Rosch 1973; Bordwell 1989: 148; Leeder 2018: 97). This chapter highlights typical horror genre content and its continuous development with examples from major literary and filmic works[3] in order to investigate how horror evokes the emotions of fear and disgust. It will be shown that especially the negotiation of oppositions, incompatibilities and incongruities is responsible for the evocation of horror feelings. Investigating these incongruities provides an avenue for inferring underlying cognitive mechanisms needed to process art-horror and thereby prepares the later (psycho)linguistic analysis of the cognitive processing of horror. This serves as the basis for the review of theories of art-horror and, eventually, this book's experimental approach to incongruity.

---

[3] For a broader overview of horror fiction up until the beginning of the 21th century in the USA and Europe, see Wisker (2005), Alpers, Fuchs and Hahn (1999) and Hahn and Giesen (2002).

Gothic origins: Combining realistic with fantasy elements

Dark, evil and scary ideas have always been part of "sagas, tales by the fire, by the bedside, in the terrors of *Beowulf*, the ogres and monsters of myth and fairy stories, and the figure of Satan himself" (Wisker 2005: 39).[4] But it was the horror (from Latin *horror* = shudder, frisson, dread, fright [cf. Stowasser, Petschenig and Skutsch 2009: 238]) of the *Gothic fiction* of 18th and early 19th century (cf. Alpers, Fuchs and Hahn 1999: 8; Hale 2002: 63; Viering 2010: 366) that "succeeded in shifting an entire paradigm" (Groom 2014: ix). It mobilized the effects of "manifestations of the Gothic past – buildings, ruins, songs and romances [. . .]" (Botting 2014: 22) with mediaeval, "geographical features (the recess, [. . .] rock [. . .], black valley [. . .]) and architectural features (priory, castle, abbey [. . .])" (Miles 2002: 41). The combination of these realistic elements with fantasy events that threateningly penetrated the realistic elements of the novel through supernatural protagonists, like the undead, witches, and mystic symbols, stimulated the affective horror reactions of the recipients (cf. Seeßlen and Jung 2006: 60; Viering 2010: 366).

Landmark novels such as Shelley's *Frankenstein; Or, The Modern Prometheus* (1818) or Lewis' *The Monk* (1796) included monstrous beings as supernatural sources of fear, disgust, and threat. Furthermore, ghost tales, like de Maupassant's *Le Horla* (1886), and vampire novels with blood sucking yet erotically seducing protagonists, like Stoker's *Dracula* (1897), or works from Russian and French authors like Tolstoi's *Upyr* (1841) were influential due to their sensual power and sexualization (cf. Brittnacher 1994: 318; Alpers, Fuchs and Hahn 1999: 11,14; Seeßlen and Jung 2006: 49f.).

Gradually, *Gothic* became a more general notion and henceforth was not only restricted to mediaeval contents but rather covered everything in prose, drama and lyrics that blurred "metaphysical, natural, religious, class, economic, marketing, generic, stylistic, and moral lines" (Hogle 2002: 8). Hoffmann (*Die Elixiere des Teufels (1816), Der Sandmann (1817)*), Poe (*The Fall of the House of Usher* (1839), *The Raven* (1845)), Lovecraft (*Supernatural Horror in Literature* (1927)), Le Fanu (*Green Tea* or *Carmilla* collected in *In a Glass Darkly* (1872)), Ewers (*Der Zauberlehrling oder: die Teufelsjäger* (1910)), and Meyrink (*Das Wachsfigurenkabinett* (1907)) gradually combined traditional elements of the Gothic with more realistic threats of mental illnesses (e.g. schizophrenia or mania) (cf. Alpers, Fuchs and Hahn 1999: 11), networks of intrigues (cf. Seeßlen and

---

[4] Direct citations will be reproduced with original formatting to retain the respective emphasis in italics or bold, unless otherwise specified.

Jung 2006: 59), and the fear of the unknown, unconscious, uncanny (cf. Viering 2010: 367), thus adding to the affective power of the genre. The uncanny became the most important element of psychoanalytical horror theories (see Chapter 1.2.2).

Besides the uncanny and abject aspects of bodily horror, the figure of the mad scientist, from Shelley onwards, became a central trope of transgression and concomitant feelings of fear and disgust (for instance through the experiments in Stevenson's *The Strange Case of Dr. Jekyll and Mr. Hyde* (1886) or Well's *The Island of Doctor Moreau* (1898)): The mad scientist's central function in the narrative structure was to broaden the skills of the human protagonists through drugs and operations so that the transformed humans became uncontrollable monsters or doppelgangers being able to exceed spatiotemporal limits (cf. Wisker 2005: 61–62).

Freud: Psychoanalysis enters the horror genre

Freud published his article *Das Unheimliche* in 1919 (see also Chapter 1.2.2) and thereby intensified the psychological trends in horror literature. Psychoanalysis allowed for readings that lumped together the monstrosity of human aggression, unconscious, infantile wishes, and psychological terror, such as in Asquith's *The Playfellow* (1929), Collier's *Green Thoughts* (1931), or Bloch's *Psycho* (1959). It treated adverse animals, such as the gulls in Du Maurier's *The Birds* (1952), and the body horror of "severed extremities, a severed head, a hand detached from the arm [. . .]" (Freud 2012 [1919]: 266; transl. LS) under the headline of fear of castration' and 'projection' (cf. Alpers, Fuchs and Hahn 1999: 20,23). Wisker (2005) emphasized how the events in *The Birds* psychologically and corporeally threatened normality, rationality, and security (cf. Wisker 2005: 84).

Modern horror: Humans threaten humans

Increasingly, the trope of the monster with its supernatural, exotic features gave way to dramatizations of the human condition, marked by deep desires and complex relationships with other humans, and became principal sources of fear, disgust, and pleasure during the 20th century. The threat humans pose to other humans was for instance shown in novels with sexual topics, such as the submission of women and their final revenge or patriarchic, sadistic figures (cf. Wisker 2005: 96,98,102), for instance in Carter's *The Magic Toyshop* (1967) or Weldon's *The Life and Loves of a She-Devil* (1983). Wisker (2005) pointed out that such novels broke "established philosophical and cultural binary oppositions, that is, male/female, good/bad, day/night, normal/Other" (Wisker 2005: 98). Horror emphasized those oppositions but covered more than the male disempowering of the desired women. Women also became the "feared Other" (Wisker 2005: 98). These transgressions challenged given ethical standards, causing defensive reactions and disgust.

From *Carrie* (1974) and *The Shining* (1977) to *Christine* (1983) and *The Green Mile (1997)*, Stephen King successfully contributed manifold horror novels, short stories and movies to the horror genre by dramatizing threatening humans. Wisker (2005) summarized the uniting narrative strategy of King's immense variety of topics as follows:

> King's world highlights the paradox of the safety of the home, the threat lurking behind Middle America's values and lifestyles, so audiences can relate to his situations, characters, and events. He explores areas of the human psyche that are usually pushed to the back of the mind [. . .] His work exemplifies the power of horror from the psychological to the social. (Wisker 2005: 119)

Magistrale (2008) also stated that the real source of fear in King's works were not only the monsters, but that "at the heart of his universe is a deep-seated awareness of American anxieties about how we live and where we are going, as nation and as individuals" (Magistrale 2008: 5). The opposition of suppressed versus liberated evil forces that hide in each of us became important to the horror genre: "The evil lurks within us and only needs to be awakened" (Alpers, Fuchs and Hahn 1999: 24; transl. LS). To point out that this evil is in us, it is appropriate to incorporate supernatural, powerful elements into the narration. This also relates to forces situated in religious contexts. Here, it is Satan who infiltrates a person's thoughts and seduces them to commit evil actions as in Levin's *Rosemary's Baby* (1967), or it is a human protagonist who exorcises the devil from a human body as in Blatty's *The Exorcist* (1971). Human protagonists as threats to other men were also shown in horror novels that treat emotional stress, such cannibalism, threatening psychiatrists, puking girls, or suits made of human skin, such as in Harris' four novels *Red Dragon* (1981), *The Silence of the Lambs* (1988), *Hannibal* (1999), and *Hannibal Rising* (2006).

Although horror can be recognized as such even without supernatural powers, the well-known, fantastic characters and monsters still exist. A prime example are vampire figures which are predestined for erotic narrations beyond heterosexual norms as it was shown in Gomez' *The Gilda Stories* (1991) with homosexual or queer characters "celebrating the black vampire women and lesbians" (Wisker 2005: 115) as well as in Brite's *Lost Souls* (1992) or *Drawing Blood*

(1993) with a "visceral, sensuous, erotic [. . . language that is] built in combinations of opposites – the oxymoron" (Wisker 2005: 108).

Horror subgenres: Limitless brutality and broken taboos

Over time, many subgenres have emerged that combine elements from *cyberpunk* and *steampunk*, with works like Jeter's *Dr. Adder* (1984) and Blaylock's *The Last Coin* (1988). Another (sub)genre, *splatterpunk*, concentrates on limitless brutality with "violent, bloody, partly orgiastically primitive" (Alpers, Fuchs and Hahn 1999: 26; transl. LS) scenes, like Barker's *Books of Blood* (1984) where he pictured "the horrors of the human condition, laying bare the suffering and doubt of the flesh" (Wisker 2005: 118). What links these diverse developments is their focus on readerly disgust, perhaps most meticulously staged in splatterpunk as an (oral) defense[5] against blood, phlegm, vomit or sweat. These subgenres, in particular, tend to extremes; taboos are excessively broken to "approach areas of socio-psychological life which offend, which are suppressed, [. . . like] relations between the sexes [. . . or] man's supposed place in the hierarchy of natural and divine life" (Punter 1980: 405).

While there are now many subgenres, horror continues to stage fear and disgust. The notion of *horror literature* turned into an umbrella term for a variety of themes and subgenres. The discussion about which works should be included in the genre is also mirrored in the different collections of general horror or Gothic reference works (see e.g. Alpers, Fuchs and Hahn (1999), Viering (2010) or Wisker (2005)).

Horror movies: Intensifying fear and disgust

The horror genre and its affective powers experienced a technical expansion with the emergence of movies in the 1920s. Initially, some Gothic novels entered the cinema (cf. Stiglegger 2007: 312), reviving vampire figures like in Murnau's movie *Nosferatu* (1922) and Browning's *Dracula* (1931), or the artificial human in Robertson's silent movie *Dr. Jekyll and Mr. Hyde* (1920). As the medium explored its technical and cineastic possibilities, it found its unique ways of staging fear and disgust, including new, more psychological content and protagonists that became more and more human and realistic while at the same

---

5 For more information on oral defense, see Chapter 4.3.

time more brutal and destructive. According to Stiglegger (2007), a broader understanding of the notion of horror needs to subsume literature and movies that are strictly thrillers (cf. Stiglegger 2007: 97). For example, Hitchcock dramatized a split consciousness and psychological violence in *Psycho* (1960). Many movies followed suit and used "narrative constructions of the psychological thriller, but exaggerated the terror moments almost into the surreal" (Stiglegger 2007: 313; transl. LS), such as Polanski's *Repulsion* (1965), which shows a young, violent woman's fears and hallucinations which force her to kill people who care for her (cf. Hahn and Giesen 2002: 176f.). The genre's borders to thrillers and crime fiction blur in the same way as they did in literary horror. According to Stiglegger (2010), this development was reinforced during the 1960s and 1970s by the Italian *Giallo* movies that contained sexualized violence like Fulci's *Lo squartatore di New York* (1982) (cf. Stiglegger 2010: 64). The reason producers were now more able to portray brutal scenes laid in the mitigated censorship regulations of the late 1960s. This opened the floor for the first splatter movies, like Reeves' *Witchfinder General* (1968). Productions became more complex, integrated special effects, and thus, contributed to gaining new audiences for known transgressors including monstrous animals, such as in Spielberg's *Jaws* (1975), exorcising pastors fighting against daemons, such as in Friedkin's *The Exorcist* (1973), or violent maniacs, such as in Kubrick's *The Shining* (1980) (cf. Hahn and Giesen 2002: 189,572; Stiglegger 2007: 314). Zombies, teen slasher and cannibalism movies grew during the late 1970s (cf. Stiglegger 2007: 314). The staging of raw brutality as well as the use of special effects within these movies stimulated the recipient's "primal fears [. . .] (e.g. the fear of the unknown depths of the sea)" (Stiglegger 2007: 314; transl. LS) on a new, sophisticated level.

In the late 1950s, horror motifs began to show in series and sequels, such as Serling's *The Twilight Zone* (episodic from 1959–2002), Carpenter and Hill's *Halloween* (1978–2021) or Barker's *Hellraiser* (1987–2018) (cf. Seeßlen and Jung 2006: 737,759). This had the advantage that characters did not have to be developed and made accessible to the recipients time and again; the movies could instead focus quickly on the atrocities committed and exert their affective powers more directly.

Real horror: Interactions of literature, movies, and real events

After the attacks of September 11, 2001, the so-called *New Horror, terror cinema* or *terror movies* dominated the cinema. Movies such as Wan's *Saw* (2004) and Roth's *Hostel* (2005) intensified the villains' potential to graphically torture their victims to death and thus forced/seduced the recipients to exceed ethical limits and even identify with the torturing slaughterer (cf. Stiglegger 2010: 21f., 60).

There is a critical debate on whether movies, which produce criminal protagonists and thereby seduce their viewers to identify with evil, guide those viewers to violence and criminal acts in real life (cf. Paik and Comstock 1994: 536–538; Johnson, Cohen, Smailes, Elizabeth M:, Kasen, Stephanie and Brook 2002: 2470; Schneider 2003: 192; Stiglegger 2006: 50; Stiglegger 2010: 17). And indeed, there were cases where individuals imitated movie characters such as the so-called *killer clowns* or *horror clowns* and became a threatening danger or – vice versa – novels and movies showed similarities to actual events (cf. Der Polizeipräsident in Berlin 2016; Rogers 2016). The horror clown character was cinematographically present recently in the movie *The Dark Knight* (2008) and in *Joker* (2019), both with realistic killer clowns represented by the figure of the Joker, as well as the novel adaptations of *It* (2017) and *It Chapter Two* (2019) both based on King's novel *It* (1986).[6] The productions blurred not only the boundaries between the neighboring genres, but also between fantasy and stories placed in a real context.

Oppositions as common denominator

This genre overview shows that art-horror covers an immense variety of characters, criminal acts, and fear triggers. Even though the concrete protagonists and technical possibilities changed over time, the "central concerns of the classical Gothic are not that different from those of the contemporary Gothic: Family dynamics, the limits of rationality and passion, the definition of statehood and citizenship, the cultural effects of technology" (Bruhm 2002: 259). What all seem to have in common is "the position of the victim – the figure under threat" (Jancovich 1992: 118). "On the playing level of the film (diegesis), human mind and body are threatened by the same human mind and body" (Meteling 2006: 28; transl. LS). Horror demonstrates the

> threat to the human mind and body [. . .] with a rhetoric of violence, terror, fear and disgust, so that this threat extends beyond the screen in the direction of the viewer [. . .] The audiovisual rhetoric of thrill [Angst-Lust] ranges from the fantastic intrusion of a foreign order into a familiar one, for example by monstrous semi-beings, to the banality of evil in the form of the mass or serial murder of people by other people.
> (Meteling 2006: 27; transl. LS)

All these supernatural beings, violent human protagonists, haunted places, and objects achieve their impact through their representation in oppositions. In

---

6 For a detailed analysis of the clown's ambiguities and how it is possible to equally scream because of and laugh about (evil) clowns, see Straßburger (2019).

the horror genre, limits are exceeded: the possible contrasts the improbable, the normal the sick, oneself the foreign; evil becomes good and good becomes evil. Internal processes are controlled externally. The opposites real/unreal, normal/abnormal, alive/dead, good/evil and own/foreign play an important role in the evocation of anxiety and disgust. Seeßlen and Jung (2006) even shorten the contrasting concepts to two oppositions (nature/magic and body/mind) and summarize them as fundaments of fear: The opposition of nature/magic, which could also be entitled rationalism/theology or real/unreal, compiles all supernatural features that influence the evil protagonists and their targets in a pre-scientific way. The opposition of body/mind concentrates on the position of the victim and summarizes all aspects of the plot where a body is deformed and thereby (metaphorically) also sickens the mind. This opposition encompasses disease in all its facets (cf. Seeßlen and Jung 2006: 31–32).

By mixing both ends of the spectrum, new categories are repeatedly created. Opposing categories like life/death or healthy/sick overlap in the concrete features of the characters, objects, and narrative strategies of the genre, as demonstrated through the living dead or the serial killer and psychiatrist Hannibal Lecter. These characters move between the worlds, damned to never fully enter either of the two spheres. Even though the horror genre had never laid claim to reality, and thus had endless possibilities for fantastic new creations (cf. Seeßlen and Jung 2006: 45), the contrasting oppositions are realized through repetitive central themes, which trigger anxiety and disgust (but also pleasure, see Chapter 1.2), and seduce the recipients to exceed ethical limits.

Classification of art-horror's oppositions

In the following, the horror repertoire and the underlying oppositions are systematically summarized (cf. Seeßlen and Jung 2006: 45–48; Stiglegger 2007: 311f.):
1. Supernatural forces and monstrous beings threaten humans. These forces can also change the human protagonist in such a way that they become the threat themselves. This category juxtaposes the concepts of reality/unreality and includes "creatures that specialize in formlessness, incompleteness, categorical interstitiality, and categorical contradictoriness" (Carroll 1990: 32),[7] which Seeßlen and Jung (2006) call "legends of blending" (Seeßlen and Jung 2006: 27; transl. LS). This category includes:

---

[7] For more details about Carroll's concept of interstitialty/impurity see Chapter 1.2.3.

- artificial humans, like Frankenstein or Golems, which unite human, mechanic, and magic features and concurrently illustrate and attack scientifically justified ideas
- beings who are neither alive nor dead like vampires, mummies, or the living dead
- hybrids and animalistic monsters like violent birds, fictional horror clowns, werewolves, or contortionists
- magicians and witches as religious and sexual motives who either represent the devil himself or close a contract with him. A witch attacks the oppressive ideas of Christianity as "wicked woman" and "perverse mother" (Seeßlen and Jung 2006: 48; transl. LS) and seduce their environment to evil actions.

2. Mystified geography, architecture, and objects, like dark castles, old houses, ruins, tunnels, and torture tools, which haunt the protagonists. This category also juxtaposes reality/unreality but focuses on the dread triggered through objects and places. This also includes an awakening evil in a place thought to be safe, lacking resources and essentials as well as natural environments like a rough, deep ocean.
3. Thoughts and emotions of psychologically abnormal humans with mental illnesses like maniacs, mad or schizophrenic scientists, doppelgangers who represent the unconscious and approaching death, or emotionally confused characters who violently threaten their environment. Abnormal dreams, infantile imaginations, and the awakening evil in a formerly good person can be embedded into this category. The contents can be subsumed to the opposition of normal/abnormal or healthy/sick.
4. Networks of intrigues, and the physical as well as psychological violence of pitiless protagonists. Even though this category cannot be separated clearly from the preceding one, these protagonists are portrayed as mentally healthy. This category includes thrilling conspiracies, violent, sexual submission, (female) revenge, and cannibalism. It opposes concepts of normal/abnormal or safety/danger.

This taxonomy and its underlying oppositions will play a role later when designing items. Beyond the incongruent characters, the narrative strategy, and the distribution of information to the recipients can also lead to incongruities and associated emotions.

Narrative strategies

In addition to these ambiguous characters and places, narrative strategies support the induction of fear and disgust. It is mainly the distribution of information about the evil characters and places that guide protagonists' and recipients' believes and emotions. Carroll (1990) introduced two main narrative structures that he called "The Complex Discovery Plot" and "The Overreacher Plot" (Carroll 1990: 99,118). While Carroll based his arguments on the concept of supernatural monsters as essential element of art-horror, his narrative structures are regarded here more generally and are adapted to the horror repertoire mentioned above.

The first of Carroll's narrative structures, "The Complex Discovery Plot" (Carroll 1990: 99), comprises four milestones that each provide important information about the narration's evil aspects: The *onset* (gradually or immediately) introduces the presence of evil while the recipients and the good protagonists do not necessarily recognize it as such. During the second phase called *discovery*, the protagonists recognize the evil element through investigation or through a sudden insight. The protagonists try to prove the existence of evil to other groups and during the third phase called *confirmation*, its presence is approved. The fourth milestone comprises the (repeated) *confrontation* with the evil element (cf. Carroll 1990: 99–103). This chronological four-step development can be varied by combining the milestones differently or by focusing on only one phase like an immediate "pure confrontation plot" (Carroll 1990: 115).

The second narrative structure called "The Overreacher Plot" (Carroll 1990: 118) stages a scientist or necromancer and their forbidden, magical or scientific knowledge. This narrative structure also develops in four phases: "[. . .] preparation for the experiment; the experiment itself; the accumulation of evidence that the experiment has boomeranged; and the confrontation [. . .]" (Carroll 1990: 120). Again, as with any artificial definition, the two narratives are not exclusive and sometimes authors purposely mix elements of the two (cf. Carroll 1990: 123).

The distribution of information to protagonists and audiences is of relevance to the extent that readers can be deliberately misled by lacking or ambiguous information. This generates narrative suspense as well as moments of surprise or shock. Again, opposites play an important role in the development and conclusion of the narration. The issue here is about competing potential storylines: The morally reprehensible confronts the good, the supernatural challenges the real. One side winning over the other changes throughout the different narrative phases (cf. Carroll 1990: 138) and "the event in the story must remain ambiguous with respect to these competing explanations for the readers" (Carroll 1990: 146).

Specifically, suspense results when the possible outcomes of the situation set down by the story are such that the outcome that is morally correct, in terms of the values inherent in the fiction, is the less likely outcome (or, at least, only as likely as the evil outcome). That is, suspense in fiction, in general, is generated by combining elements of morality and probability in such a way that the question that issue in the plot have logically opposed answers – x will happen/x will not happen – and furthermore, that opposition is also characterized by an opposition of morality and probability ratings.

(Carroll 1990: 137f.)

Based on the distribution of information, viewers can also deliberately be seduced to a certain semantic interpretation or cognitive model of the ongoing narration. They are kept ignorant until the sudden revelation of an ambiguous context offering an evil reading.

(1) You get home, tired after a long day's work and ready for a relaxing night alone. You reach for the light switch, but another hand is already there. (Hall 2013)

(2) The audience at Hollywood's Dolby Theatre was spellbound when the disguised moderator opened the golden envelope. 'Row 1. Seat 9.' was written on the card. She pulled out the gun. (adapted from Meimberg 2011: 34, transl. LS)

In example (1), the reader is seduced to assume that the protagonist comes back to a safe home and that the darkness in the flat can easily be lightened through turning on the light switch. In example (2), the award ceremony audience does not expect the winner will be murdered. But at the end of these tiny plots, the correct resolution of the ambiguous elements is given. The threat is revealed only at the last moment, when it seems to be too late for the victim. The late revelation as "cruel punchline" (Seeßlen and Jung 2006: 57; transl. LS) can lead to the emotion of surprise which, in turn, can cause fear in the protagonists and audience (cf. Ekman 2010 [2003]: 206). This mechanism of ambiguous information distribution and the late ambiguity resolution is called *garden path effect* (GP) (cf. Rehbock 2016: 220,273). We will come back to the latter in Chapter 2.

The repertoire of horror and the narrative strategies trigger a series of emotions both in the characters and in the recipients. The victims of the narration are threatened by supernatural beings, haunted places, and cruel actions. They lose their minds, parts of their bodies, or die eventually. They are anxious and disgusted, suffer pain, cry, and are forced to change their ethical codex to survive. They scream because of incongruity. However, as previously mentioned, identification with the aggressor is also possible, further facilitating potential reactions and emotions from the viewers. The following chapters deal with the emotions of fear and disgust triggered in the recipients and the theories that try to explain those horror effects.

1.2 Horror theories: Why fear and disgust?

Horror texts and movies not only show the emotions of fear and disgust but also aim to induce them in the recipients (cf. Baumann 1989: 219). As an introductory overview, this chapter first describes these emotions. By referring to "the paradox of painful art" (Smuts 2009: 511) and the more specific concept of "the paradox of horror" (Carroll 1990: 159), the introductory part raises the question why viewers expose themselves at all to texts and movies that trigger ostensibly negative emotions. Subsequently, theoretical approaches are summarized that explain why the emotions of fear and disgust occur during the consumption of horror material, why their evocation is addressed in the form of the horror genre, which further emotions may also play a role for the experience of being horrified and which conditions define art-horror sufficiently with special reference to incongruity.

1.2.1 Art-horror's emotions

What are emotions, and how are fear and disgust defined?

Kleinginna and Kleinginna (1981) condensed an interdisciplinary working definition from over a hundred emotion theories spanning affective, physiological and cognitive approaches. According to their multifactorial definition, an emotion is:

> a complex set of interactions among subjective and objective factors, mediated by neural/hormonal systems, which can (a) give rise to affective experiences such as feelings of arousal, pleasure/displeasure; (b) generate cognitive processes such as emotionally relevant perceptual effects, appraisals, labeling processes; (c) activate widespread physiological adjustments to the arousing conditions; and (d) lead to behavior that is often, but not always, expressive, goal-directed, and adaptive. (Kleinginna and Kleinginna 1981: 355)

The subjective components of an emotion comprise the temporary, psychic experience and the cognitive evaluation of a stimulus as either positive or negative. The objective, measurable factors include physiological reactions like sweating, raised heart rate or blood pressure. An emotion is also a motivation to adapt one's behavior towards an incoming stimulus, thereby satisfying a need. Such behavior, in turn, aims to gain positive and avoid negative emotions. While some approaches concentrate on the description of emotional dimensions like their activating potential or intensity, categorical approaches classify emotions qualitatively to distinguish individual emotions from each other. From the latter approach of qualitative distinction comes the description of basic emotions (cf. Brandstätter, Schüler, Puca and Lozo 2018: 164–169), among them amusement, anger, fear, surprise, disgust, and relief (cf. Ekman 2005 [1999]: 55; Ekman 2010 [2003]: XVIf.).

Emotion, affect, feeling
In the current book, the terms *affect* and *feeling* cannot always be sharply separated from *emotion*, since both are sometimes used synonymously with *emotion* in the research literature (e.g. in Brandstätter, Schüler, Puca and Lozo 2018), are interchangeably used to describe one another, or are part of superordinate emotion definitions. Their interchangeability is also due to their long-lasting use in the interdisciplinary research tradition that has not yet arrived at a universal definition. Because of this, all three notions appear in the current work when it reviews research literature of art-horror (and later of humor). Generally, however, differences between *emotion*, *affect* and *feeling* are recognized: Contrary to emotion, a *feeling* is often understood as not being goal-directed; it equals a longer lasting mood. *Affect* is understood as the subconscious visceral reaction to a stimulus (corresponding to component (a) of Kleinginna and Kleinginna's definition above).[8] This book focuses on *emotion* with a competence-oriented understanding of art-horror reception. Even though the physical and psychic reactions are automatic, the recipients are aware of them, make cognitive (except to startle responses) and physical adjustments to the stimuli, and can actively describe the qualia of this experience. Determining basic emotions is helpful to reduce the complexity of and define art-horror. However, it also raises serious issues: Since art-horror is fictitious, the questions arise how the recipient's reaction reflects a reaction to natural, real horror, and how accurately basic emotions describe this reaction. Thought Theory (see Chapter 1.2.3) offers an explanation of these questions. Ultimately, the distinction between affect and emotion does not play a role in the later experiments concerning reading time, FACS and EEG (Chapters 4.2 to 4.4) since the subjects do not have to consciously reflect on their emotions. The assignment of the visceral reaction to a (single) emotion actually contains risks of interpretation inaccuracies or ambiguities. In turn, questioning consciously perceived emotions (as it is important for the ratings in Chapter 4.1) holds similar risks and further challenges, such as the possibility that participants could claim they were not frightened, even though they in fact were.

---

[8] For a comprehensive discussion of the philosophical research literature see Scarantino (2016). For details on the differentiation between *affect*, *feeling* and *emotion*, see for example, Scherer (2005) who understands *feeling* as the individual experience of the qualia of an emotion with regulative functions.

The emotions of fear, disgust, and surprise

As we have seen in Chapter 1.1, the research literature suggests that the emotions of fear and disgust are of central relevance to the description of art-horror and its reception. Therefore, they are depicted here in more detail from a psycho-physiological perspective, supplemented by some phenomenological considerations:

Fear

Fear is a consciously, individually experienced, and negatively evaluated state of arousal, threat, tension and concern associated with heightened activity of the autonomic nervous system (cf. Spielberger 1972: 30–31; Krohne 1996: 5; LaBar 2016: 751). The person involved evaluates the qualia of fear as agonizing, frightening and oppressive and tries to rapidly cope with fear provoking situations or objects (goal-directedness) or avoid them entirely (cf. Stöber and Schwarzer 2000: 189,195; Hanich 2010: 19). Fear activates physiological adaptation mechanisms like raised blood pressure (cf. Stöber and Schwarzer 2000: 190), widened eyes and increased blood flow to the legs (cf. Ekman 2010 [2003]: 221). It motivates the person involved to adapt to the situation and activate protecting coping strategies. These involve the logical reanalysis of the threatening situation by concentrating on the appraisal (e.g. psychic re-appraisal as challenge, considering alternatives), the problem (threat's elimination e.g. through information seeking, fleeing, freezing or fighting), and the subjective emotion (regulation of the occurring emotion e.g. through taking a deep breath, verbal expression, tranquilizers) (cf. Billings and Moos 1984: 882; Stöber and Schwarzer 2000: 195; LaBar 2016: 752–754). From a psychological point of view, two forms of fear play a role during the consumption of art-horror texts or movies: 1) fear as a temporary affective state (*state anxiety*) directed at a threatening situation, object or just to a symbolic threat as well as 2) fear as a non-directed intuition of an imminent danger (cf. Baumann 1989: 220–223; Stiglegger 2007: 366; LaBar 2016: 751), also called *trait anxiety* (cf. Stöber and Schwarzer 2000: 190).

From a phenomenological perspective, art-horror can even evoke five different sub-types of fear which Hanich (2010) calls "direct horror, suggested horror, cinematic shock, cinematic dread and cinematic terror" (Hanich 2010: 19). This differentiation shows that different art-horror narrative strategies lead to (rather small) differences in "intentionality, appraisal, action tendency, physiological change and phenomenological experience" (Hanich 2010: 19) while at the same time the notion of fear might be too general to grasp the different, emotional phenomena in art-horror (cf. Hanich 2010: 19).

Disgust
Disgust is psychologically, phenomenologically as well as physiologically described as oral, nasal, aural and visual rejection which serves to protect against contamination through bad or poisoned food and odors, excreted bodily substances like sweat, feces, or saliva, the touch of a nasty object or morally questionable behavior. Physiologically, disgust can cause nausea and vomiting (cf. Rozin and Fallon 1987; Hennig and Netter 2000; Ekman and Friesen 2003; Rozin, Haidt and McCauley 2016). Disgust motivates the persons involved to adapt to a disgust triggering situation with an "aversive reaction" (Hanich 2010: 297) by protecting their body or psyche against "obtrusive nearness" (Hanich 2010: 295). This is done either by closing the perception channels like nose wrinkling and narrowing of the eyes, or opening them to repel the object just touched, like tongue extrusion or a raised upper lip (cf. Rozin, Lowery and Ebert 1994: 870). Ekman and Friesen (2003) enumerate a large portion of the horror repertoire by describing disgust triggered through humans:

> People can be offensive in their appearance; to look at them may be distasteful. Some people experience disgust when seeing a deformed, crippled person, or an ugly person. An injured person with an exposed wound may be disgusting. The sight of blood or the witnessing of surgery makes some people disgusted. Certain human actions are disgusting; you may be revolted by what a person does. A person who mistreats or tortures a dog or cat may be the object of disgust. A person who indulges in what others consider sexual perversion may be disgusting. A philosophy of life or way of treating people that is considered debasing can make those who regard it that way feel disgusted.
> (Ekman and Friesen 2003: 67)

From a phenomenological perspective, Hanich (2011) enumerates five factors that influence the qualitative experience of disgust: temporality (sudden or anticipatory confrontation), presence (perception or imagination of disgust), character engagement (empathy or sympathy), sensual experience, and simultaneously evoked emotions (cf. Hanich 2011: 12). Research literature also sheds light on the fact that three specific circumstances allow for enjoyment of disgust, namely romantic situations, art (-horror), and humor (cf. Strohminger 2014: 485–487; Rozin, Haidt and McCauley 2016: 828).

Surprise
According to the narrative strategy of the garden path (GP, see Chapter 1.1) in which the threatening object is detected only at a late, surprising moment, the emotion of surprise also plays an important role during the reception of art-horror. Even though surprise does not belong to negatively evaluated emotions per se, it is nonetheless important for the stimulus detection and its evaluation.

Surprise occurs when an unexpected stimulus (object-direction) arises that needs to be compared with previously given information about a situation. The qualia of surprise itself has neither a positive nor negative valence and, the cognitive component of the emotion predominates (which, in turn, leads to discussions of whether surprise is a (basic) emotion at all [cf. Meyer, Reisenzein and Niepel 2000: 260]). Meyer et al. (2000) describe surprise as a four-stage cognitive process, of which the visceral emotion of surprise is only one part of the second processing stage: (1) detection of the unexpected, incoming stimulus, (2) interruption of previous activities and focus on the unexpected stimulus, (3) evaluation of incoming stimulus through verification, search for its reasons, estimation of stimulus influence on well-being, and estimation of stimulus influence on given situation/activity, and (4) adaption to stimulus according to evaluation through control and prediction of future events, avoidance, or ignorance (cf. Meyer, Reisenzein and Niepel 2000: 255–257). The stage of evaluation reveals whether the incoming stimulus is positive or negative so that further emotions like fear or disgust can occur and accompany the adaptation phase. Ekman (2010) summarizes the facial expressions associated with the visceral reaction. The accompanying facial expression of surprise includes widened eyes, raised eye brows, and an opened, o-formed mouth (cf. Ekman 2010 [2003]: 210). Surprise needs to be distinguished from the startle reflex which does not count as an emotion because of its uncontrollability and different facial expression including narrowed eyes, lowered eye brows and tightened lips (cf. Ekman 2010 [2003]: 210–211).

The paradox of horror
If both fear and disgust are emotions that we try to avoid and which make us suppress their triggers, why do recipients consume horror books or movies at all? Why are they interested in voluntarily experiencing negative emotions which they would evade in real life? And why do they even like it?

Carroll addressed these questions under the heading "paradox of horror" (Carroll 1990: 158) with a special focus on art-horror. However, since this paradox also concerns all genres that induce negative audience emotions like tragedies or thrillers, Smuts (2014) deduced the problem logically for all pain-triggering texts and movies and renames the concept "paradox of painful art" (Smuts 2014: 8):

1. People voluntarily avoid things that provide painful experiences and only pursue things that provide pleasurable experiences.
2. Audiences routinely have net painful experiences in response to putatively painful art (PPA), such as tragedies, melodramas, religious works, sad songs, and horror films.

3. People expect to have net painful experiences in response to PPA.
4. People voluntarily pursue works that they know to be PPA.   (Smuts 2014: 8)

Early explanations for the question why recipients consume art-horror come from philosophy. Burke (1757), Kant (1790), and Schiller (1793) found philosophical reasons for the consumption of the terrible in the sublime (from Latin *sublimitas* = sublimity [cf. Stowasser, Petschenig and Skutsch 2009: 488]) which they understood to be the aesthetics of dread and are separate from the pleasure of beauty. The sublime arises precisely from the imagination of dread and sensually inconceivable greatness. The mind feels superior to the physical senses as it is separated from them. While Burke emphasized the immunity of the mind to physical threat as source of delight and astonishment (cf. Burke 2014 [1757]: 53,248), Kant differentiated in *Kritik der Urteilskraft* (1790) between the mathematically and dynamically sublime. The former refers to the impression of size that exceeds all the units of measurement humans can grasp with their senses. The dynamic sublime refers to the realization that our mind is independent of nature and its power and thus also of our survival instinct and physical deprivation of liberty (cf. Kant 2011 [1790]: §24). Schiller further developed Kant's dual distinction in his treatise *Vom Erhabenen* (1793) into the theoretically and practically sublime, with the theoretically sublime outlining more generally everything our mind is unable to grasp and the practically sublime encompassing everything beyond our physical power. In particular, by imagining an attack of the practical, terrible nature on our physis (which Burke called terror compared to the mind's pain [cf. Burke 2014 [1757]: 247]), the sublime is awakened as an element independent of nature (cf. Schiller 1793: 325). Schiller developed a three-step path to sublimity: imagination of physical power, notion of powerlessness to that power, moral elevation above physical power (cf. Schiller 1793: 348). Through the concept of the sublime, the consumption of art-horror can be understood as the representation of the terrible that awakens the ability of the audience to rise morally above their physical constraints and above threatening nature.

Today, a multitude of different disciplines and perspectives try to answer the paradox of horror. The following two chapters summarize the modern theoretical approaches from a psychoanalytical angle, with a particular focus on the uncanny, the repressed but returned unconscious, and the abject (Chapter 1.2.2), as well as from a cognitive prospect focusing on mechanisms of conversion, control, and compensation (Chapter 1.2.3). Both approaches will help to provide a number of potential explanations why audiences feel fear and disgust, why they consume art-horror at all, and if there is more than negative emotion.

1.2.2 Psychoanalytic horror approaches

Back to Freud: The uncanny

Freud is considered the first author in the scholarly analysis of the uncanny, although his work was preceded by Jentsch's reflections (1906) on the etymological origin of the uncanny from the unfamiliar, on causes like doubts about the (in-)animacy of an object or being, and on defense mechanisms against the unfamiliar. Freud's psychoanalytic approach attempted to attribute the emotions that overcome us in the dark or through the imagination of spirits, animated machines or separated body parts to psychological roots of repressed infantile complexes which return from the unconscious and surmounted beliefs (cf. Freud 2012 [1919]: 271). For this purpose, Freud used the notion of *unheimlich* (English: uncanny), a term he explains both etymologically and through concrete example. The German adjective *heimlich* (English: secret, belonging to a home, familiar, intimate) and its potential negation *unheimlich* (English: uncanny, creepy) etymologically show an overlapping meaning insofar as they signify something that belongs to a home (*heim*), but both can also mean secret or hidden (cf. Kluge and Schirmer 1957: 299; Freud 2012 [1919]: 250). Notably, Freud also listed stories like Hoffmann's *The Sandman* and Heine's *The Gods in Exile*, in which the most familiar things (sight, religion) are taken away from the protagonists. This loss was understood by Freud as a representation of the infantile fear of castration, which was repressed into unconsciousness and returns in uncanny moments. The repression of emotion belonging to the *heimlich*, or the familiar, into the unconscious alienates us from it and makes it appear frightening, sinister, and *unheimlich* (cf. Freud 2012 [1919]: 271), no matter which emotion or desire was repressed.

Besides a set of key topoi and elements, such as animated dolls and machines[9] or the motif of the doppelganger, Freud's essay "identified the particular effects of defamiliarization, where the familiar becomes strange and the strange more familiar, where whole bodies seem mechanical, sick, uncontrollable; where boundaries between what we take for granted and strange events destabilise our sense of solid reality and communication through language" (Wisker 2005: 231).

Freud's approach is not only important for the present work with regard to horror motifs and their effects on the recipients. He also described that in order

---

9 Interestingly, robotics adapt these findings to the construction of real robots to prevent them from being perceived as uncanny. Mori (2012 [1970]) develops a model called the *uncanny valley* that disentangles human affinity to robots as a function of the robot's human likeness.

to evoke the uncanny, it is necessary for the viewer to identify with the victim. If there is a lack of identification potential with the victim, the protagonist would quickly be drawn into comedy (cf. Freud 2012 [1919]: 274). This suggests that the uncanny and humor are similar and have a common foundation.

The uncanny can also be reinforced by narrative strategies in which the audience is only informed about the conditions of the depicted, fictitious world at a late stage of the story plot (cf. Freud 2012 [1919]: 273). We have already encountered this kind of narration under the term *garden path* (GP) in Chapter 1.1.

Kristeva and the abject
Contrary to Freud's claim of identification, Kristeva (1982) added the concept of the *abject* to psychoanalytical horror analysis, which is precisely determined by the fact that it neither defines a clear object of desire nor belongs to the subject/the self. Kristeva emphasized that the threatening element of horror was its indefinable quality, the revelation of the insufficiency of human language, and "the limits of the human universe" (Kristeva 1982: 11). The abject "disturbs identity, system, order [. . .] The in-between, the ambiguous, the composite. The traitor, the liar, the criminal with a good conscience, the shameless rapist, the killer who claims he is a savior" (Kristeva 1982: 4). Kristeva enumerated exuded "urine, blood, sperm, excrement" (Kristeva 1982: 52) as examples of the abject which threaten one's "own and clean self" by breaking human, cognitive categories – a component which will be discussed in cognitive terms in Chapter 1.2.3 – through a "collapse of the border between inside and outside" (Kristeva 1982: 52). Hogle (2002) summarized Kristeva's concept of abjection as a human mechanism of throwing off

> whatever threatens us with anything like this betwixt-and-between, even dead-and-alive [. . . .] into defamiliarized manifestations, which we henceforth fear and desire because they both threaten and reengulf us and promise to return us to our primal origins. Those othered figures reveal this deeply familiar foundation while 'throwing it under' the cover of an outcast monster more vaguely archaic and filled with contradictions than supposedly normal human beings, as in the cadaverous creature *Frankenstein,* the aristocratic vampire in *Dracula,* or the shrunken and gnarled other-self-*in*-the-self of Robert Louis Stevenson's *Dr. Jekyll and Mr. Hyde.* (Hogle 2002: 7)

The monster between superego and id
In psychoanalysis, the monster in particular serves as an "actual dramatization of the dual concept of the repressed/the Other" (Wood 1986: 75) and as a symbol for "the battle of supremacy between the ravenous id and the controlling superego [which] translates in myriad ways into the conflicts of the Gothic"

(Bruhm 2002: 262). The monster equates "the superego [that] takes monstrous form in the ultrarational, cultured figures of Hannibal Lecter, Damien Thorne, and Anne Rice's blood-drinking literati" (Bruhm 2002: 261–262). King (1981) emphasized that the psychoanalytical approach offered the possibility to interpret the superego as torturer and the id as the attacker's and audience's "free will to do evil or to deny it" (King 1981: 83). King claimed that "we're all mentally ill" (King 1981: 173), that "the potential lyncher is in almost all of us" and that "anticivilization emotions doesn't (sic!) go away, and they demand periodic exercise" (King 1981: 174). In his view, "the best horror films [. . .] manage to be reactionary, anarchistic and revolutionary all at the same time" (King 1981: 175). Wood (2012) underlined the psychoanalytical potential to comprehend the monster as representations of the id and superego through his claim that in a "traditional horror film [. . .] the monster was in general a creature from the id, not merely a product of repression but a protest against it, whereas in the current cycles the monster, while still produced by repression, has essentially become a superego figure" (Wood 2012: 195).

Taking up King's double function of progressive and reactionary horror elements, Wood claimed that the traditional horror films "invited, however ambiguously, an identification with the return of the repressed, the contemporary horror film invite[d] an identification (either sadistic or masochistic or both simultaneously) with punishment" (Wood 1986: 195).

Psychoanalysis answers the paradox of horror

Art-horror not only serves as a dramatization of the evils of superego and id but also offers a solution to the paradox of painful art: Art is reframed in therapeutic terms as gratification. In psychoanalysis, objects of disgust and fear are also interpreted in terms of sexual desires or rejections. These lead, on one hand, to oedipal confrontations and, on the other hand, to what is called the "pleasures of horror" and the "pleasures of restoration" (Hills 2005: 68): The former comprise symbols for castration, such as the son's attack against the father who, in turn, expels the son (Bruhm 2002: 263). The latter are represented through the art-horror plots of incest, patricide, or revenge on women. Even though psychoanalytical research argues for therapeutic goals to 'heal' these desires, critical voices claim that there is nothing wrong or unhealthy in art-horror emotions and that the audience searches exactly for these emotions instead of healing them (cf. Hanich 2010: 9).

Carroll (2004) complained that "many of the psychoanalytic ideas available to filmmakers and their audiences are extremely general, rather vague, and even inchoate" (Carroll 2004: 259) and that a standardized "symbolic expression of a repressed wish" (Carroll 2004: 262) was not possible. However, Hills (2005) summarized the psychoanalytical approaches to a master narrative strategy for art-horror by reviewing them according to their different foci on the return of the repressed, on the reconfirmation of the surmounted beliefs, or on the purification of the abject (cf. Hills 2005: 60):

(1) 'X' is lost via civilizing processes (whether repressed Oedipal complexes, repressed fears of castration, primitive animistic beliefs or the pleasures of reveling in filth and muck):
(2) This 'X' is restored temporarily and narratively via horror texts.
(3) 'X' is then repelled again, returning us to our starting point, and ritualistically restoring civilized society (repression/the mature cognitive self/the symbolic order).

(Hills 2005: 61)

The frequent repetition of art-horror motifs and the summary of narrations to a master structure pays tribute to the human compulsion to repeat (cf. Bruhm 2002: 272). As we will see in Chapter 2, the mechanisms of repetition, mechanical movement, liberation of drives, and (de)familiarization (as mentioned above) are also treated in psychoanalytical humor theory.

Psychoanalysis provides interesting insights into the roots of our emotions, especially fear, and the extent to which they control cognition. Ultimately, however, psychoanalysis of the uncanny results in the cognitive processing of oppositions, which requires cognitive mechanisms of uncovering and dissolving to overcome the emotions evoked. For this reason, cognitive horror theories are given priority in this book.

1.2.3 Cognitive horror approaches

Cognitive approaches to horror include a whole range of different theories such as Conversion Theory, Control Theory, Power Theory, Enjoyment or Evaluation Theory, and Compensation Theory. What they all have in common is that they try to attribute the reasons for fear and disgust, and also the audience's attraction to art-horror, to cognitive mechanisms: "Their key assumption is: emotions involve cognitions. Apart from a bodily feeling (a) and an object to which the person is intentionally directed (b), there must be a thought, belief, evaluation, or judgment involved that connects a) and b)" (Hanich 2010: 12–13).

They aim, on one hand, to define the nature of (supernatural) triggers of fear and disgust and, on the other, to explain which role the audience's cognition plays in the evocation of the emotions mentioned. This chapter briefly depicts these approaches with a special focus on Compensation Theory.

Conversion theory
Conversion approaches claim that the audience is interested in negative emotions because the experienced pain belongs to the beauty of the reception and turns into pleasure through the eloquence of the text. According to this approach, the audience is able to contemplate fear and disgust in the overall context of art, beauty, and passion (cf. Hume 1996 [1985]: 3–4) and thereby convert "the pain [. . .] into a larger, more pleasurable experience" (Smuts 2014: 8). The rich-experience approach is similar to conversion theory: Even though it admits the idea that there can be more reasons than (the transformation into) pleasure that attract viewers, the pain is described as "valuable, and, as such motivating" (Smuts 2014: 8) so that a positive experience eventually emerges.

Control and power theories
According to Control Theory, viewers enjoy painful art as long as they cognitively and mechanically control the arising emotions and know how to cope with them (cf. Morreall 1985: 97). The pain-inducing stimuli therefore must not be too strong and there must be ways of controlling the art-horror consumption individually or stopping it entirely:

> Control is usually easiest to maintain when we are merely attending to something which has no practical consequences for us, as when we watch from a distance some event unrelated to us. Here our control requires our ability to pay attention when we want, to stop paying attention when we want, and to direct our attention to those features of the event that interest us. When we have this ability to start, stop, and direct the experience, we can enjoy a wide range of experiences, even 'unpleasant ones'. (Morreall 1985: 97)

The loss of the familiar and of control, on the other hand, often cause fear and disgust in art-horror. Such forms of loss, however, are accompanied by a desire for control in the form of the "hope that the fear can be tolerated and mastered [. . .] This mixture of fear, pleasure and confident hope in the face of an external danger is what constitutes the fundamental elements of all *thrills*" (Balint 2018 [1959]: 23). According to Seeßlen (1995), *thrill* is excitement that follows a dramatic structure: The audience starts in a phase of rest, which gradually turns into increased arousal, and finally returns to the resting phase (cf. Seeßlen 1995: 13). The initial state of rest lets the audience yearn for something new; it is a state of cognitive boredom. The subsequent increase in danger, the unknown and morally and socially unexpected leads to an experience of fear, combined with the hope of a secure return (cf. Seeßlen 1995: 11,15,28). Similar to Morreall (1985), Seeßlen stated that the effect of fear had to be at a low level and easier to cope with than real fears of social or psychological threat, in order to satisfyingly overcome the fear (cf. Seeßlen 1995: 11) and to be strengthened for subsequent phases of rest and further thrills. Like the Aristotelian catharsis through tragedy (cf. Aristotle, Halliwell, Fyfe, Russell, Innes and Rhys Roberts 1995 [ca. 335 BC]: 1449b), Seeßlen spoke of a purification of the character, the attainment of a new self-confidence (cf. Seeßlen 1995: 15,28), and of "pleasure in one's own progress" (Seeßlen 1995: 19; transl. LS).

Theories that focus on power mechanisms link up with control approaches and assert that it is precisely the (cognitive) overcoming of fears and the awareness of human superiority over the threat that attract audiences to art-horror (cf. Smuts 2014: 8). Shaw (2003) and Stiglegger (2010) explained the audience's attraction to art-horror through a "dual identification with both the threatening antagonists and human protagonists" (Shaw 2003: 11) and the opposition of sovereignty and submission. While on one hand, art-horror seduces its audiences to identify with the "aggressor" (Stiglegger 2010: 25) and (virtually) feel sovereign to the foreign, other, and abused body (cf. Stiglegger 2010: 24–25), the audience on the other hand identifies with the victims of the plot and considers its own fears as "masochistic enjoyment" (cf. Stiglegger 2010: 25). "Our ambivalence is grounded in this tension between our guilty enjoyment [. . .] and the true terror [. . .] as well as this dual identification with both the monstrous force and with those who seek to conquer it" (Shaw 2003: 11). Stiglegger stated restrictively that these two proposed explanatory approaches needed the recipients' cognitive ability to distance themselves from reality and to enjoy the sadism while concurrently reflect the fictional status of art-horror and avoid their own traumatization (cf. Stiglegger 2010: 26).

It becomes evident that the pain of fear and disgust is not the sole characteristic of art-horror reception, but that moments of enjoyment and pleasure are added, triggered by cognitive control, power, or art.

Compensation theory

Another cognitive approach, called Compensation Theory or Hedonic Compensatory Solution, also searches for pleasurable aspects in art-horror. However, this approach claims it is not about enjoying (parts of) negative emotions themselves. Instead, it is about compensating them cognitively (cf. Smuts 2014: 8) by the aforementioned pleasurable elements, like an artistically valuable implementation of the art-horror content that outweighs the negative experience and turning art-horror into a worthy candidate for reception. "We get more pleasure than displeasure, or pain, from watching horror movies. The pleasure compensates for the pain" (Smuts 2014: 8).

Carroll (1990) has established the most cited, but also most criticized, theory of compensation. He claimed the audience was, by nature, curious and inclined to learn more about potentially impossible objects such as are found in the repertoire of horror described above. The revelation of new information during the horror plot therefore means pleasure to the audience. However, the newly introduced objects in horror fictions blurred features that would normally belong to different categories and thereby cause cognitive processing challenges for the audience. Referring to Douglas (1970 [1966]), Carroll deduced the idea of categorical impurity or interstitialty of the art-horror objects. A crawling lobster in the ocean served as an example for beings that transgress cultural categories and are therefore regarded as impure. The lobster is both an aquatic animal and thus semantically assigned to [+ swimming] as well as a terrestrial animal as he uses the seabed to move [+ crawling]. It is an animal that cannot be clearly sorted into a single cultural category and is therefore impure (cf. Carroll 1990: 31–32). Carroll emphasized that impurity is about unifying "categorical oppositions such as me/not me, inside/outside, and living/dead" (Carroll 1990: 32). He enumerated opposing concepts by referring to excreted body fluids which, on the one hand, belonged to man but, on the other hand, had already left the body and were therefore no longer categorically pure: feces, "spittle, blood, tears, sweat, hair clippings, vomit, nail clippings, pieces of flesh" (Carroll 1990: 32). The clash of opposing concepts culminates in Carroll's definition of the supernatural monster, which he even understood as the distinctive moment of art-horror. Monsters are equated with impurity since they are "creatures that specialize in formlessness, incompleteness, categorical interstitialty, and categorical contradictoriness" (Carroll 1990: 32).

Similar to the already shown repertoire of horror where the relation of a part to its whole is an integral part of the horror repertoire (cf. Seeßlen and Jung 2006: 77–79), Carroll's monsters are an in-between where parts of different totalities form a new whole. Indeed, the characters and places of the repertoire of horror frequently combine oppositional structures or contradictory concepts: The werewolf is both wolf and man, zombies and mummies are simultaneously dead and alive, and Frankenstein is both newborn and old (see Chapter 1.1). Impurity breaks cultural norms, categories, concepts, and schemata, and thereby cognitively challenges the audience. In art-horror, danger, and harmfulness poison impurity, which thereby becomes fearsome itself. Carroll called this process "toxification" (Carroll 1999: 158).

The bodily reaction to fearsome impurity consists of fear and disgust which accompany the revelation of the unknown and hardly understandable. But to satisfy curiosity, the audience is willing to accept these negative emotions as adverse effects (cf. Carroll 2003: 8–9). The experience of art-horror is the "price we are willing to pay" (Carroll 1990: 186) for the cognitive pleasures of discovery. Indeed, Zuckerman's work on sensation seeking supports the curiosity approach experimentally. While sensation seeking is defined as "the need for varied, novel, and complex sensations and experiences and the willingness to take physical and social risks for the sake of such experience" (Zuckerman 2015 [1979]: 10), it is primarily understood as seeking for "sensory effects of external stimulation" (Zuckerman 1994: 10). Yet, "it is not incompatible with intellectual curiosity" (Zuckerman 2015 [1979]:10) and correlates with "attendance at 'X'-rated movies" (Zuckerman 2015 [1979]: 248).[10] Aldana Reyes (2016) also supported Carroll's theory by claiming that "fear-inducing stimuli are also the ones that most consistently capture human attention and for which there is most rapid target detection, a fact that is probably connected to evolutionary developments" (Aldana Reyes 2016: 101). In Chapter 3.4 and 4, we will learn more about how emotions influence audience's reactions (e.g., processing speed).

Thought theory
The corporeal reaction also shows that the audience's thoughts about threatening objects and the challenge to cognitively process them suffice to cause emotions (Thought Theory). This explains why it is possible at all to be afraid of fiction, and thus, of something that does not exist (cf. Carroll 1990: 80; Smuts 2014: 13). Carroll's reflections correlate with findings from studies on motor imagery which show that the mere thought or mental simulation of a movement features the same temporal activation characteristics (cf. Decety and Michel 1989) and neuronal patterns (cf. Sirigu, Duhamel, Cohen, Pillon, Dubois and Agid 1996; Jeannerod 2001; Savaki and Raos 2019) as the actual execution of that movement. To transfer these findings into emotional reactions during art-horror reception, Smuts (2003) derived a circular feedback system in which the physiological reactions triggered by visual stimuli and the awareness of them (thought) reinforced the emotion experienced and vice versa (cf. Smuts 2003: 161).

Furthermore, although each viewer's reaction is unique and subjective, the reactions and emotions of the fictious characters visually prime[11] the audience to

---

[10] The so-called X-rating refers to movies that are intended specifically for adults because they explicitly stage violence and sexuality. Many horror movies are included in this category. In Germany, today, such movies would receive a recommendation of FSK (Freiwillige Selbstkontrolle der Filmwirtschaft, Self-Regulatory Body of the Movie Industry) for the age of 18 or above.

[11] In cognitive psychology, so-called *priming* refers to the memory effect in which a first stimulus passively and unconsciously influences the reaction to a second stimulus by invoking implicit knowledge (cf. Brandstätter, Schüler, Puca and Lozo (2018): 108) through "perceptual, semantic or conceptual stimulus repetition" (Hsu and Schütt (2012): vii). For example, priming can influence cognitive processing through previously evoked emotions.

evaluate a painful, threatening art-horror situation and subliminally influence[12] the emotions of the audience (cf. Baumann 1989: 285; Carroll 1999: 149; Smuts 2003: 161; Rymarczyk, Żurawski, Jankowiak-Siuda and Szatkowska 2016: 6). Since Carroll assumed that the biggest identification potential for the recipients was provided by the threatened, human victims, he argued that spectators were scared and disgusted concurrently with the victims: "The character [. . .] is horrified, while the audience member is art-horrified" (Carroll 1990: 91). At this point, Smuts (2003) contributed to Thought Theory that the fictitious scenario had to be authentic and credible to seduce the audience into consuming art-horror. As this was ideally done by denying the knowledge of the fictitious, non-real characters, Smuts referred to it as "disbelief mitigation" (Smuts 2003: 158).

Art-horror, monsters, and impurity

Eventually, Carroll defined art-horror through the entity of a monster (at least one). According to him, this monster had to be impure, that is lying in-between two categories, and threatening. It scared the recipients if they believed in its potential existence and if they were physically agitated. Carroll summarized the elements of art-horror as follows:

> Assuming that 'I-as-audience-member' am in an analogous emotional state to that which fictional characters beset by monsters are described to be in, then: I am occurrently art-horrified by some monster X, say Dracula, if and only if 1) I am in some state of abnormal, physically felt agitation (shuddering, tingling, screaming, etc.) which 2) has been *caused* by a) the thought: that Dracula is a possible being; and by the evaluative thoughts: that b) said Dracula has the property of being physically (and perhaps morally and socially) threatening in the ways portrayed in the fiction and that c) said Dracula has the property of being impure, where 3) such thoughts are usually accompanied by the desire to avoid the touch of things like Dracula. (Carroll 1990: 27)

Carroll's focus on the supernatural monster has been widely criticized for "overintellectualiz[ing] a rather somatic experience" (Hanich 2010: 5) while excluding horror narratives based on more realistic threats like serial murders, psychic

---

[12] In neurocognitions, the term *emotional contagion* describes the phenomenon that the emotional facial expressions, voices, postures, and movements of a human sender can be transmitted to receivers. The transfer, in which mirror neurons play an important role, takes place in three steps: (1) Imitation/Mimicry of the observed; (2) Feedback as an attribution of imitation and associated emotion; and (3) Infection as an empathetic, conscious reliving of the other's emotion (cf. Hatfield, Carpenter and Rapson 2014: 114). Wróbel and Imbir (2019) subsume emotional contagion to priming.

disorders, and "diegetic evil, transcendent forces that the audience must imagine" (Hills 2003: 143) – among them horror classics like *Psycho* or *The Shining*. While Carroll initially summarized the latter cases under a new, disgust excluding category, called *art-dread* (cf. Carroll 1990: 42; Freeland 2004), he later responded to the critique by adding the art-horror component called "science fictions of the mind" (Carroll 1995: 68). This category includes mental disorders such as those of Norman Bates or Hannibal Lector and differs from the already established art-horror component of "science fictions of the body" (Carroll 1995: 68) with a focus on the known supernatural monsters. Carroll argued that there was no need to develop a new approach like Gaut's Enjoyment Theory or Evaluation Theory (cf. Gaut 1993; cf. Gaut 1995), since his theory was able to adapt to the criticized shortcomings (cf. Carroll 1995: 68) through the new category of mind fiction. His differentiation between art-horror components of mind and body fictions agrees with Baumann's idea that the emotion of fear occurred as reaction to a psychic threat, while disgust was a reaction to a physical threat (cf. Baumann 1989: 219,239). However, it ignores that disgust can also be caused through morally inacceptable behavior. Carroll countered criticism that stereotypical, well-known plots could not satisfy curiosity by stating that plots were stereotypical because they functioned so well (cf. Carroll 1995: 69).

In line with Smuts' claim "that fear is precisely what we seek from a good horror movie [. . . and that fear] is not the price, but the reward" (Smuts 2014: 9), Gaut (1993) criticized Carroll's analogy between a negatively evaluated object and a subsequent negative emotion. Gaut claimed that even though people stereotypically did not enjoy negative emotions, the relation between object, evaluation, and emotion was not contingent. Thus, a negatively evaluated object could cause positive emotions. This conceptual redefinition included the possibility of enjoying negative emotions and neglected the paradox of art-horror (cf. Gaut 1993: 343–344):

> The evaluative theory holds that emotions are individuated in terms of their evaluative contents, and to say that something is disvaluable does not entail that it is unpleasant. So what makes emotions negative is not their feeling unpleasant, but their involving negative evaluations[.] Hence as far as concerns its individuation-conditions, it is possible to enjoy having a negative emotion. (Gaut 1995: 287)

Elaborating on the potential enjoyment of negative emotions like fear and disgust, Feagin (1991) argued that it also comprised three meta-pleasures consisting of (1) the pleasure of expressing the negative emotion, (2) the pleasure of experiencing this pleasure, and (3) a moment of pride that one was able to have such pleasures (cf. Feagin 1991: 83–84). According to Feagin, Carroll's monster is not necessary for the enjoyment of being art-horrified. The monster triggers art-horror but is not itself the actual object of fear or disgust. Feagin illustrated this consideration with an example of discarded clothing in the dark that were draped like a silhouette of a man: While the illusion of the man was triggered by the clothing, it was not the clothing itself that was feared (cf. Feagin 1991: 78). Carroll's focus on monsters was further critiqued by Hills (2003) who widened the art-horror definition through an event-based approach (cf. Hills 2003: 138–139) albeit ignoring Carroll's own extended art-horror scope. He expanded the idea of the monster into "entities that 1) violate cultural categories, 2) inspire revulsion and disgust, and 3) cue a sense of threat" (Hills 2003: 142). The latter threatening effect was only possible through "the representation of narrative events such as the victim shrinking away from the monster" (Hills 2003: 142). According to Hills, the events are the *"only necessary and sufficient conditions of art-horror"* (Hills 2003: 143). He contrasted events with coincidental happenings without the agency/action of an entity (cf. Hills 2003: 148). Most recently, Aldana Reyes (2016) summarized Feagin's and Hill's critiques by arguing that "the monster is not the marker of the emotion of horror, but [. . .] a mere catalyst that can be replaced by events, situations, objects and even the mutilation or dismemberment of the body in isolation" (Aldana Reyes 2016: 98).

Despite all criticisms and extensions, it is Carroll's transfer of Douglas' concept of impurity to art-horror that has made an important contribution to the understanding of how art-horror is processed cognitively. By emphasizing broken categories and the union of opposing concepts (real/unreal, possible/impossible, normal/abnormal and certain/threatened), Carroll initiates a cognitive art-horror model that explains how these concepts come together (through the repertoire of horror) and which challenges they cause to cognition. The understanding of art-horror as representation of oppositions makes it possible to create sequential models which explain art-horror sources and predict its effects on recipients systematically from a cognitive, psycholinguistic perspective. Furthermore, his concept of categorical interstitiality bridges the gap to research fields which investigate similar processing mechanisms. In the course of this book, we will see that incongruity theories in humor research investigate the same cognitive mechanisms.

Art-horror and cognition: Cognitive dissonances
From a cognitive perspective, further research on art-horror oppositions came from Grodal (2000) who deepened the understanding of oppositional structures and the cognitive processing of art-horror through his concept of *cognitive dissonance*. He abstracted the horror repertoire with its characters, places, and actions by entirely attributing it to the opposition of cognitive models. Even though

Grodal did not clearly define his understanding of mental models as reference systems for incoming information, according to him, art-horror lacks cognitive consistency since "the protagonists are caught between two different models and interpretations of a given set of facts" (Grodal 2000: 245). These facts were brought together, for example, through "'false causality', combining the effect of the fictively established 'causality' and a strongly motivating emotion (fear of death, or loss of body/mind autonomy), and, further, by undermining the 'belief in science'" (Grodal 2000: 249). Thus, the protagonists (and the audience) were not able to integrate the experienced situation into "consistent representations of the world" (Grodal 2000: 245). This dissonance, which could already be called incongruity in terms of a later comparison of art-horror and humor, allows more than a single interpretation of the ambiguous experience; it is subsequently defined as "an arousal state with aversive emotional properties" (Grodal 2000: 246). Grodal illustrated cognitive dissonance using Crichton's movie *Coma* (1978) as an example, where a friend of the protagonist dies during a minor, non-dangerous operation. According to the narrative strategy of the garden path (see Chapter 1.1), only later does it turn out that her death was a planned murder to sell her organs. As such, two contradictory mental models and their emotional association collapse in the concept of the hospital including the reading of a healing, potentially life-saving operation and an immoral, profit-oriented homicide (cf. Grodal 2000: 246). The protagonist and the audience are mentally confronted with "[. . .] two opposed functions coupled to the two opposed intentions, to cure and to kill, and with two opposed emotional values [. . .]" (Grodal 2000: 247). Grodal argued that the dissociation was the detection that the initially assumed reading of the hospital as a safe and good place was actually evil (cf. Grodal 2000: 247). Rejecting psychoanalytical theories, Grodal reinforced his cognitive approach by claiming that "the basis of fear in thrillers and horror stories is therefore, in some respects, rational" (Grodal 2000: 249). He showed that the different approaches mentioned at the beginning of this chapter (control, compensation, evaluation) are not mutually exclusive: On one hand, he combined Carroll's reflections (subsumed to compensatory theory) with control theories; "the explicit motivation for horror fiction is [. . .] a desire for cognitive and physical control: the problem is choosing the appropriate schemata" (Grodal 2000: 249). On the other hand, in line with Smuts (2014), he highlighted the importance of cognitive evaluation[13] of input information to trigger emotional reactions; "arousal is dependent on a cognitive evaluation, which can either be positive, in which case a further increase in arousal is experienced

---

[13] For more information on Appraisal Theory, see Chapter 3.4.

as positive, or negative, in which case only a decrease in arousal is pleasurable" (Grodal 2000: 252).

So far, there are no experimental approaches that attest the cognitive art-horror approaches presented here. However, there are studies that deal with the emotional reaction to art-horror. These are presented in Chapter 3 in the light of psycholinguistic models of language comprehension and in comparison with analogous humor models that have already been investigated experimentally.

1.3 Intermediate results

Art-horror is a cross-art, cross-media genre aimed at triggering emotional reactions of fear, disgust, surprise, and pleasure. Starting as Gothic Novels during the 18th century, art-horror today comprises a great variety of dark contents and thrilling, narrative strategies. The repertoire of horror includes supernatural monsters and interstitial, impure beings (including vampires, zombies, hybrids, or witches), mystified geographies like dark castles, and realistic threats through psychically abnormal protagonists, conspiracies, violent sexuality, and cannibalism. The repertoire can be understood through the union of oppositions like normality/abnormality, reality/unreality, safety/danger, health/sickness, or good/bad. Potential narrative strategies include complex discovery plots, with onset/discovery/confirmation/confrontation, overreacher plots, with preparation/implementation/escalation/confrontation, or garden paths with seduction/late discovery/resolution.

Emotions are generally defined as an interacting, motivating system of subjective, temporary, psychic experiences with cognitive, goal-directed evaluations; they are objectively measurable physiological reactions like sweating, heart rate or blood pressure. A qualitative distinction describes basic emotions including the art-horror emotions of fear and disgust:

Fear comprises an agonizing, oppressing affective state of consciously, intraindividually experienced arousal, threat, tension, and concern with a heightened activity of the autonomic nervous system. The person who experiences fear stereotypically tries to avoid fearsome situations by adapting to the given situation and activating coping strategies. In addition to state anxiety as a directed emotion to a threatening situation, object or symbol, trait anxiety describes non-directed intuition of an imminent danger.

Disgust is an emotion of oral, olfactory, aural, and visual rejection that psychologically as well as physiologically protects against bodily (through bad food or excretions) and psychic (through unethical behavior) contamination. The emotion of disgust can cause nausea and the motivation to close all bodily channels by, for example, nose wrinkling, narrowing of the eyes, or opening them to repel the contaminated material.

The emotion of surprise is understood more cognitively. It is itself perceived neither positively nor negatively, but prepares the more concrete, emotional processing of art-horror. After a phase of incongruity detection and interruption of the ongoing activity, the moment of surprise contributes to the positive or negative evaluation of the input and the adaptation to the stimulus so that further emotions, like fear or disgust, can occur and accompany the adaptation phase.

Smut's paradox of painful art and especially Carroll's paradox of horror describe the question of why recipients like to consume art-horror even though they would avoid threatening, fearsome and disgusting situations in real life.

Psychoanalytical theories trace the art-horror experience back to a return of repressed emotions or surmounted beliefs, to infantile complexes and a competition of the drive-controlled id and the rational instance of the superego. Exploring the term uncanny, psychoanalysis describes human relations to familiar, trustworthy situations and how this relation is disturbed through death, animistic superstition, uncertainty about reality, and human repetition compulsions. Psychoanalytical approaches also discuss how identification with the victims of art-horror is crucial for a frightening reception and note that art-horror can also evoke fear through the lack of identification potential and staging of ambiguity in the abject. Monsters are understood as the dramatized repression and a master narrative is defined as the loss of civilizing processes, their restoration through horror, and the repelling/return to the starting point. On one hand, psychoanalysis aims to describe unhealthy desires and create adequate therapies, but on the other hand, offers insights into how far art-horror's broken taboos, like incest, patricide, or revenge, can be enjoyed. Even though psychoanalysis offers possibilities for art-horror interpretation, it effectively finds that cognitive processing of oppositional concepts precedes a potential therapeutic effect. Therefore, cognitive horror theories are given priority in this work.

In addition to determining horror content in the sense of a comprehensive outline of the genre, cognitive theories attempt to trace the causes of the triggered emotions back to cognitive mechanisms and answer the question to what extent viewers are willing to expose themselves to stimuli that trigger negative emotions (paradox of painful art). Conversion Theory claims that humans are able to view anxiety and disgust causing stimuli in a larger, artistic context and enjoy the transformed content. Control Theory claims that the extent to which the content can be controlled by the audience influences the degree of triggered horror. The Power Approach shows strong similarities to Control Theory while focusing on feelings of superiority through a dual identification with the attacker and victim. The Enjoyment and Evaluation Theories separate the evaluation of a stimulus from the evaluation of an emotion and deduce that negative stimuli can be experienced positively, negating the horror paradox.

Compensation Theory, in particular Carroll's approach, attributes the audience's interest in art-horror to the stimulation and satisfaction of curiosity and fascination and regards the negative feelings of art-horror as the price to be paid for this satisfaction. Carroll also transfers Douglas' concept of impurity to the art-horror repertoire, claiming that characters break cultural categories by uniting contradictory concepts. This impurity causes cognitive effort and leads to the negative emotions of fear and disgust. Gaut, Feagin, and Hills refine Carroll's theory adding more realistic threats to the initially distinctive features of the supernatural monster. Grodal then deepens the idea of oppositional structures and abstracts the mechanisms that trigger art-horror entirely to the confrontation of mental representation systems. According to him, it is not possible for the art-horror recipients to create cognitive consistency between the opposite models combined through, for example, false causality.

In this book, I pursue a cognitive definition of art-horror and interpret it as the union of incongruous, cognitive concepts like life/death, normality/abnormality, reality/unreality, or safety/danger which break cultural categories and, thereby, cause cognitive processing costs and the negative emotions of, in particular, fear and disgust, as well as surprise and pleasure. A cognitive art-horror model which explains and predicts stages of a chronological or incremental processing attested by empirical data does not yet exist. Experimentally attested processing models involving incongruity do exist for the phenomenon of humor which shares crucial contents, narrative strategies, and cognitive mechanisms with art-horror. To make insights of humor research theoretically and methodologically fruitful for art-horror, the following chapter identifies similarities between the two phenomena and transfers humor findings and methodological merits to art-horror; it addresses the question of how it is possible that two genres, which trigger such opposing emotions, show similar underlying cognitive mechanisms.

2 Humor: How to smile about incongruity

> The audience at Hollywood's Dolby Theater was spellbound
> when the disguised moderator opened the golden envelope.
> 'Row 1. Seat 9.' was written on the card.
> She pulled out the golden raspberry.
> (adapted from: Meimberg 2011: 34; transl. LS)

Funniness, hilariousness, laughter, amusement, joy, exhilaration[14] – the notion of *humor* evokes a variety of positive associations and emotions.[15] To establish an initial common ground, humor can be understood as a communication mode and the individual ability to make use of it, as a source of laughter and positive emotions. For example, the positively evaluated emotion of exhilaration as a short-term facet of joy is directly connected with successful humor. The physiological reaction is comprised of, in particular, laughter – an adapted respiration of high frequency and low amplitude with facial expressions including (inter alia; further details in Chapter 4.3) raised corners of the mouth, tense muscles around the eyes, and raised cheeks (cf. Ruch 2000: 231–232; Ekman 2010 [2003]: 288). The understanding of humor will be sharpened in the course of this chapter.

Why compare art-horror and humor

Reviewing existing art-horror and humor comparisons makes evident the role humor plays in this work. Since, as Carroll emphasized, "it appears that these two mental states – being horrified and being comically amused – could not be more different" (Carroll 1999: 147), this chapter sets out to ask, to quote Carroll, how "such broadly opposite affects can attach to the same stimulus" (Carroll 1999: 145) and to what extent humor and art-horror resemble each other. Despite the different emotional reactions, similarities between humor and art-horror are often observed in horror research. Not only because there are special genres such as splatstick[16] or

---

[14] English dictionaries present two meanings for *exhilaration*: "to make cheerful, merry" and "to invigorate, stimulate" (Collins Dictionary 2021). The latter meaning is not included in the German translation of *Erheiterung* (cf. Ruch 1993). According to its Latin origin (Latin: ex-hilarare = to cheer), the notion of exhilaration is understood in this book as a raise in cheerfulness.
[15] Unless one suffers from gelotophobia – the fear of being laughed at (see Chapter 4.3).
[16] In reference to the genre of slapstick, this amalgamation refers to horror films, which drive the element of bloody splatter to extremes and thereby achieve comic effects.

black humor that intentionally combine the two phenomena, but also because humor and art-horror merge into each other in unintended situations.

An example of humor and art-horror merging was identified by Aldana Reyes (2016). He observed that the drastic body exploitation in art-horror could cause more than fear and disgust, "because of their histrionics, may bring it into contact with comedy and 'gross out' Horror or 'splatstick'" (Aldana Reyes 2016: 88). He also claimed that the monster could be more than threatening by demonstrating that in horror-comedies, such as Henenlotter's *Basket Case 2* (1990) or Craig's *Tucker and Dale vs. Evil* (2010), monsters served as a "source of laughter, depending on treatment" (Aldana Reyes 2016: 92).

Paul (1994) had previously touched on the comparison between humor and art-horror and highlighted that the crucial comparative moment between the two phenomena was ambivalence. It is the ambivalence of both the monster, as "anarchic force that is worth celebrating as much as it is worth fearing, something we want to embrace and pull away from at the same time" (Paul 1994: 418–419), as well as of gross-out, "as an art of inversion" (Paul 1994: 420), that unites the two genres. He further observed that gross-out "is a mode moving in two directions at once, the horror films may invoke comedy, while the comedies take on suddenly nightmarish imagery. Gross-out vacillates between extremes within each individual work, much as these two allied genres of horror and comedy travel in seemingly opposite directions" (Paul 1994: 419).

Following the idea of a common, superordinate mechanism bridging art-horror and humor, Carroll (1999) argued that the two phenomena "share one condition" (Carroll 1999: 157), namely their categorical interstitialty. This criterion has already been discussed for art-horror and Carroll claimed that it also applied to humor to the same extent. Carroll found that only the fearsomeness of the stimulus decided the content's genre: "horror equals categorical transgression or jamming plus fear; incongruity humor equals, in part, categorical transgression or jamming minus fear" (Carroll 1999: 157). The harmless figure of Chewbacca in Lucas' *Star Wars* (1977) served to illustrate the observed proximity of horror and comedy characters, as Carroll compared it to the similar-looking but menacing monster in Landers' *The Return of the Vampire* (1943) (cf. Carroll 1999: 149): "the same figure – say the monster [. . .] can look and act in exactly the same way; they can be perceptually indiscernible. Yet, one provokes horror and the other provokes humor" (Carroll 1999: 147). Subtracting the fearsomeness from art-horror or adding it to humorous incongruity, Carroll thereby offered a solution to how art-horror and humor merge (cf. Carroll 1999: 156,158).

These comparisons show that humor and art-horror not only easily turn into each other but that they are even comparable regarding their implementation of incongruities. "On the map of mental states, horror and incongruity amusement are adjacent and partially overlapping regions" (Carroll 1999: 156). Humor research already offers important contributions to explain incongruity mechanisms which – as I will show in Chapters 2.3 and 4 – are also suitable to explain art-horror cognitively. Therefore, the incongruity mechanisms are examined in more detail in the course of this book to comprehensively grasp linguistic similarities and differences between humor and art-horror and to make humor findings applicable to art-horror theory.

In this chapter, the historical origins of humor theory are illuminated as well as its social and psychoanalytical conditions (Chapter 2). The following section sheds light on the notion of incongruity and cognitive processing of humor, from a psycholinguistic perspective (Chapter 2.2). Finally, theoretical and experimental findings are transferred to art-horror with the notion of incongruity serving as tertium comparationis between humor and art-horror (Chapter 2.3). This transfer serves as the foundation for an experimental comparison of humor and art-horror, regarding cognitive processes, and costs for incongruity and its resolution.

2.1 Humor theories: From antiquity to modern approaches

In contrast to art-horror, humor research has a long tradition and goes back to antiquity, starting with Greek philosophers writing about the ridiculous and comedy. This chapter explores the history of philosophical humor theory through the work of important authors from antiquity until modern approaches.[17]

Humor theories in antiquity

In one of the earliest records mentioning comedy, Plato (427–347 BC) wrote in Philebus (50) about laughter as a combination of pleasure in and envy of (thus pain) the comedy on stage and in life. Although the ambivalent emotions of pleasure and pain seemed to exclude each other, they appeared simultaneously (Plato, Fowler and Lamb 1925: 339–341). This early explanatory approach already revealed a relation between incongruent emotions and circumstances; therefore, it is considered to be the prototype of ambivalence theories, a theoretical family which only differs from modern incongruity theories (see Chapter 2.2) in its focus on emotions instead of ideas (cf. Keith-Spiegel 1972: 10). Plato called those people

---

[17] For a broader overview of ancient humor theory see Attardo (1994).

ridiculous, who did not know themselves, were weak and could not fight aggressors who laugh at them (cf. Plato, Fowler and Lamb 1925: 337). Frede speculated (that based on Plato's definition of humor), an interest in someone's harm and comic was therefore to be interpreted as negative and unfair (cf. Plato, Frede and Heitsch 1997: 287–288) and should be shown only towards enemies; this insinuated the exclusiveness of a deriding group. Plato's theory is therefore also prototypical for humor explanations focusing on aggressions and the opposition of a strong and a weak person (cf. Attardo 1994: 19).

Succeeding Plato, Aristotle (384–322 BC) enhanced comedy theory and described it as "mimesis of baser but not wholly vicious characters" (Aristotle, Halliwell, Fyfe, Russell, Innes and Rhys Roberts 1995 [ca. 335 BC]: 45). For him, the ridiculous was ugly, erroneous and deformed. Being the incongruent adversary, the ridiculous was opposed to the pleasant and right. Unlike Plato, Aristotle neglected that the ridiculous caused pain and thus laughter was regarded as positive feeling (cf. Aristotle, Halliwell, Fyfe, Russell, Innes and Rhys Roberts 1995 [ca. 335 BC]: 45). Aristotle countered Plato by stating that the soul was not overwhelmed by laughter but that the laughter stimulated the soul and even evoked benevolence (cf. Plebe 1952: 15–16; Attardo 1994: 19). He described the unexpected as another source for laughter in which words with several readings or metaphors could be used by the speaker for surprise effects (cf. Aristotle 1984: III, 111412b; Attardo 1994: 20). Thereby, Aristotle highlighted the role of surprise and of ambiguity for the evocation of laughter. He located the ridiculous in comedy and separated it from tragedy. He described the comedy with regard to its realistic content and standardized the three unities of action, time and place (cf. Plebe 1952: 14; Attardo 1994: 21).

Aristotle's work is preserved in the *Tractatus Coislinianus* (10th century) in which he differentiated between verbal and referential sources of laughter: "Laughter arises (I) from the diction [= expression] (II) from the things [= content]" (Aristotle and Cooper 1922: 224; square brackets in the original). For verbal humor, Aristotle enumerated "homonyms, synonyms, garrulity [repetitions], paronyms formed by addition and clipping, diminutives, perversion by the voice [or] by other means of the same word, grammar and syntax" (Aristotle and Cooper 1922: 225). Referential humor, he claimed, was evoked

> by the things from assimilations, employed toward the worse [and] toward the better, from deception, from the impossible, from the possible and inconsequent, from the unexpected, from debasing the personage, from the use of clownish (pantomimic) dancing, when one of those having power, neglecting the greatest things, takes the most worthless, when the story is disjointed, and has no sequence (Aristotle and Cooper 1922: 225)

We already saw in Chapter 1 that elements of these enumerations, like repetitions, the opposition of possible/impossible, the unexpected or humiliations, are also crucial for the evocation of art-horror.

At approximately the same time, Hippocrates (460–370 BC) developed the medical theory of *humorism* to which the etymological origin of the word humor can be attributed. In *On the nature of men* and *On the humors* in *Corpus Hippocraticum*, Hippocrates medically defined four bodily fluids known as *humores* that determined as person's health. These four fluids were blood, yellow bile, black bile, and phlegm. According to Hippocrates, these fluids corresponded to a cosmic element (air, water, earth, fire) and a quality (hot, cold, dry, wet), and they dominated each in one season of the year (spring, summer, autumn, winter) and during an age of life (childhood, youth, prime and old age) (cf. Hippocrates, Heraclitus of Ephesus, Jones and Potter 1931: 19–27; Stelmack and Stalikas 1991: 258–260). Surplus quantities of one fluid deranged the fluid balance, lead to diseases and should be removed (cf. Hippocrates, Heraclitus of Ephesus, Jones and Potter 1931: 7,11; Golder 2007: 136–137).

Several centuries later, Galen (~125–215 AC) enhanced Hippocrates' theory by linking medical symptoms to the (combination of) body fluids. Galen developed four temperaments (from Latin *temperare*: combining in a balanced manner) to describe a person's susceptibility to illness, their constitution and physiognomy. He called the temperaments according to the dominant fluid: sanguine, choleric, phlegmatic, and melancholic (cf. Stelmack and Stalikas 1991: 259). Although Galen's theory was primarily a medical one, he and his followers started to associate a person's character (as symptoms for a disease) with the temperaments. For example, the melancholic temperament with a dominance of black bile was associated with depression and anxiety (cf. Stelmack and Stalikas 1991: 260). Later on, Kant 1912 [1798] described the behavioral components of a temperament in detail so that the humour theory became an anthropological one. Henceforth, "humour referred to a more or less predominant mood quality either positive (good humour) or negative (bad humour)" (Ruch 1998: 8). Eysenck and Eysenck (1987) developed the temperament theory further and included the temperaments into their dimensional personality system. Here, the temperaments were distributed over two axes, one representing stable/instable and the other extraverted/introverted, each with numerous characteristics (cf. Eysenck and Eysenck 1987: 45): People considered to have an overload of the fluid blood had a sanguine temperament, characterized by carelessness, agility and a good ability to respond. Sanguine people showed an extraverted and stable personality. An excess of yellow bile was considered to lead to a choleric temperament described as active and optimistic and extraverted but also aggressive, disquieted, and affected by a high instability. The third personality type was the melancholic, dominated by black bile, which was considered to lead to pessimism, fearfulness, a dark mood, introversion, and instability. The patients with an excess of phlegm was peaceful, calm and controlled, they were introverted and instable (cf. Eysenck and Eysenck 1987: 45; Kagan 1994: 2–3). Along this line, it will be shown that the notion of *mood* or *atmosphere* evolved from this theory.

Humor theories and the Latins

Latins, above all Cicero (106–43 BC) and Quintilian (35–100 AC) investigated the nature of humor (as a phenomenon). In his work *De Oratore*, Cicero discussed the to what extent humor was important for appropriate rhetorics of a speaker and which genres could be deduced subsequently (cf. Cicero, Sutton and Rackham 1942: 373). He elaborated on the difference between verbal and referential humor: People laughed about both, the words (*in verbo*) and the facts (*in re*) (cf. Cicero, Sutton and Rackham 1942: 377, 383). If people laugh about something said, they laugh about ambiguities, something unexpected, a word play, quotations of verses or proverbs, taking a figurative expression literally, allegories, metaphors, irony, or antithetical expressions (cf. Cicero, Sutton and Rackham 1942: 385–397). The activation of an appropriate and less appropriate interpretation lies, per definition, in the ambiguity so that an incongruity easily arises between the two readings. Similarly, an opposition occurs in literal readings of a figurative expression that manifests itself between the intended speech figure and the literal meaning of the word. If someone intends to laugh about *re*, anecdotes and caricatures are suitable. Cicero even elaborated on the controllability of verbal and referential instances, by proposing the translation of a certain passage in a foreign language to test if the reader laughed about a translatable concept or if the source for laughter was the exact wording. Cicero focused, here, on the wittiness of concrete words; paraphrases and conversion of the precise wording could suffocate the laughter quickly (cf. Cicero, Sutton and Rackham 1942: 389). This hypothesis was later criticized by Attardo who argued that a professional translator would find equivalent expressions for the target language, and thus, the *in verbi* would become translatable (cf. Attardo 1994: 29).

These antique discussions about the phenomenon of incongruity and the differentiation between the sources of laughter are the foundation for modern incongruity theories (see Chapter 2.2). Quintilian, who is additionally considered as one of the first authors of relaxation theories, developed the incongruity theories further:

Quintilian wrote about laughter in the context of pedagogical education and adapts and expands Cicero's ideas. He was the first to write about the importance of relaxation both as a physical and psychic source of laughter (cf. Attardo 1994: 30; Quintilian and Russell 2002 [1 AC – 100 AC]: 65 [VI-3–1]). With a focus on the social functions of laughter and who is being laughed at, Quintilian claimed that one laughed either about others, one's own group or something neutral; if one laughed about others, the laughter would function either as reproach, refusal, praise, or aversion. Quintilian interpreted laughter about one's own group or about oneself as either blunder or play. Laughter about a neutral topic comprises "deceiving expectations, taking words in a perverse sense, and other procedures which do not affect either party" (Quintilian and Russell 2002 [1 AC – 100 AC]: 75). Quintilian argued that laughter arose through (hypothetical) similarities or dissimilarities, which could be presented physically, in narrations or through remarks (cf. Quintilian and Russell 2002 [1 AC – 100 AC]: 81,95,107). He included linguistic phenomena, like different figures of speech (tropes, irony, metaphors, allegories or emphasis), into his list of sources of laughter (cf. Quintilian and Russell 2002 [1 AC – 100 AC]: 97–107).

Quintilian's texts laid the foundation for a modern understanding of linguistic incongruity. Attardo (1994) showed this by comparing Quintilian's understanding of ambiguity and the humorous opposition of possible and impossible events within script-based humor theories (cf. Attardo 1994: 32; Quintilian and Russell 2002 [1 AC – 100 AC]: 111) which will be elaborated in detail in Chapter 2.2. We have already seen that these oppositions are also crucial for the evocation of negative emotions and Quintilian recognized this. He acknowledged the darker side of humor through jokes that could have a bitter, cruel and aggressive character and could be used for derision (cf. Quintilian and Russell 2002 [1 AC – 100 AC]: 67,77,79).

Humor theories during Renaissance

Building upon the work of the Greeks and the Latins, the discussion about comedy continued during Renaissance. Vincenzo Maggi (Madius 1550) countered Aristotle's equation of comedy and ugliness, claiming ugliness alone did not suffice to cause laughter, as it rested when the laughter ended. He added that ugly but known circumstances did not provoke laughter, because a supplemental, surprising moment of incongruity was needed (cf. Maggi 1970 [1550]: 99; Attardo 1994: 37–39). During this period, physiological and psychological laughter were differentiated. Trissino (1562) countered that joy came from the senses and did not suffice to generate laughter. He repeated Aristotle's comment about the surprising moment and insisted that the appearance of something unexpected offended the senses and hopes; he equated humor with human malignity (cf. Trissino 1970 [1549]: 69–70; Attardo 1994: 40). In doing so, Trissino foreshadowed that malice can also lurk in the mechanism of surprise, and humor not only suits positive emotions but can also be used for or turn into effects of evil, fear and violence.

Hobbes (1739) then combined the surprise factor and negative effects of laughter showing they were both compatible in his laughter theory. He stressed the negative side of laughter and traced it back to the humorist's sudden impression of being superior to the person laughed at:

> The passion of Laughter is nothing else but *sudden Glory* arising from a sudden conception of some Eminency in ourselves, by comparison with the Infirmity of others, or with our own formerly: for men laugh at the Follies of themselves past, when they come suddenly to remembrance, except they bring with them any present Dishonour. It is no wonder therefore that men take heinously to be laughed at or derided, that is, triumphed over. Laughing without Offence, must be at absurdities and infirmities abstracted from persons, and when all the company may laugh together: for laughing to one's self putteth all the rest into jealousy, and examination of themselves. (Hobbes 1812 [1739]: 65)

In his perspective, laughter is part of a competition between the humorist and the person laughed at whereas the triumphant humorist degrades the opponent. These findings, which advanced Plato's ideas of laughter, led to Hobbes' also being regarded as the founder of the superiority theory.

Early modern approaches

The meaning of *humor* shifted to its modern use through Scottish moral philosophy during the 18th century. The humores of Hippocrates' humorism and Galen's temperament theory became understood as mood or temper allowing for the consideration of their instability and fugacity. Humor's meaning shifted from eccentric speech and extravagant behavior to a positive human ability with focus on its personal and interpersonal merits (cf. Preisendanz 2010b: 100). The notion of *humor* was revalued based on its positive effects in overcoming mockery and derision: it became a communication mode of creativity offering the possibility to actively refer to oneself and to reality. Humor became a non-binding communication mode and reflected the relation between ideality and reality, finiteness and infinity, and objective borders and subjective imagination (cf. Preisendanz 2010b: 101) "through the infinite diversity of subjective refraction of the real" (Preisendanz 2010a: 11144; transl. LS). Preisendanz even claimed that this new understanding of humor replaced the opposition between sublime and comic, since it alternatingly included pain and laughter. Simultaneously, he criticized that humor idealized negativity, adversity and imperfection (cf. Preisendanz 2010b: 101).

Through their claim that opposing ideas unexpectedly came together, Kant (2010 [1790]) and Schopenhauer (2010 [1819]) supplied the earliest of the modern incongruity approaches. Kant defined laughter as "an affect resulting from the sudden transformation of a heightened expectation into nothing" (Kant 2010 [1790]: §54; transl. LS). Thus, Kant focused on the suddenness of the incongruity and the respective resolution of tensions within the expectations of the listeners. Schopenhauer countered that it was to a lesser extent a matter of disappointed expectations and more importantly the surprising explanation. He disagreed with the idea that an affect dissolved into nothing and rather proposed that the affect transformed into the unexpected, incongruent stimulus (cf. Morreall 1983: 15). For Schopenhauer, "all laughter is occasioned by a paradoxical and hence unexpected subsumption, irrespective of whether it is expressed in words or deeds" (Schopenhauer 2010 [1819]: 84). He recognized that unexpectedness, surprise, the opposition real/unreal, and ambiguity played an important role in evoking laughter:

> *laughter* arises from nothing other than the sudden perception of an incongruity between a concept and the real objects that are, in some respect, thought through the concept; in fact laughter itself is simply the expression of this incongruity. It often occurs when two or more real objects are thought through a *single* concept that transfers its identity to them; but their very great difference in other respects makes it conspicuously obvious that the concept only applied to the objects in a very one-sided way.
> (Schopenhauer 2010 [1819]: 84)

The ambiguity of a concept allows for analogies between two signified concepts, even though one of them would normally not be interpreted in this way. Thus, unexpected und surprising interpretations occur through this combination of incongruent ideas.

Interdisciplinary perspectives on humor

Nowadays, humor is researched from separate disciplines (even though the single disciplines try to recognize interdisciplinary results). Literature studies, philosophy, psychology, cultural sciences, neurosciences, and linguistics all contribute to humor theory and aim at explaining causes and functions of humor and laughter. However, although they all stem from ancient and Latin ideas, they focus on different, intradisciplinary aspects and therefore offer different humor definitions and explanations – with varying foci on its social and psychological functions as well as on its cognitive processing. Thus, humor is not a consistently described phenomenon and the definitions of the core phenomenon vary in detail between disciplines. From a literary and philosophical perspective, humor is defined as a "fundamental aesthetic term of the modern age exerting and integrating every variety of comic" (Preisendanz 2010b: 100; transl. LS) with *comic* being defined as "objects, events, circumstances and expressions that cause laughter; or the property that produces this effect" (Kablitz 2010: 289; transl. LS). Humor covers both a communication mode and the individual ability or perspective of the world; it "is not a supratemporal, but a historically locatable phenomenon" (Preisendanz 2010b: 100; transl. LS), manifested through humor research lasting millennia. Literature studies use the notion of *humor* to classify text corpora categorically and find related or subordinate phenomena like comedy, irony, or sarcasm. Some definitions are even more general by determining *humor* as "a word that today is coined in colloquial language on everything that stands in relation to laughter" (Preisendanz 2010a: 11143; transl. LS). The research area of linguistics also bases its humor definition on the ancient foundations of ambivalence and adjoins psychological and neurocognitive ideas. Here, the phenomenon of incongruity is considered a precondition for laughter and is understood as the contrast between two combined cognitive concepts like surprisingly conjoined oppositions of normal and abnormal, real, and unreal, expectations and reality. Finally, from a psychological perspective, fundamental social functions described since the antiquity are discussed in detail, such as social correction to socially accepted behavior, relaxation from a tense emotional state, aggression, and superiority versus a threatening or unacceptable other.

Humor families

To categorize the numerous contributions to humor theory including ancient and modern approaches, Keith-Spiegel (1972) classified them into eight categories including biology/evolution, superiority, incongruity, surprise, ambivalence, release/relief, configuration, and psychoanalysis. "With emphasis on those aspects that are most important from a linguistic point of view" (Attardo 1994: 46), Attardo (1994) instead summarized the contributions into three, interdisciplinary families (see Table 1):

Table 1: Humor families (Attardo 1994: 47).

Social	Psychoanalytical	Cognitive
Hostility	Release	Incongruity
Aggression	Sublimation	Contrast
Superiority	Liberation	
Triumph	Economy	
Derision		
Disparagement		

Social humor theories

The first family of theories focuses on social humor mechanisms of degradation including mockery, disparagement, and triumph. It assumes that the person being laughed at – called the target or victim, analogous to art-horror terminology – is disparaged through a superior, aggressive, and hostile humorist or a social instance that aims at correcting the unwelcome person or their behavior: "our laughter is always the laughter of a group" (Bergson 1988: 15) illustrating the exclusiveness of the deriding group (cf. Attardo 1994: 50). The potential to identify with the aggressing, superior group is as seducing for the consumers as in art-horror. Beside the derided person, the recipients of the humorous instance can also be the target of a joke because they are faced with the challenge of understanding the joke and not become the ridiculous object of the humorist (cf. Sherzer 1985: 219). Humor contributes to the management of a social group by instrumentalizing norms and controlling deviant, tabooed behavior or circumstances through aggressive behavior (cf. Attardo 1994: 323), a social mechanism which was also observed for art-horror. Aggressive jokes also include dark motives such as "drollery in death, destruction, and disaster" (Gruner 1997: 41), which all belong to art-horror, too.

Laughter serves as expression for a sudden triumph and marks the rhetorical winner of a conversation (cf. Martin 2007: 45). Humor also conduces to the management of a discourse by marking the start and end point of a conversation. It is used to "establish common ground" (Attardo 1994: 324) implying the social corrective achieves more than degradation; if the additional cognitive processes to understand humor are mastered through an elevated cleverness, humorist and recipient are equal. "The ability to 'get the joke' gives the listener a feeling of superiority and victory, presumably over hypothetical others who might not be able to understand it" (Martin 2007: 46) and it enables "the listeners to share feelings of mastery and superiority along with the joke-teller" (Martin 2007: 46). In this context, the aspect of social play becomes important because the application of humor can establish comradeship, the affinity to the group and intimacy. Thus, humor can even repair a mislead conversation and is able to cancel displeasing expressions in a conciliatory way by exploiting its non-binding mode and focusing on play through phrases like 'It was just a joke!' (cf. Attardo 1994: 324, 328).

Emphasizing the negative mechanisms of humor, Bergson (1988) excluded emotions from the topic of humor because empathy for a derided person could not work in a humorous situation. He hypothesized that tragic incidents could become humorous by "isolating them from the accompanying music of sentiment" (Bergson 1988: 15). His emotional approach showed weaknesses due to its neglection of exhilarating humor effects, but he interestingly described humor stimuli which also play a role for art-horror. For example, Bergson described "mechanical inelasticity" (Bergson 1988: 17) as a source of humor, but in psychoanalytical art-horror theory the inanimacy of an object, like a stiff, human-like doll, is one of the uncanny triggers for fear and disgust (cf. Jentsch 1906: 197; Carroll 1999: 146).

Psychoanalytic humor theories

The second humor family concentrates on psychoanalytic relaxation theories. Here, it is again Sigmund Freud (2012 [1905]) who included the phenomenon of humor in his theories of id, ego, and superego and thus established the psychoanalytical approach to explaining humor. He not only associated the joke with a momentarily unconscious processing of a pre-conscious thought (which made it available for conscious perception [cf. Freud 2012 [1905]: 155]) but also explained humor through an economical perspective, claiming it originated in an emotional saving, in "*erspartem Gefühlsaufwand*" (Freud 2012 [1905]: 219). According to this reasoning, the recipients save mental effort through an awaited but missing effect of a speaker and a subsequently awaited but also missing reaction with the same effect of the recipient. The humorist economizes this reactional expenditure by making a joke which produces pleasure as a narcissistic phenomenon. The transformation of the situation induces a psychological shift of interpretation from the ego to the responsibility of the superego, which undertakes the tasks of parental welfare and reassuring the frightened ego (cf. Freud 2012 [1927]: 278–279); Freud called this a "triumph of narcissism" (Freud 2012 [1927]: 278–279; transl. LS). Consequently, the ego can satisfy its infantile needs and energy releases and discharges in the laughter of the recipient. Thereby, humor regulates tensions between the urges of the ego and cultural requirements and is accompanied by a pleasure gain. Freud differentiated between harmless, hostile, and tendentious jokes. The latter is most appropriate to release emotional tension by laughing about something desired which, thereby, becomes ridiculous. This relieves inhibitions and regulates the perspective on the ideal (cf. Freud 2012 [1905]: 92,113).

In addition to the effects of pleasure gain, which have been described both for the consumption of art-horror and of humor, some psychoanalytic structural and functional similarities between humor and art-horror have been worked out. Seeßlen and Jung (2006), for example, compared the mechanisms of Freud's dirty, obscene jokes with art-horror via their function of excluding an absent, third party, such as parents, partners or something desired: "as with the dirty joke, the narrative falls silent when the absent person shines into it. One may suspect that someone is listening behind the door, but it must not open" (Seeßlen and Jung 2006: 89).

The discipline of psychology has made crucial contributions in this family of approaches that go far beyond psychoanalysis. Psychologists have developed humor therapies assuming that humor can be learned; in this context, the 7 humor habits program by McGhee (2010) is of particular importance. Furthermore, psychology contributed to the understanding and measurement of individual differences in humor preferences, behavior and styles like benevolent and corrective humor in a worldwide context (cf. Heintz, Ruch, Platt, Pang, Carretero-Dios, Dionigi, Argüello Gutiérrez, Brdar, Brzozowska, Chen, Chłopicki, Collins, Ďurka, Yahfoufi, Quiroga-Garza, Isler, Mendiburo-Seguel, Ramis, Saglam, Shcherbakova, Singh, Stokenberga, Wong and Torres-Marín 2018). At the intersection of hostility approaches and the psychological humor family, the fear of being laughed at, called gelotophobia (cf. Proyer 2014; Ruch, Hofmann, Platt and Proyer 2014), has been investigated.

The third humor family regards humor as an interplay of contrary concepts and cognitive models. Since it is of crucial relevance for this book, it is described in detail in Chapter 2.2.

To sum up, humor theories originated in ancient theories on ambivalence. While Plato understood humor negatively as unfair, deriding, exclusive and aggressive, Aristotle wrote about laughter as a positive and benevolent stimulus. Aristotle emphasized that the ridiculous was ugly, erroneous, and deformed and that unexpectedness, surprise, and ambiguity played an important role in its evocation. He differentiated between verbal and referential stimuli. Following Hippocrates's theory of four bodily fluids (humores, humorism), which led to the etymological origin of *humor*, van Galen developed those ideas to a personality theory preparing the later understanding of humor as mood or temper. Cicero repeated the importance of ambiguities and the difference between verbal (in verbo) and referential (in re) sources of laughter, including their correct use in rhetorics. Quintilian then advanced the understanding of humor's physical and mental relaxation ability. He described the social function of laughter and distinguished between laughter at others (to chide, refuse or praise), at one's own group (as blunder or play), or at a neutral category (such as deceived experiences). He shed light on different figures of speech which were acceptable as trigger for laughter. Hobbes illuminated the negative effects of humor and claimed that laughter arose through the humorist's impression of being superior to an opponent. During the 18th century, the meaning of *humor* shifted to mood, atmosphere, and temper and was understood as a positive ability, active reflection, and non-binding communication mode; humor considered the relation between ideality and reality, finiteness and infinity, possibility and impossibility. Oppositions also played a role in Kant's and Schopenhauer's incongruity theories, in which unexpected combinations of and analogies between concepts led to laughter and an emotional tension release. Nowadays, contributions to humor research come from separate disciplines including literature studies, philosophy, and psycholinguistics. And while they aim to provide a comprehensive understanding of humor, they complicate a uniform definition. Contributions from all disciplines can be categorized into three theory families (social, psychoanalytical, cognitive) with different foci on humor's social mechanisms, its psychoanalytical aspects, and its cognitive processing.

The following chapter is dedicated to the third family of cognitive theories. With its emphasis on cognitive incongruity from a linguistic perspective, it plays a decisive role in this book.

2.2 Cognitive approaches: Incongruity and humor

The third family of humor theory describes humor through the phenomenon of incongruity and receives contributions from the disciplines of linguistics, philosophy, psychology, and neurosciences. Incongruity theories repose on a long, interdisciplinary research tradition. Since Plato's ancient concept of a combination of pleasure and pain and Aristotle's description of the unexpected, incongruity has been discussed as a crucial source of laughter. In order to approach the phenomenon as the basis of the third family of humor theory, incongruity, its cognitive creation, and processing are examined here in the context of higher-order mechanisms of the human brain, information structure, and language processing.

The brain enables a person to perceive their environment, process incoming stimuli (such as information coming from an interlocutor), adapt and respond to them. It is assumed that speakers and hearers of a discourse permanently establish discourse representations (such as mental models [cf. Johnson-Laird 2010] or situation models [cf. van Dijk and Kintsch 1983]) of their world and the incoming information, which are fed by the individual experiences of the recipients, their world knowledge or schemata (cf. Schank and Abelson 1977), the extra-sentential and intra-sentential context. Recipients update the discourse representation dynamically in the course of the incoming information. In doing so, on one hand, the recipients can better process and structure the discourse and, on the other hand, make better predictions for expected future information and sensory inputs. These incrementally updated, expectation-based predictions rely on the discourse representation and facilitate the recipients' cognitive processing of the incoming material and a forward-directed parsing (cf. Federmeier 2007; Friston 2010;

Bornkessel-Schlesewsky and Schumacher 2016; Heusinger and Schumacher 2019). Thus, the recipients unconsciously calculate a probability with which the predictions become true. However, if the predictions do not eventuate and unexpected content is received instead, we speak of a prediction error, surprise, or incongruity (cf. Levy 2008; Levy 2011).

During the reception of humor, the brain is challenged by precisely this alignment of prediction and incongruous input, because the punchline of a joke presents surprising information that was not expected by the recipient. Successful humor reception therefore requires the application of cognitive mechanisms that enable the recipient to detect the incongruity and reconcile the given mental model with the input to resolve the incongruity, extract a coherent meaning, and understand the joke.

In the following, models are presented that are dedicated to the cognitive processing of humor. They describe the particular connection of incongruent contents in humor and show how the recipients uncover and solve the incongruity.

Incongruity in humor models

Koestler's model of *bisociation* (1966) strengthened the detection and resolution of incongruity. Koestler illustrated that a parallel association of two incongruent facts, called *bisociation*, emerged during the humorous expression and that any two systems could be combined by a suitable connective (cf. Koestler 1966: 52); "the sudden bisociation of a mental event with two commonly irreconcilable systems entails that the train of thoughts is transferred abruptly from one association context to another" (Koestler 1966: 52, transl. LS). For example, ambiguous words producing a literal and figurative meaning can act as a connective between two systems. Furthermore, different logics and scales or similarities in sound serve as an adhesive. At this point, reference may be made to later models of the *Semantic Script Theory of Humor* (SSTH) and the *General Theory of Verbal Humor* (GTVH) (see Chapter 1.1.1 and 4.2.1.1), and their cognitive script oppositions which are already approximated by the bisociation of "trains of thoughts pulling peacefully in the opposite direction" (Koestler 1966: 60, transl. LS).

Suls (1972) integrated the concept of incongruity systematically in his *Two-Stage Model* which explained humor, in the form of jokes and cartoons, as information processing in two stages. Suls pursued the idea that the recipient had to pass two crucial stages to understand a joke (cf. Suls 1972: 82–89):

(1) read the stimulus, (incrementally) store context as reference model/narrative schema, predict further input, recognize incongruity at the punchline of the joke, react surprised
(2) search for a cognitive rule that combines the incongruent parts of context and unexpected input in a problem-solving manner using motivational, emotional, and situational cues to resolve the incongruity and enable a congruent reading of the joke or cartoon.

Suls pointed out that an incongruent ending was a necessary but not a sufficient condition for humor since incongruity without resolution led to a non-humorous nonsense reading and puzzlement (cf. Suls 1972: 83). Therefore, non-felicitous conditions are also included in his humor appreciation model (see Figure 1):

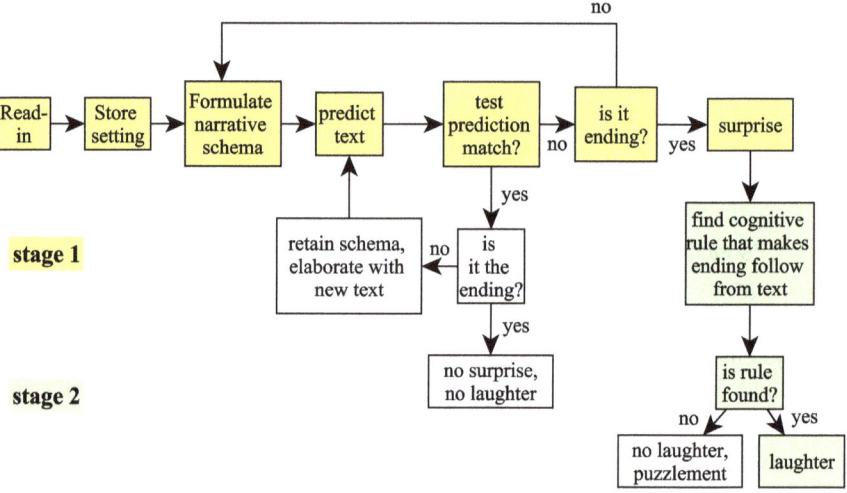

Figure 1: Information-processing model of humor (adapted from Suls 1972: 85).

Four factors which act as further predictors for a successful humor appreciation are defined: incongruity type which indicates the degree of expectation violation, complexity of the two-stage processing and subsequent cognitive load, time needed, and salience of the cognitive rule according to motivational, situational or emotional setting (cf. Suls 1972: 92).

Suls' model is the predecessor of linguistic theories like the SSTH, its successor GTVH and subsequent extensions. With a focus on the cognitive mechanisms that combine the contrasting concepts, and how they are processed in the human brain, SSTH and GTVH explain the interface between stage 1 and 2 and relate humor processing to higher-level cognitions. They are examined in the following chapters.

2.2.1 Script-based theories of humor

At the interface of linguistics, psychology, Gestalt theory, and artificial intelligence, theories of perception and thinking, cognitive problem-solving, learning and understanding are developed that contribute to humor theory by describing its cognitive mechanisms in a superordinate model of thinking and understanding. These approaches try to answer the question of how information is in general cognitively processed, stored, retrieved, and adapted. In the 1970s, Minsky, Rumelhart and Norman, and Schank and Abelson form the notions of *schema*, *frame*, and *script* which denote a very similar phenomenon and are examined here with regard to their later application in humor theories.

Schema, frame, and script
To describe the visual perception of a scene, its actions, causes, transformations, and mental representations, and to apply the findings to linguistic questions of memory, knowledge acquisition and retrieval, Minsky (1974) defined the notion of *frame* as a memorized "data-structure for representing a stereotyped situation, like being in a certain kind of living-room, or going to a child's birthday party" (Minsky 1974: 1). Every frame contains information about default features of the situation, predictions about potentially further incoming material, and details about how to use the frame for felicitous or after nonfelicitous applications. A frame is structured hierarchically with higher levels containing information about a situation that stay fixed and true, and lower levels including changing *terminals* which need to be adapted to a given instance. Through sharing terminals, a frame is related to other frames so that a frame-system emerges (cf. Minsky 1974: 2). Minsky transferred his understanding of frames to linguistic discourse analysis, emphasizing the function of terminals, which helped to answer questions about agents, intentions and instruments in a discourse by filling empty slots with stereotypical information (cf. Minsky 1974: 40). With the help of frames, it is possible for the participants of a discourse to create expectations about incoming material, to develop them further or replace them, and to thereby, learn how memory can be stored and retrieved efficiently in a global scheme (cf. Minsky 1974: 43). Today, the concept of frames is still understood as a universal, functional, recursive representation system of human cognition (cf. Barsalou 1992; Löbner 2015).

On a similar note, Rumelhart and Norman (1976) developed the notion of *schema* which encompasses generalized knowledge about backgrounds, situations and activities as an organized, active unit of information. A schema is linked to other schemata and activates itself whenever it becomes relevant to understanding and predicting incoming material, or designing a model for a particular situation (cf. Rumelhart and Norman 1976: 7–12). Rumelhart and Norman explained the schema concept using the example of farming with the variables "land, crops or animals, some person, machinery, products, specialized buildings" (Rumelhart and Norman 1976: 9) which could be filled with (culturally limited) details in concrete situations so that, for example, carrots replaced crops. The selection and verification or rejection of appropriate schemata is important to understand and correctly represent a given situation and incoming material. Finally, "the schema that is selected will determine the interpretation of the situation and will direct processing attention to selected aspects of the situation" (Rumelhart and Norman 1976: 10–11). Incoming material influences the development of a schema and its link to other schemata by activating three learning mechanisms: accretion, the input is accumulated under a schema without changing it. Tuning, the input modifies a schema and thereby adapts it to enable a congruous interpretation of the input. Restructuring, new cognitive structures are created to understand and interpret new (but also old) knowledge in a better way (cf. Rumelhart and Norman 1976: 3–4).

A final term, *script*, developed by Schank and Abelson (1977), also captures established knowledge about recurring everyday situations in cognitive information units that facilitate the understanding of incoming material as well as its production, for example, in the form of language. A script, however, focuses on event sequences in certain situations and facilitating the completion of elliptical event narratives in order to quickly develop a complete set of well-known, individual elements. Thus, an invoked script activates the sequential framework of the incoming material so that all its details do not all have to be named individually. Examples of such stored event sequences are a restaurant visit, a bus ride, or a birthday party (cf. Schank and Abelson 1977: 41).

Raskin (1985), Attardo and Raskin (2017), and Attardo (2020) claimed that the different notions of frame and script labeled the same phenomenon (cf. Raskin 1985: 81; Attardo 2020) and were "true notational variant[s], because frames are the same as scripts" (Attardo and Raskin 2017: 56). In this work, frame and script are used synonymously, along with the notion of schema so that the following theories are subsumed to script-based approaches. The theories themselves emphasize the one or the other notion.

2.2.1.1 Semantic Script Theory of Humor

The *Semantic Script Theory of Humor* (SSTH) by Raskin (1985) and its successor, the *General Theory of Verbal Humor* (GTVH) apply the insights of script theory to humor and the questions of how incongruent, semantic elements come together in verbal humor and through which cognitive mechanisms this incongruity is resolved in felicitous humor conditions. Even though Raskin and Attardo (1991) initially did not incorporate their approaches into the family of incongruity theories because of divergent terminology, they later claimed that "SO [script oppositions] and incongruity are different conceptualizations of the same phenomenon" (cf. Attardo 1997: 401). In the current book, they are both subsumed under the incongruity theories because they model the union of oppositional elements with the peculiar innovation that they do so through a script-based approach. Before we apply scripts to humor, some details about the nativist and communicative/pragmatic context of SSTH and GTVH are provided.

The SSTH emerged in the context of the transformational grammar and postulates innate humor competence for every human being. It assumes that if speakers can assess a sentence for grammar, they can also say whether or not it is humorous. To describe a text as humorous means to recognize its perlocutionary effects and goals. It is not about uniform judgments of the speakers concerning the wit of a sentence but about a basic competence to process humor. For the substance of a humorous text, the performance is less relevant as the humorous potential (cf. Attardo 1994: 196). As such, the SSTH starts with an ideal humor recipient who is receptive to any humorous content. Thus, the humor recipient must have no racial or gender affiliation, must behave undisturbed against pornographic, obscene or disgusting material, should not be affected by boredom and must have never heard the corresponding joke before (cf. Attardo 1994: 197). The SSTH tries to theoretically grasp the semantic competence of a native speaker (cf. Raskin 1985: 59).

Even though the SSTH primarily focuses on semantic mechanisms in humor, it tries to integrate the humorist's pragmatic abilities in a (Neo-)Gricean way and treat the communication style of joking as a mode of violating truthfulness. Following the cooperative principle, the SSTH bases itself on the four Gricean maxims of quantity, quality, relevance, and manner. It reformulates the maxims of conversation and integrates them in the concept of a non-truthful communication mode called *non-bona-fide mode* (NBF) or *non-observance* (cf. Raskin 1985: 100; Attardo 2017a: 182):

> Maxim of Quantity: Give exactly as much information as is necessary for the joke
> Maxim of Quality: Say only what is compatible with the world of the joke
> Maxim of Relation: Say only what is relevant to the joke
> Maxim of Manner: Tell the joke efficiently   (Raskin 1985: 103)

In order to derive the semantically necessary and sufficient conditions for the humorous success of a joke, SSTH and its successor GTVH use insights from script theory. They understand scripts as sets of semantic information provided through cognitive structures and memory about relationships between objects and events, typical processes and established routines, hierarchies, and global networks. Two types of script are distinguished in these two humor theories: macroscripts and complex scripts. While macroscripts are understood as clusters of several chronologically sorted scripts, such as stored knowledge about procedures for dinning in a restaurant, complex scripts are linked information chunks without chronological sorting like knowledge about wars with components like weapons, attacks, or victims (with each representing a further subordinate script). Attardo refined the concept of scripts by semantically distinguishing between lexical knowledge of the word itself and encyclopedic knowledge of the relation of the object to the world. He illustrated this with the example of the word *beer*: Although beer lexically has the characteristic [+ liquid] and is thus initially difficult to stow in a refrigerator, the encyclopedic knowledge provides enriching information about the usual bottling of the liquid in bottles [- fluid], so that the storage in a refrigerator can succeed (cf. Attardo 1994: 200–201). Further semantic associations of information emerge, for example, through synonymy, antonymy or hyponymy. Thus, the scripts, including all their links and combinatorial rules in the mental dictionary, constitute a global network of all the known information of the speaker. Scripts are of large scale and multi-dimensional (cf. Attardo 1994: 202) and their sum results in a semantic network which comprises every detail a person remembers of their culture and experiences as permanently available knowledge (cf. Attardo 1994: 198–199). To ensure a coherent reading of a text, all relevant script combinations must be stored and retrieved until each text element is processed. As soon as a coherent and well-formed reading of the textual material becomes accessible to the reader, this is "licensed as 'the meaning' of the text" (Attardo 1994: 203).

The SSTH claims that humor arises through a combination of opposed yet overlapping scripts. It postulates two hypotheses are necessary and sufficient for the humoristic success of a "single-joke-carrying text" (Raskin 1985: 99):

(i) The text is compatible, fully or in part, with two different scripts.
(ii) The two scripts with which the text is compatible are opposite [. . . and] are said to overlap fully or in part in this text. (Raskin 1985: 99)

Humor arises if the second script contains contrasting information (opposition) but still shares some information with the first script (overlap). For example, ambiguous words that have multiple meanings, negations or antonyms offer such an opposition interface (cf. Raskin 1985: 108). Attardo emphasized the necessity of opposition and overlap since alternative script combinations without overlap led, for example, to a conflict (cf. Attardo 1994: 204). In the case of script overlap without conflict, metaphors or allegories emerge (see Table 2).

Table 2: Possible script combinations (Attardo 1994: 204).

scripts	opposed	non-opposed
overlapping	humor	metaphor, allegory, figurative, mythical, allusive, obscure
non-overlapping	conflict (possibly tragic)	plain narrative

Possible script combinations

Raskin described three basic, script-based oppositions that led to humorous success through their combination in a joke (cf. Raskin 1985: 111,127):

1. **Script opposition actual/non-actual, also called real/unreal:** Humorous material initially invokes unreal, improper content, and only later reveals the actual, real situation. Raskin illustrated this opposition with a joke about an archdeacon claiming to have drudged all night long and hoping he did not catch anything. The unreal but initially evoked situation refers to an abstinent, busy clerical life whereas the last statement of the joke reveals the real situation and alludes to him having sex all night long.
2. **Script opposition normal/abnormal:** The second opposition normal/abnormal refers to the expectations of the recipient. Depending on the initially invoked script, the recipient creates an expectation for further incoming text. A joke disappoints this expectation and causes a switch to an abnormal situation. This opposition can also be illustrated by the example of the archdeacon where the normal would be the observance of celibacy turning into an abnormal state of the archdeacon's sexually active night.
3. **Script opposition possible/impossible:** Raskin illustrated the third fundamental opposition in a joke of a chauffeur with the surname Darling. The woman being chauffeured is forced to break her rule of not calling chauffeurs by their first name because it would suggest to her surroundings to have an affair with her chauffeur.

Raskin listed five common and, for him, essentially human oppositions which were subsumed to the three basic categories including good/bad, life/death, obscene/non-obscene, money/no money, and high/low stature (cf. Raskin 1985: 113–114,127).

The recipient of the humorous material is directed from a first to a second script by means of the so-called *script switch trigger* (cf. Raskin 1985:114): This trigger can be of various nature: it can be a grammatical or lexical hint, an ambiguous or contradictory stimulus. If a trigger is ambiguous, the overlap of two scripts is large. Raskin differentiated between six subtypes of ambiguity with regular, auxiliary, metaphorical, syntactic, situational, and phonetically activated pseudo-triggers. If the trigger is a contradiction, the script change succeeds by depicting the opposite of reality. Raskin illustrated this with a joke about a man who on a Monday on his way to his gallows said that the week was off to a good start (cf. Raskin 1985: 116). Recognizing the trigger as compatible with several scripts, the recipient has to re-scan the text, identify an NBF mode, switch to the second script, and generate a new, humorous meaning (cf. Raskin 1985: 114–117,125).

Although the oppositions presented are fundamentally important for the analysis of humorous material, the SSTH lacks the potential to analyze different humor genres (verbal vs. referential) and systematic criteria to compare different humorous materials (cf. Attardo 2017b: 127).

2.2.1.2 General Theory of Verbal Humor

The *General Theory of Verbal Humor* (GTVH) further developed the ideas of the SSTH in order to fundamentally grasp humor and cover all humor types. Although semantic properties of humor continue to be the theory's most important element, it also implements situational, social, narrative, and linguistic features of the humorous input (cf. Attardo 2017b: 126). The GTVH extended the SSTH's scope by establishing a system of six knowledge resources (KR) which are depicted here according to their initial hierarchical importance and determination:

1. *Script oppositions* (SO), which have already been established in the SSTH, and their partial overlap emerge unaltered in the GTVH as the highest KR, applicable to every humorous material.

2. *Logical mechanisms* (LM) connect two scripts and (completely or partially) resolve foregrounded incongruities (cf. Attardo, Hempelmann and Di Maio 2002: 25; Hempelmann and Attardo 2011: 125,140). Attardo, Hempelmann and Di Maio (2002) clustered possible LMs in syntagmatic relationships that concatenate the scripts through a spatial proximity (see Figure 2), and in mechanisms of reasoning that comprise script connections arising from correct, faulty or meta inferences (see Figure 3).

Syntagmatic LMs contain script links that suggest a semantic proximity due to a spatial proximity of scripts, like a juxtaposition of two scripts, or an explicit or implicit parallelism. The syntagmatic relationships also include so-called reversals, in which the script concatenation is achieved through permutation of a text element, like a chiasm that repeats words in reverse order and thereby creates a new, humorous perspective (cf. Attardo, Hempelmann and Di Maio 2002: 18).

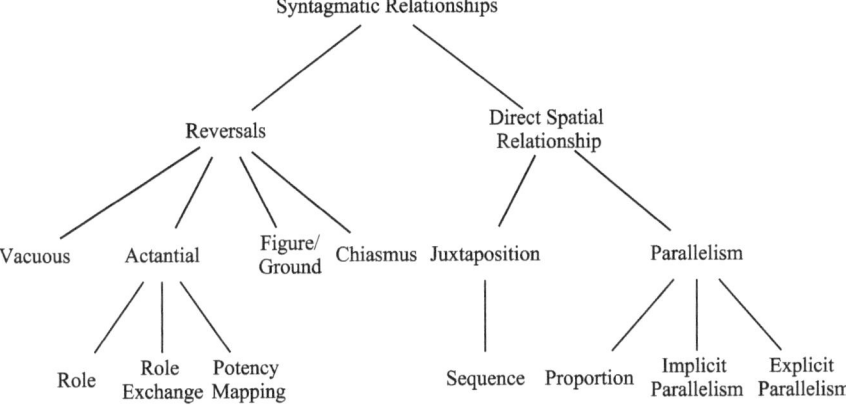

Figure 2: Syntagmatic LM (adapted from Attardo, Hempelmann and Di Maio 2002: 18).

The second group of LMs includes inference processes, which in turn are subdivided into the three groups of false, correct, and meta-conclusions. The correct inferences include analogies in which characteristics of one concept are transferred to another, as well as correct assumptions based on a false premise. In addition, the correct inferences cover almost situations, that is moments in which an alleged fact is almost true, but in actuality not completely or at all (cf. Attardo, Hempelmann and Di Maio 2002: 18–19).

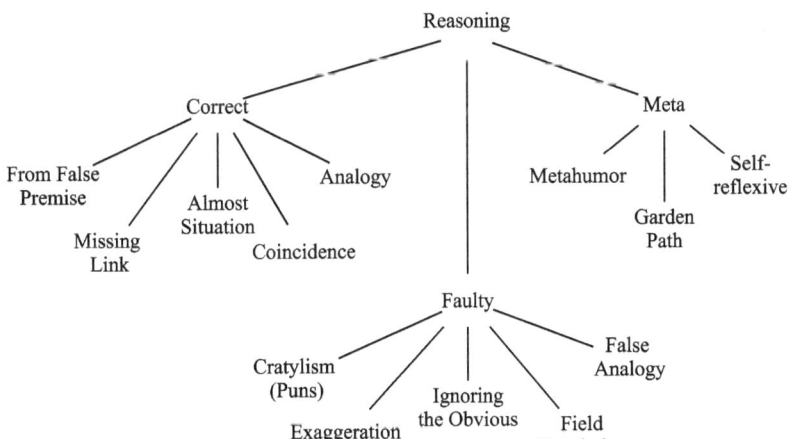

Figure 3: Reasoning LM (adapted from Attardo, Hempelmann and Di Maio 2002: 19).

The faulty inferences include five subtypes; puns, restrictions of an expression's scope, exaggerations, false analogies that equate two entities to a situation X (although they have little in common in the proper sense), and moments when the obvious is ignored. Reasoning LM also cover the subgroup of meta-conclusions including metahumor, self-reflexives and garden paths (GP). Metahumor, for example, comprises cases where humor is itself used humorously. In contrast, the LMs of the GP, which is also known for threatening readings in art-horror, describes the case of a meta-level where the recipient is deliberately misled to the false assumption of the first script, which is revealed shortly thereafter and therefore must switch to the second script (cf. Attardo, Hempelmann and Di Maio 2002: 5,18).

Attardo, Hempelmann and Di Maio (2002) complemented the LMs by a further group called *verbal humor*. This group includes the referential ambiguity which is omnipresent in humor and triggers a script change through the lexical ambiguity of a term based on homonyms in the form of homographs and homophones, as well as on paronyms (cf. Attardo, Hempelmann and Di Maio 2002: 15).

Finally, despite their high position in the KR hierarchy, LMs are optional because some humorous texts, like absurd humor or nonsense jokes, are humorous exactly for their lack of resolving mechanisms (cf. Attardo 2017b: 133). Incongruity-resolution theories therefore seem to only explain certain subclasses of humor (cf. Ritchie 2014: 314–315).

3. Background information as macroscripts of the humorous situation (e.g. person X walks into a bar) are tackled through the third knowledge resource called *situation* (SI). It should be noted that SI is often confound with contextual circumstances of the joke communication, including pragmatic abilities of speaker and recipient which are not part of the competence-oriented GTVH (cf. Attardo 2017b: 131). SI defines the joke's diegetic objects, participants, tools, and actions. Ultimately, every kind of humor contains a situational framing, but its importance varies and so, it is enriched to different degrees (cf. Attardo 1994: 225). Even though SI has initially represented the third hierarchical position, Ruch, Attardo and Raskin (1993) showed through their empirical rating study of joke similarities that the SI is a candidate of ranging at higher levels parallelly to SO and LM (cf. Ruch, Attardo and Raskin 1993: 131).

4. Since jokes often work at the expense of a person being laughed at, the GTVH uses the fourth, optional KR to incorporate the *target* of an aggressive joke (TA). Objects or victims of humor can be stereotypes such as Poles or names of individuals. These stereotypes change according to given cultural background and current trends. The recipient of the joke, too, can become a target of humor by, among other things, testing his intellectual abilities to process humor. Yet still,

TA can remain empty in case of non-aggressive humor (cf. Attardo 1994: 224–225). Since the victims of a humorous instance represent (part of) the participants or objects that have already been described in the third KR, they could also be subsumed to SI.

5. The fifth knowledge resource covers the *narrative structure* of the humorous material (NS) and defines the format of the text as dialogue, puzzle, riddle or "three-step sequence frequently used in jokes" (Attardo 2017b: 130). NS determines the distribution of information throughout the text, like the position of the punchline (at the of a text) or the jab line (not at the end but somewhere else in the text), and whether there is a "narrative disruption and [. . .] a humorous central complication" (Attardo 2017b: 130).

6. Finally, the GTVH also introduces a KR for the linguistic resources of a humorous text including its syntactic, phonological, morphological, and lexical features (LA for *language*). LA appears in the last position in the hierarchy of the KR. LA is responsible for the concrete formulation of a text, the exact word order and well-formedness of the sentences. Attardo (1994) pointed out that each sentence could be modified, for example, by a paraphrase or synonym, thus giving a very large pool of possible phrases that do not attack the semantics of the statement. This also includes the difficulties of translating into other languages (cf. Attardo 1994: 223; Attardo 2017b: 128–129).

The following criteria catalogue results for the analysis of a humorous text (see Figure 4):

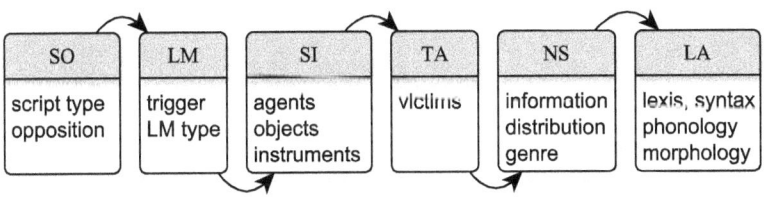

Figure 4: GTVH's six Knowledge Resources in hierarchical order.

With the help of the GTVH, the joke (3) that also precedes this chapter can now be analyzed comprehensively:

(3) The audience at Hollywood's Dolby Theater was spellbound when the disguised moderator opened the golden envelope. 'Row 1. Seat 9.' was written on the card. She pulled out the golden raspberry.   (adapted from Meimberg 2011: 34; transl. LS)

The macroscript of winning an honorary award opposes the macroscripts of winning an embarrassing, ridiculous prize (SO) with the underlying opposition winner/loser or good/bad. The scripts overlap in the situation (SI) of an award ceremony with the audience eagerly awaiting which name is hidden in the envelope of the moderator and who will receive the prize (TA). The script switch trigger consists in the lexical item *raspberry* as metaphor (LA) for the worst contribution of that year which links the two scripts. The readers are seduced to assume a positive prize and to focus on the question of who wins the prize instead of what the prize comprises. The narration follows a three-step (where – who – what) with the surprising revelation of the punchline at the very end of the text (NS), so that the readers are led down the garden path (reasoning LM) and need to retrieve their encyclopedic knowledge concerning different awards and their honoring meaning to resolve the incongruity.

2.2.1.3 GTVH revis(it)ed: Pragmatics and context

Even though the GTVH is still an influential, interdisciplinary theory of humor research today, it lacks important theoretical components concerning contextual factors and pragmatic abilities of the humor recipients. Recent Neo-Gricean literature therefore attempts to update the GTVH (revisionist approach) and to expand it (extension approach). Although the authors of the SSTH and GTVH reduce pragmatic speaker abilities to Grice's maxims for the theory's competence orientation and would prefer a separate theory for humor pragmatics (cf. Attardo 2017b: 138), the GTVH is suitable to address precisely these deficiencies by means of an extension.

New knowledge resources: Meta-knowledge and context

Canestrari (2010) developed a seventh KR called *Meta-Knowledge Resource* (Meta-KR) that accounts for humorous interactions, the contextual framing and processing of humorous signals between communicators in a dialogue in the GTVH model. The addition of this seventh KR to the GTVH offers the advantage of modelling "external indexes" (Canestrari 2010: 339) and increasingly incorporating the recipient's perspective. Canestrari defined an interaction as humorous if at least one participant was aware of the humorous conversation's content and used different signals to meta-communicate the playful mode aiming at a humorous resonance of the other participant (cf. Canestrari 2010: 330; Canestrari 2012: 59). The signals that support the humorous speaker intention and its reception go beyond laughter and can be expressed through verbal expressions like 'Do you already know that one?', non-verbally through facial expressions such as blinking, or para-verbally through a certain emphasis or pitch range (cf. Canestrari 2010: 339–340). Hay (2001) concretized the verbal signals and listed the following strategies: "contributing more humor, echoing the humor, offering sympathy or contradicting self-deprecating humor, and using overlap or other strategies to show heightened involvement in the conversation" (Hay 2001: 76). These signals may refer to the humorous material itself, the genre or the situation (cf. Canestrari 2010: 340). The Meta-KR comprises the total of all meta-communicative signals between the participants of a humorous interaction (cf. Canestrari 2010: 339–340).

Tsakona (2013) developed an independent, eighth KR for the integration of ideal recipients and their socio-culturally influenced and negotiated humor preferences (cf. Tsakona 2013: 25,29–30). She called this *Context* (CO) and placed it at the top of the KR hierarchy (cf. Tsakona 2013: 42). However, the factors she defined, to investigate whether the meta-communicative signals are sufficient for a humorous text interpretation and what happens if these signals, SO and LM are ignored or misinterpreted (cf. Tsakona 2013: 29), rather complement the Meta-KR. She redundantly listed multimodal factors and (non-)verbal recipient reactions as contextual framing which are already enumerated through the Meta-KR. Nevertheless, she contributed ideas of sociocultural factors as well as individual parameters of the speakers and recipients. CO is fed by components of discourse analysis and anthropological linguistics (cf. Tsakona 2013: 44) and covers the socio-cultural influences on humor production/reception formalized through two mutually-dependent information resources, when and to whom a text is humorous:

(1) Sociocultural presuppositions: they form the "social, historical and cultural context in which a communication comes to be defined as funny" (El Refaie 2011: 104) and determine the "production and interpretation of script oppositions, logical mechanisms and humorous targets" (Tsakona 2013: 42).
(2) Metapragmatic stereotypes of speakers: this type comprises information at the level of speakers and their "ideological assumptions and stances on whether a specific text can be considered humorous or not, why, how, when, and to whom" (Tsakona 2013: 42) and formalizes "the background knowledge, values and opinions of the participants" (El Refaie 2011: 104). This factor involves the influence of "age, gender/sexual orientation, ethnicity, religion, social class, political affiliation, profession, etc. of individuals" (Chovanec and Tsakona 2018: 5) on humor preferences.

The eighth KR is an important interface to the humorous family of social theories. It incorporates the reasons for humor and its social functions such as the creation and revelation of a community's identity and its moral values, the creation of a certain atmosphere and emotions like empathy but also aggressive disparagement, attention control, and the management of a speaker's or group's popularity (cf. Chovanec and Tsakona 2018: 6). Chovanec and Tsakona added that the genre importantly influenced humor's functions as well as the speakers' and recipients' preferences, performances, and identities (cf. Chovanec and Tsakona 2018: 7).

Tsakona (2013) and Chovanec and Tsakona (2018) argued that the expanded GTVH was able, through Meta-KR and CO, to model why the same text material could be perceived as humorous, (in)felicitous, distasteful, or aggressive "depending on each recipient's perspective and value system" (Tsakona 2013: 30). "Finally, social roles, identities, norms, and restrictions usually determine whether humor is going to be used or perceived as aggressive, critical, affiliative, mitigating, supportive" (Chovanec and Tsakona 2018: 7). These indications are taken into account in this work to distinguish between humor and art-horror.

Since the seventh and eighth KR highly overlap and are dependent on each other in many ways, here they are grouped in one KR called Meta/CO; it encompasses both metapragmatic factors, humor signals, and sociocultural context aspects. Thus, the extended model of the GTVH involves the following analysis criteria (see Figure 5):

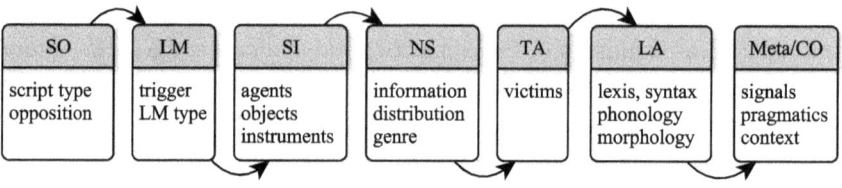

Figure 5: Expanded Knowledge Resources of the GTVH.

Meta-KR and CO have been developed to account for felicitous humor conditions, but they can also be used to describe failed humorous interactions. Hay (2001) listed the following meta-pragmatic reasons for infelicitous humor:

(1) Insufficient contextualization
(2) Being too late, or reviving 'dead' humor
(3) Assuming too much background knowledge
(4) Misjudging relation between speaker and audience
(5) Negatively teasing someone present
(6) Trying to gain membership of an exclusive sub-group
(7) Disrupting serious conversation
(8) Portraying oneself inappropriately for one's status or gender   (Hay 2001: 71)

Marszalek (2013) emphasized that narrative texts could lose their humorous potential due to a missing context. A lacking CO aggravates felicitous humor conditions of some humorous texts since "they are parts of patterns of extended humor, and their appreciation requires the ability to look for a humorous interpretation in the wider narrative context" (Marszalek 2013: 417).

Meta-KR and CO increasingly show how important the recipient's pragmatic abilities are for successful humor appreciation. Hay (2001) shed light on humor processing through four pragmatic implicatures: (1) recognition of a humorous attempt, (2) understanding as a cognitive test, resulting in face maintenance, (3) appreciation of a humorous instance as funny and (4) agreement or rejection of subtle messages sent to the recipient via the humor material (cf. Hay 2001: 67–72). The first three implicatures are scalar insofar as "understanding entails recognition, and appreciation entails both recognition and understanding" (Hay 2001: 67).

Canestrari (2012) used these ideas to develop a seven-stage model that depicts the failure and success of a humorous interaction (see Figure 6). Assuming that the speaker wants to communicate a humorous stimulus, which includes SO and LM using meta-communicative signals, the success of a humorous interaction is determined by the (non)accomplishment of the three implicatures mentioned by Hay (2001).

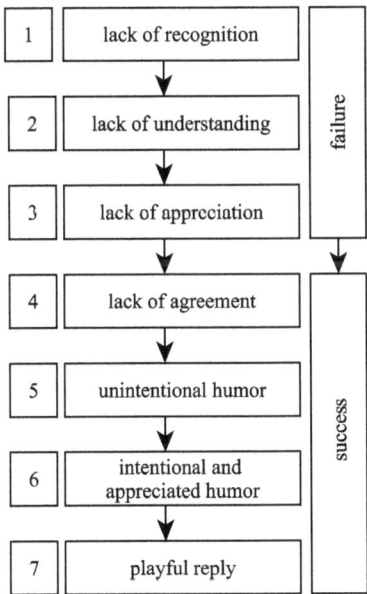

Figure 6: Humor implicatures on 7 levels (based on Canestrari 2012: 65–73).

A humorous interaction fails if one or more of the first three implicatures (recognition, understanding, appreciation) are not performed. In contrast, humor can succeed in the interaction if only the fourth implicature (agreement) is not performed (cf. Canestrari 2012: 65). The success of the humorous interaction is measured by the performance of the implicatures. It gradually becomes larger with the humoristic intention of the speaker, the performed appreciation of the intended humor and the playful answer as continuation of the humorous situation (cf. Canestrari 2012: 65–73).

Incongruity types: Global, additive, intermediate, pure

The GTVH also requires a more precise definition of incongruity types. Although Canestrari and Bianchi (2013) did not explicitly understand their research as an extension of the GTVH, their literature review and findings highlight and solve its weaknesses.

Canestrari and Bianchi (2013) continued to approximate incongruity through the lens of psychology of perception. They experimentally attested that basic perceptual mechanisms, like the connection of stimuli parts to a harmonic whole, are applicable to the processing of humorous incongruity (cf. Canestrari and Bianchi 2013: 6). They described three types of contrariness, which they applied later to humor reception:

- Global contrariety: This opposition is immediately recognizable and consists of two characteristics of the same unit (e.g. tall/small in matters of the unit *size*). The evidence of an opposition is as necessary as the invariance of other features of the contrasted stimuli, to detect the relevant opposition and maintain the stimulus type (cf. Canestrari and Bianchi 2013: 7).
- Additive contrariety: This type of incongruity describes the case of multiple oppositions between two stimuli. The intended opposition only becomes apparent after an analytical comparison (e.g. tall/small AND white/black AND thick/thin). If all of the characteristics of a stimulus turn into their opposite (high variance), the stimulus might change so intensely that it cannot be recognized as such anymore (cf. Canestrari and Bianchi 2013: 7).
- Intermediate contrariety: This concerns weak oppositions which are hardly recognizable (e.g. small/medium). The second indicator indeed varies in the direction of the opposite pole but it does not reach a sufficient value on the scale (cf. Canestrari and Bianchi 2013: 8).

Hence, they develop a continuum of incongruity strength with the intermediate incongruity at the weakest position and the additive at the strongest (see Figure 7).

Continuum of contrariety

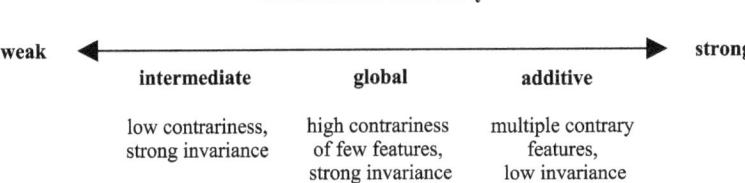

weak ←——————————————————————→ strong

intermediate	global	additive
low contrariness, strong invariance	high contrariness of few features, strong invariance	multiple contrary features, low invariance

Figure 7: Continuum of contrariety depending on contrariety type and invariance of further feature (based on Canestrari and Bianchi 2013: 17–18).

Against this background, Canestrari and Bianchi (2013) broadened the continuum and applied it to humorous incongruities. They claimed that the humorous success depended on the type of incongruity. Thus, their adapted continuum correlates incongruity type and humorous potential (see Figure 8).

Humor success depending on the type of incongruity

weak ←——————————————————————→ strong

pure	intermediate	additive	global
unresolvable incongruity	low contrariness, strong invariance	multiple contrary characteristics, low invariance	few contrary characteristics, higher invariance

Figure 8: Correlation of incongruity type and humorous success (based on Canestrari and Bianchi 2013: 20).

Pure incongruity (nonsense), that is not resolvable and therefore offers a weak humor potential, occupies one extreme of the continuum (cf. Canestrari and Bianchi 2013: 17–20). Intermediate and additive incongruity are in the middle of the continuum with additive incongruity having a higher humor potential. Global incongruity, with an easily recognizable incongruity, highly facilitates the humorous appreciation of a text. However, it must be noted that nonsense humor attracts its very own fandom so that it is conceivable that pure incongruity ranges above intermediate incongruity.

Overall, SSTH and GTVH explain humor and its mechanisms by superordinate innate, cognitive mechanisms of information processing. Their script-based approach suggests that recipients can rely on memorized, networked knowledge about stereotypical situations, agents, and action sequences (scripts) during humor processing. A connection between two incongruent yet overlapping scripts, whose opposition can (partly) be resolved through logical mechanisms, enables a humorous reception. Further resources comprise intratextual situations, agents and targets, narrative structures as planned distributions of information, and linguistic aspects such as concrete lexical, syntactical, and phonological elements. The GTVH extensions provide insights into the influence of the pragmatic abilities of speakers and recipients as well as the effects of extra-diegetic, socio-cultural contexts on the success conditions of humor. The (meta)pragmatics include meta-communicative signals as (non)verbal support of a humorous interaction and four implicatures (recognition, understanding, appreciation, and agreement) that highly influence the success of a humorous instance. The contextual framing involves information about the sociocultural background of the participant's culture as well as about the participant's individual preferences, both which affect the success and appreciation of humor. The notion of incongruity is split into the subtypes global, additive, intermediate, and pure incongruity, which correlate from high to low potential to facilitate a humorous interpretation of a text.

Advantages of the (expanded) GTVH lie in their potential to explain humorous instances that cannot be reduced to a semantic level and exceed the text form of jokes. Additionally, "a degree of similarity between any two jokes" (Attardo 1994: 228) can be described through the number of equal KRs.

2.2.1.4 Space structuring model

In the introduction of Chapter 2.2.1, the notions of script, schema and frame are traced back to the same theoretical origins of psycholinguistics, artificial intelligence, and language processing. They all model information and their cognitive processing in mental networks fed by memory and learning procedures. Those stored networks support the mental enrichment of incoming material. They rely strongly on the same theoretical, complementary basis, while the focus of script and frame differ in detail. Thus, Coulson's understanding of frames and her concept of *frame-shifting* correspond to the already established scripts, aside from a few details (dynamics of the mutual meaning enrichment of input, long-term memory and context (cf. Coulson, Urbach and Kutas 2006: 230; Coulson 2001: 34; Brône 2017: 251–252) which will not be elaborated here). However, the cohesion between scripts/frames is not without criticism. Coulson criticized that in the GTVH, a script was not enough to represent language processing and humorous challenges. The GTVH is "unable to compute the relationship between unexpected and normal events, because its inferencing capacity is based on knowledge represented in the script itself" (Coulson, Urbach and Kutas 2006: 232). She, therefore, designed a superordinate model called *Space Structuring Model* which "appeals to processes proposed in cognitive semantics for the creative combination of frames and the construction of novel frames in response to contextual demands" (Coulson, Urbach and Kutas 2006: 232). Based on Fauconnier's mental spaces, Coulson's model seeks answers to the connections between frames. Her Space Structuring Model contains three assumptions that capture the dependence of language to physical body conditions, rapid information integration and its further elaboration into cognitive models (cf. Coulson, Urbach and Kutas 2006: 231). The three assumptions are:

(i) the embodiment assumption, that the structure of language at least partially reflects bodily constraints on perception and action;
(ii) the immediacy assumption, that the integration of linguistic and non-linguistic information occurs rapidly, and does not (necessarily) require the prior construction of a propositional representation of sentence meaning;
(iii) the elaboration assumption, that language comprehension involves animating the cognitive models constructed by the listener
(Coulson, Urbach and Kutas 2006: 231)

The cognitive models are superordinate to frames but are informed by them and interlink them. The models contain the same hierarchical structure as frames and standardized placeholders for unspecified attributes; "though schematic and partial, these models are detailed enough to enable small-scale simulations of the scenarios they represent" (Coulson, Urbach and Kutas 2006: 231). Coulson based her model on neurocognitive findings that assume incoming information, like a sentence, is split into parts (partitioning) that are processed parallelly as individual strands. Strong connections between subsystems enable a continuous updating and exchange of the individual pieces of information allowing for an adequate representation of the incoming material to a complete message (cf. Coulson, Urbach and Kutas 2006: 247).

Ultimately, frame-shifting and the space structuring model do not offer added value to the aforementioned theories and are not sufficiently innovative to be understood as a superordinate script. Coulson's approach is, therefore, taken up again in Chapter 3 for its merits in empirical verification, but theoretically it is equated with the script-based approaches described above.

2.2.2 Graded informativeness, optimal innovation, and relevance

Cognitive linguistics provides alternatives to script-based theories which are conceptually different from the idea of incongruity processing but can ultimately be understood as complementing rather than competing with the GTVH model.

Giora's approach of *Graded Informativeness* examined the information structure of funny stimuli and set the following conditions for a well-formed joke (cf. Giora 1991: 470):
1. Jokes serve the discourse and are therefore relevant (relevance requirement).
2. Jokes do not gradually build up their information content from an unmarked to the new, marked information, but suddenly come to the marked information by means of the punchline (marked informativeness requirement).
3. In jokes, readers have to complete a linear shift from an unmarked reading, which is to be deleted, to a marked reading.

Giora incorporated the humorous interpretation of a text into the concept of a lexical set of information. This lexical set includes different, possible readings but occupies only one entry in the mental lexicon. The reading of the punchline is the least salient meaning and unlikely for the discourse continuation. According to *prototype theory* (Rosch 1973), this reading is therefore marked (cf. Giora 1991: 471). Giora defined salience as the interplay of "familiarity, frequency, conventionality, or prototypicality" (Giora 2004: 117) and argued that it needed to be in balance with innovation in order to achieve a good sense of humor (cf. Brône 2017: 254). Thus, Giora (2004) developed the *hypothesis of optimal innovation*, claiming that "pleasurability is sensitive to optimal innovation" (Giora, Fein, Kronrod, Elnatan, Shuval and Zur 2004: 116). This optimal innovation is achieved through the involvement of qualitatively and quantitively new information which "allows for the automatic recoverability of a salient response related to that stimulus[,] so that both responses make sense" (Giora 2004: 116). The title of her article *Weapons of mass distraction* (2004) served as a humorous example to demonstrate that a relevant but less expected input (here the noun *distraction*) leads to humor; if the information is introduced through a non-gradual distribution and at the same time easily reanalyzable (here through its phonological similarity to the noun *destruction*), it enables a transition from an expected, unmarked to a marked reading (cf. Giora 2004: 117).

Even though Giora's approach is developed as an alternative to the script-based theories, it parallels and complements them in several aspects: The unmarked and marked information can be understood as two sources of information (such as scripts) that overlap (in the same entry in the mental model). The idea of switching between pieces of information (condition 3) is also similar to script-switching in SSTH/GTVH. As an eclectic enrichment between the different approaches to humor, the hypothesis of optimal innovation can also be understood as a qualitative supplement to the GTVH, since it specifies the characteristics of SO.

Relevance theory
The pragmatic approach by Wilson and Sperber (2004) also emphasized the relevance of a stimulus and the recipient's cognitive effort in processing it. In their post-Gricean *Relevance Theory*, they formulated principles guiding the general, cognitive processing of a stimulus that also apply to humor reception:
1. "Human cognition tends to be geared to the maximization of relevance" (Wilson and Sperber 2004: 610) with relevance as a "positive, cognitive effect" (Wilson and Sperber 2004: 608) during the processing of a stimulus.
2. "Every ostensive stimulus conveys a presumption of its own optimal relevance" (Wilson and Sperber 2004: 612) with the ostensive stimulus being "designed to attract an audience's attention and focus it on the communicator's meaning" (Wilson and Sperber 2004: 611). The stimulus is relevant to the recipient if it is worth the "processing effort [. . . and] compatible with [the] communicator's abilities and preferences" (Wilson and Sperber 2004: 612).
3. By following "the path of least effort in computing cognitive effects" (Wilson and Sperber 2004: 613) and applying interpretation strategies such as disambiguation or implicatures depending on availability, a pragmatic economy of processing can be derived. Here, recipients cease processing at the time the "expectations of relevance are satisfied (or abandoned)" (Wilson and Sperber 2004: 613).

Recipients also follow these general principles while processing a humorous stimulus, such that information is not further processed (immediately) after the stimulus is thought to be relevant.

According to Yus (2016), Relevance Theory can be combined with the approaches that describe humor through an incongruity and its resolution:

> IR [Incongruity Resolution Theory] relies on a linear cumulative processing of the joke and on the predicted inferential steps towards an acceptable interpretation of the text. These steps are both predicted and manipulated for the sake of humour. In this sense, RT [Relevance Theory] can provide a valid cognitive explanation of why certain senses of words are selected (and eventually rejected), or why certain framings of the situations depicted in the joke can be manipulated for the sake of incongruity (together with the manipulation of the inferential steps to turn the text into full-fledged interpretations) in order to generate humorous effects. (Yus 2016: 66)

Relevance Theory can be understood as complementing the GTVH by describing in more detail why the first script is assumed until the punchline of a humorous text.

2.3 Incongruity in humor and art-horror

In art-horror theories as well as in cognitive humor approaches, it has been shown that the phenomenon of incongruity is of great importance for the evocation of the intended effect: In art-horror, unexpectedly combined stimuli lead to frightening interpretations, while in humor opposing stimuli are described as fundamental for an exhilarating effect. Even though the cognitive art-horror theories by Carroll and Grodal used a different terminology to tackle the source of the frightening effect, they basically described the same underlying mechanisms as humor theories. To concretize Grodal's notion of cognitive dissonances and Carroll's categorical interstitialty and to unify the terminology of both phenomena, the concept of scripts is transferred to art-horror: In art-horror, two stored memories of default routines and situations (scripts) are combined; this combination is first experienced as incongruent but later processed to a congruent reading via a connecting mechanism.

This observation correlates with critics of humor theories which point out that incongruity alone is not enough to explain humor revealing intersections to art-horror. Already Bain (1876) described cases in which incongruent stimuli do not cause pleasure, but rather displeasure or even anxiety:

> There are many incongruities that may produce anything but a laugh. A decrepit man under a heavy burden, five loaves and two fishes among a multitude, and all unfitness and gross disproportion; an instrument out of tune, a fly in ointment, snow in May, Archimedes studying geometry in a siege, and all discordant things; a wolf in sheep's clothing, a breach of bargain, and falsehood in general; the multitude taking the law into their own hands, and everything of the nature of disorder; a corpse at a feast, parental cruelty, filial ingratitude, and whatever is unnatural; the entire catalogue of vanities given by Solomon, – are all incongruous, but they cause feelings of pain, anger, sadness, loathing, rather than mirth. (Bain 1876: 256)

Critics of the script-based approaches showed that final criteria for a clear definition of humor are still missing and that humor theories are also suitable to explain fiction in general and genres with threatening characteristics: Oring (2011) even rejected the three basic oppositions of SSTH/GTVH for the fact that not only jokes included them but that they were generally found in fictive situations dealing with unreal, abnormal and impossible beings, objects and situations. He claimed that humor appreciation was linked to adequate incongruity, that is the right opposition between the scripts (cf. Oring 2011: 218). Morreall (2004) further criticized the SSTH/GTVH by explaining that switching between opposing, overlapping scripts worked without the emergence of humor. He exemplified his observation with a text which uses the same mechanisms as jokes, but which ends with a scary reading. His example is about extraterrestrials and their serving relationship to human beings. While the readers are initially seduced to a positive reading of the altruistic subordination of the extraterrestrials, they later have to change to the script of cannibalism. The script switch trigger is the ambiguous lexical item of the English verb *(to) serve* which provides the interpretations of a subordinated person fulfilling the superior person's wishes but also of offering a meal. Morreall's example shows that the script change between opposing, overlapping scripts can also lead to a reading of an existential threat of the human beings (cf. Morreall 2004: 394–385). Likewise, Coulson pointed out that frame-shifting is not only accomplished in jokes which she illustrated at the example of Shyamalan's *The Sixth Sense* (1999): "The frame-shifting [. . .] can also be prompted by other situations. For example, in The Sixth Sense, Bruce Willis plays a child psychologist treating a disturbed boy who 'sees dead people.' At a critical moment in the film, it becomes apparent that Willis, himself, is dead, prompting the viewer to reevaluate Willis' relationship with the boy" (Coulson 2006: 233).

From a literary perspective, Triezenberg (2008) also contributed to the discussion on how other genres work with script oppositions and to what extent they (do not) differ from humor. She pointed out that the GTVH also applied to other genres: "A modified version of the GTVH has been found to successfully describe many aspects of the standard murder mystery" (Triezenberg 2008: 541).

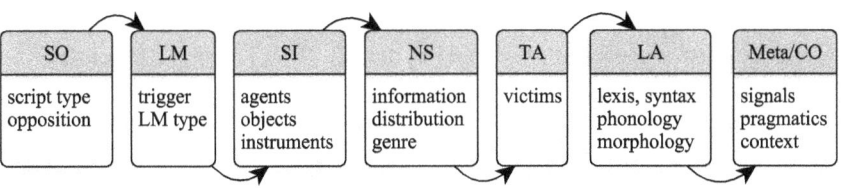

Figure 9: Expanded Knowledge Resources (equals Figure 5).

Thus, the GTVH's (extended) criteria catalogue (here again in Figure 9) should not only be able to describe humorous situations but should also be suitable for the analysis of art-horror scenarios.

Against this background, the following passage analyzes three short art-horror examples, which include the basic oppositions of normal/abnormal, real/unreal, and possible/impossible with different LMs through the seven KRs:

1. SO normal/abnormal with LM of referential ambiguity

Coming back to the art-horror example (2) (here again in (4)), the GP is analyzed with the terminology of the GTVH:

> (4) The audience at Hollywood's Dolby Theater was spellbound when the disguised moderator opened the golden envelope. 'Row 1. Seat 9.' was written on the card. She pulled out the gun. (adapted from: Meimberg 2011: 34; transl. LS)

The cognitive macroscript of the award ceremony is combined with the macroscript of an assassination (SO normal/abnormal with the underlying oppositions life/death and safety/danger). The scripts overlap in the referential ambiguity of the word *disguised* (LM). The readers are seduced to a certain first script established in the context and expect a certain outcome of the plot. The information distribution follows a three-step (where – who – what) with the surprising revelation of the punchline at the very end of the text (NS), so that the readers are led down the garden path (LM of reasoning). The ambiguity of the trigger adjective *disguised* is uncovered (detection of incongruity) at the punchline position with the noun *gun*. The readers need to reanalyze the text and update their initial default interpretation of the situation through retrieving their encyclopedic knowledge concerning different meanings of masks to resolve the incongruity. The readers understand that the moderating person does not represent a stylish anchorwoman but a hired, masked assassin (SI) and that the selected person in Row 1 does not win a prize but loses his/her life (TA). The readers switch to the threatening reading and react emotionally (art-horror). The text contains main and subordinate clauses as well as direct speech without lexical or syntactical peculiarities (LA). The Meta/CO-KR depends on the reader's context but in this book, the chapter's transfer of humor theories to art-horror signalizes and facilitates an art-horror reading. In the course of this chapter, the importance of CO is further highlighted.

2. SO real/unreal with LM of reversals

Recipients are led down the garden path in most jokes so that the initially assumed script turns out to be wrong (or unreal). Thus, the script opposition real/unreal needs to be verified for art-horror, too.

> (5) The soap bubbles floated over the Champs-Elysées. Many passersby smiled movedly. The bubbles spread slowly and extensively. They contained poison gas.
> (adapted from Meimberg 2011; transl. LS)

In example (5), the macroscript of a busy luxury avenue in Paris (SI) where rich costumers (agents and victims [TA]) are pleased through soap bubbles (objects) collides with the script of homicide (SO real/unreal as well as safety/danger). Even though readers know that bubbles contain gas, they assume that this gas is oxygen and not lethal. Here, the function of the bubbles is reversed since they are not distributed to please people but to kill them (syntagmatic LM of (object) reversal). The pieces of information are again provided in three steps with details about place and agents, the ongoing event, and the surprising revelation of the cruel punchline at the very end (NS). The text contains main clauses without lexical or syntactical peculiarities even though the noun poison is negatively connotated (LA). The context (Meta/CO) depends on the reader's circumstances but, again, in this book, the chapter's content signalizes an art-horror reading.

3. SO possible/impossible with LM of correct reasoning from false premise

With art-horror's tendency to integrate supernatural characteristics, the opposition possible/impossible is fundamental to the genre. The following example therefore does not include magic, impossible features but describes a situation where a (potentially real) diver (agent and victim) tries to safe his life by throwing his diving bottle (object) away to reach the surface of the water a faster way (SI).

> (6) The empty diving bottle trundled into the black depth. Timo fought his way to the surface with his last ounce of strength and hit the ice.
> (adapted from Meimberg 2011: 139; trans. LS)

The readers initially assume that the protagonist arrives at the surface of liquid water and that it is therefore possible for the diver to breath once he has reached the surface. Only at the position of the last word (NS), the readers receive the information that the water is frozen and that it is not possible for the diver to reach the life-saving oxygen (SO). The language of the text contains main clauses without lexical or syntactical particularities (LA). The context (Meta/CO) depends again on the reader's circumstances and this chapter's signals beforehand.

GTVH: A general theory of humor and horror?

These examples show that the GTVH and especially its SO and LM equally apply to the analysis of art-horror. In examples (2/4) to (6), a first script is replaced by a second through a connecting mechanism that links the two overlapping scripts. In more general, the examples support the claim that art-horror can contain the same sequential processing steps of detecting the incongruity at a punchline, resolving it by switching to a second script and elaborating/reacting emotionally. However, in line with Jancovich's observation that art-horror is universally about "the position of the victim – the figure under threat" (Jancovich 1992: 118), it must be noted that the second script of all three examples is always about the protagonist's injury which facilitates the threatening reading. To avoid this particularity of identification with the victim, Straßburger (2015) examined the series *Dexter* (2006) which suggest to identify with the cruelest of all shown murderers. Again, it was possible to equally apply the six KR from the GTVH applicable to the analysis of art-horror, especially with regard to SO and LM. Straßburger showed that all basic oppositions of the SSTH/GTVH including normal/abnormal, real/unreal, possible/impossible and the sub-incongruities of good/bad, life/death, obscene/non-obscene, money/no money, high/low stature as well as all LM (see Figures 2 and 3) can also be used to trigger fear and disgust. It turns out that both humor and art-horror scenes combine oppositional scripts in the same way and yet trigger feelings that could not be more conflicting. Furthermore, in line with the observations by Carroll (1999), Aldana Reyes (2016), and Paul (1994) that humor and art-horror easily merge into each other and that the same figures sometimes trigger amusement and sometimes fear or disgust, Straßburger (2015) confirmed this claim through her corpus analysis and concluded that incongruities represented the common denominator and tertium comparationis between humorous and scary texts and thus linked them (cf. Straßburger 2015: 62–63).

While the combined oppositions cause fear and disgust in art-horror, they lead to amusement and laughter in humorous stimuli. The incongruity, its detection and resolution are the common denominator so that the sequential steps of both phenomena can be modeled as follows (see Figure 10):

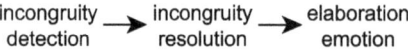

Figure 10: Incongruity processing steps in art-horror and humor.

With this sequential model, we are now facing for the first time an experimentally verifiable model of art-horror that captures the individual steps of cognitive processing, and on the other hand, we are simultaneously confronted with the problem that the same model explains humor processing.

If there are no differences between the oppositions and their LM of art-horror and humor, then the pragmatic abilities of the recipients or the context (Meta/CO) could cue the interpretation possibilities of an incongruent input. So far, only Meta/CO of the expanded GTVH can model why the same text material can be perceived as humorous, felicitous, distasteful, aggressive or similar "depending on each recipient's perspective and value system" (Tsakona 2013: 30). Thus, El Refaie (2011) emphasized the recipient's pragmatic abilities and that

> [. . .] enjoyment of a multimodal joke depends to a large extent on the background knowledge, values and attitudes of the individual. If, for instance, a cartoon is too threatening to someone's core sense of identity, it is likely to create anger and alienation rather than amusement. Humor appreciation is also shown to depend on the broader sociocultural context in which the cartoon is encountered. (El Refaie 2011: 87)

However, with a further look on the syntony model by Canestrari (2012) (see Figure 6), the seven implicatures of humor appreciation can be transferred to art-horror, too: If the recipient does neither recognize nor understand the threat and its sources, the stimulus only triggers a mood or a feeling but not an object-directed emotion. If the recipient cannot appreciate the input, art-horror does not satisfy the fandom and fails. Furthermore, art-horror is successful no matter if the recipients agree with the events or not, and no matter if the diegetic danger is intentional or not. Even the playful reply of the seventh implicature can be transferred to art-horror. For example, in the first season of the series *Dexter*, the protagonist (with whom the recipients identify) plays a cruel game with his brother who also is a mass murderer and equal in terms of cruelty and bloodlust (like playing humorists are equally concerning the humorous intention). The playful reply can also be associated with the game *hide and seek* or with murderer's wishes to play with their victims like in the above mentioned movie *Saw* (2004) with Jigsaw playing murderous games with his victims (cf. Wan 2004). Thus, if even the same pragmatic abilities are required to successfully enjoy art-horror, the contextual framing of the received incongruity has to contain details about differences between humor and art-horror.

Rothbart's model of affective responses to incongruity

Rothbart (2017 [1976]) argued that the intensity of the triggered arousal is a major factor in the interpretation of the incongruent stimulus. Further, her model allows the conclusion that unexpected stimuli and their processing have to be reflected in the context of higher-level mechanisms of problem-solving. According to her, the stimulus interpretation depends on the questions of

whether the (context of a) stimulus is dangerous, whether the stimulus challenges the recipients and whether the incongruity can be resolved (cf. Rothbart 2017 [1976]: 38). Rothbart separated the incongruent input in four categories according to affective arousal level the stimulus triggers (see Figure 11 for a reduced version of Rothbart's model without redundancies):
1. If the input only reaches a minimal level of arousal, it is ignored.
2. If the stimulus activates a low arousal level, the recipients approach it with the question whether the stimulus is challenging with respect to known schemata. If it is not challenging, the recipients' tension releases and they smile.
3. If the stimulus activates a medium arousal level, the recipients first evaluate it and verify whether it is dangerous. If it is, its processing switches to the mechanisms reserved to the fourth category of high arousal leading to defensive reactions, fear, and flight without further engaging in a problem-solving way. If it is not dangerous, the recipients verify whether known schemata are challenged by the stimulus. If they are not challenged, the recipients tension releases and they show a big smile or laugh. If the stimulus does challenge the recipients' schemata, problem-solving strategies are activated. If these are successful, the tension releases and the recipients show a smile or laugh. If the stimulus activates a high arousal level, the recipients try to avoid the stimulus and react with fear. They try to remove the stimulus. If this is not possible, the recipients approach the stimulus with the question whether it is dangerous. If it is, they remain in a fearful state and continue trying to remove the stimulus. If it is not, the recipients engage in problem-solving strategies. After successfully resolving the challenge, the recipients' tension releases and they laugh.

Cognitive reactions thus do not seem to depend on the incongruity (of a certain genre) per se, but on the strength of arousal and the input's dangerousness. Applied to art-horror, Rothbart's model would predict that it is only processed with problem-solving strategies if avoidance is not possible, the stimulus was not too intense, and no danger was present. Otherwise, fearsome recipients flee or show typical art-horror reactions consisting in facial expressions of avoidance like narrowed eyes or a raised upper lip. Rothbart's model is thus not completely compatible with a three-stage art-horror model, as it is suggested in the current book (see Figure 10). Even though it makes an important contribution to fearful incongruity reactions, it ignores, first, that art-horror's reaction of fear can be elicited after or even through the resolution of the incongruity, and, second, that fear in art-horror can be enjoyed (paradox of painful art from Smuts (2014), see Chapter 1.2.1).

2.3 Incongruity in humor and art-horror — 79

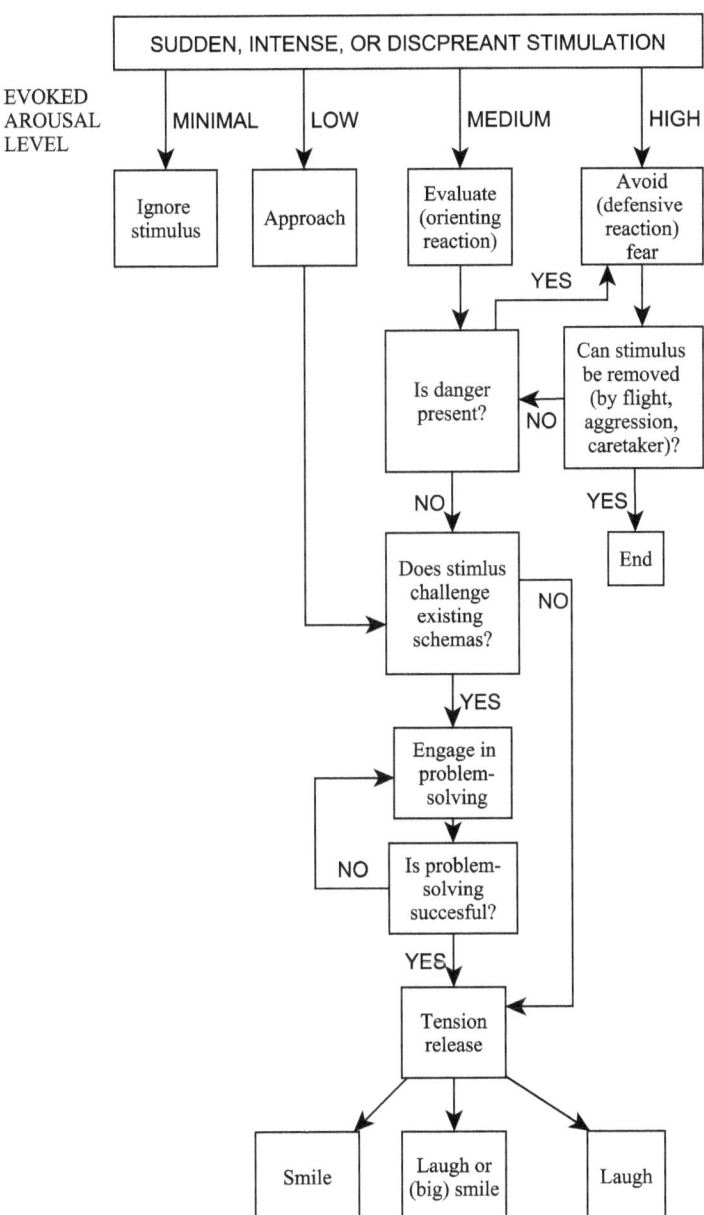

Figure 11: Rothbart's model of affective responses to incongruity (adapted from Rothbart 2017 [1976]: 39).

Canestrari and Bianchi's incongruity continuum (2013) and the idea that the incongruity type can be correlated with a potential humor success can also be reconciled with art-horror. While global incongruity (followed in descending order by intermediate, additive, and pure incongruity) promises the highest facilitating effect in humor, this continuum can be applied to art-horror in nearly the same order (depending on the dangerous context). It can be assumed that a quickly and unambiguously identifiable opposition is more likely to lead to art-horror than several opposites, which must first be analyzed. Unsolvable incongruities have a bad chance of humorous and frightening success since they are not recognizable within a genre intention. However, it is conceivable for art-horror that exactly these unresolvable incongruities (correlating with unresolvable nonsense humor), according to Rothbart (2017 [1976]) are experienced as highly arousing and dangerous and are thus avoided. As shown for humor, incongruity-resolution theories therefore seem to only explain certain subclasses of art-horror, such as garden paths.

2.4 Intermediate results

The phenomenon of humor as a communication mode, individual ability, source of laughter and positive emotion, has been examined since ancient times. Initially, it was discussed in questions about morality and rhetorical utility due to its aggressive, ugly, negative, but also motivating potential. The word humor has its origin in humorism, in which (the quantities of) the bodily fluids of yellow bile, black bile, phlegm, and blood were medically correlated with a patient's state of health. In British philosophy, the term was understood as the ability to actively reflect, a non-binding mode of communication. Schopenhauer and Kant also recognized that surprises, unexpectedness, and suddenness play a role in successful humor. Today, the phenomenon of humor is examined in an interdisciplinary manner with contributions from philosophy, literary studies, medicine, psychology, and linguistics.

The modern approaches to describe humor are divided into three families; social theories that focus on triumph, degradation, mockery and hostility, psychoanalytic approaches with a focus on infantile causes of suppression into the subconscious, and incongruity theories. Contributions to humor theory also emerged at the interface of linguistics, psychology, and artificial intelligence; theories of perception, thinking, cognitive problem-solving, learning and understanding highlight humor's cognitive mechanisms in a superordinate model of thinking and understanding. These approaches tried to answer the question of how information is cognitively processed, stored, retrieved, and adapted; from them, the notions of schema, frame, and script (which all denote a very similar phenomenon) are deduced. All of these approaches held the basic assumption that humans could enrich an (elliptic) input through established memories and knowledge about recurring default situations and routines. Thus, frames, schemata or scripts help the parsers to create expectations about incoming material of a discourse which facilitates the completion of elliptic event narratives and a faster, more accurate understanding and production of a discourse.

Raskin's and Attardo's SSTH and GTVH used the notion of scripts to trace humor and its mechanisms back to innate, cognitive mechanisms of information processing. They assumed that recipients could rely on memorized, networked knowledge about stereotypical situations, agents, and action sequences (scripts) during humor processing. The union of two incongruent yet overlapping scripts whose opposition can (partly) be resolved through logical mechanisms activates humor. The criteria catalogue for the humor analysis comprised six KR including information about the opposition, its link, the diegetic situation, its agents and victims, narrative structures as information distribution, and linguistic aspects. SSTH/GTVH were expanded upon by two further KR: Meta-KR and CO; these focus on the influence of pragmatic abilities of discourse participants including meta-communicative signals and pragmatic abilities as well as on effects of extra-diegetic, socio-cultural contexts of the success conditions of humor. The notion of incongruity was correlated to the potential to be humorous and split into subtypes (global, additive, intermediate, and pure incongruity), ranging from the highest probability of successful humor appreciation to the lowest.

The aforementioned humor models were complemented by a further frame-based approach by Coulson: the space structuring model. This model is very similar to the other script-based models and, namely, only contributes to the connection of frames, the partitioning of incoming material in favor of parallelly processable strands and continuous updating of the discourse.

Two alternatives to script-based theories that conceptually differ from incongruity processing were Giora's approach of Graded Informativeness as well as Relevance Theory by Sperber and Wilson. Giora claimed that humorous stimuli broke the requirement of optimal innovation and turned suddenly (instead of developing sentences gradually) to the marked information at the punchline. Therefore, the recipients have to shift from an unmarked to a marked reading. The approach by Wilson and Sperber (2004), Relevance Theory, formulated principles that guide cognitive stimulus processing in more general but that also apply to humor reception; it emphasized that human cognition searched for the maximization of relevance with every ostensive stimulus being conceptualized to attract recipients' attention. A stimulus is only worth being processed in an effortful way if it is relevant to the recipients. Relevance Theory claimed that recipients also applied these principles during humor processing so that information is not further processed if the input is recognized as irrelevant. Relevance Theory complemented incongruity resolution approaches by explaining why particular interpretations, like an initial script, are selected.

In this book, the notion of humor is not only defined as a communication mode, individual ability and character trait (sense of humor), a social intention (derision, superiority), a psychoanalytical phenomenon (release) or source for laughter and exhilaration as an "umbrella-term for *all* phenomena of this field" (Ruch 1998: 6). It is mainly regarded through a cognitive, linguistic perspective. Here, I define a humorous source similarly to my definition of art-horror: the union of incongruous, cognitive concepts like life/death, normality/abnormality, reality/unreality, or safety/danger which are linked through connecting mechanisms; while these mechanisms do cause additional cognitive processing costs, they result in positive emotions of exhilaration.

This chapter has shown that a unified terminology between art-horror and humor enables detailed insights into similarities of the two phenomena. The tertium comparationis is incongruity which consists in the combination of two opposing yet overlapping scripts, which are connected through a logical mechanism. The GTVH's KRs have successfully been applied to art-horror instances with the SO normal/abnormal, real/unreal, and possible/impossible with different LM. Following this transfer, it has been concluded that art-horror is also processed in a three-step procedure of incongruity detection, resolution, and emotional response. Furthermore, the required recipient's pragmatics, including seven implicatures for humor appreciation, have also successfully been transferred to art-horror, allowing one to assume that the necessary pragmatic skills for enjoying art-horror are the same as in humor.

Rothbart's model contributes to an incongruity understanding that includes more than an exhilaration reaction, emphasizing the influence of the recipients' arousal level and the dangerousness of the stimulus. While her model can explain why some incongruities are experienced as fearsome and are thus avoided (high arousal, danger, non-removeable stimulus), it ignores that fear can arise after problem-solving strategies, such as the resolution of art-horror garden paths.

In line with humorous incongruity types of global, additive, intermediate, and pure incongruity, the facilitating art-horror effect follows the same continuum (depending on the dangerous context): While global incongruities promise the highest facilitating effect in humor, additive incongruities are harder to recognize and analyze. Intermediate incongruities only cause low arousal, since the crucial opposition is difficult to grasp. Pure incongruity can be interpreted in two ways: On one hand, they are hardly recognizable since a link between the opposing scripts is missing and on the other hand, exactly this effect can lead to nonsense humor (or in art-horror, to high level arousal and avoidance).

The theoretical comparison of art-horror and humor concepts not only highlighted a bridge between the research fields and how they can profit from each other, but it also revealed that distinctive criteria are still missing in given art-horror and humor theories. So far, known theories are not yet able to explain art-horror and humor comprehensively. This book searches for a cognitive incongruity model that explains humor *and* art-horror, and that predicts processing stages, verified by empirical data. It aims at determining peculiarities that are related to only one of the phenomena and underlying, higher-level mechanisms of incongruity processing. The next chapter shows to what extent an experimental approach helps to differentiate between humor and art-horror and how the theoretical concepts of humor and art-horror research can be transferred into experimental correlates.

3 Humor & horror: Processing incongruity

In Chapter 2, it was shown conceptually that it is fruitful to compare humor and art-horror to better understand distinct criteria of each phenomenon but also similarities and shared mechanisms. This chapter focusses on attesting the humor and art-horror models experimentally. While experimental research in art-horror is still in its infancy, the cognitive humor models described in Chapter 2.2 have been extensively attested experimentally. This chapter recapitulates the understanding of incongruity and its resolution from a psycholinguistic perspective and describes how the theoretical concepts of the humor models can be transferred into measurable correlates of experiments. To this end, the relationship between language and cognition will be discussed first. Then, the extent to which incongruent texts induce additional costs in cognitive processing and how these can be measured indirectly via reaction times or electrophysiological reactions is explained (Chapter 3.1). This will then be illustrated using different types of incongruity as examples (Chapter 3.2). Subsequently, studies are presented that address incongruity processing in humor and discuss correlates for the humor phases of incongruity detection and resolution (Chapter 3.3) and emotional reaction (Chapter 3.4). Finally, the extent to which recipients' individual characteristics and abilities influence processing (Chapter 3.5) is discussed. All subchapters deduce an analogous art-horror analysis, transferring findings and methodological merits from humor research to a deeper investigation of art-horror processing.

Language and cognition

Using the notions of prediction error, disambiguation, and processing costs, psycholinguistic research also discusses incongruity and its resolution from an experimental perspective, embedding them into more general cognitive models of language comprehension. Here, language is understood as part of cognition: "Language is seen as a specific mental system within cognition, relying on principles of its own, which at the same time strongly interacts with the other mental subsystems (such as the perceptual, the emotional and the conceptual system)" (Schwarz-Friesel 2015: 160).

Psycholinguistic research on language comprehension is still ongoing, so that different comprehension models exist. Serial, syntax-first models (e.g. Frazier and Rayner 1982) compete with interactive constraint-satisfaction models (e.g. Warren 1995) and cascaded processing models (e.g. Bornkessel-Schlesewsky and Schlesewsky 2016). All models try to classify how language-related information such as semantic, syntactic, or prosodic input is processed temporally and spatially, and aim to understand their interaction. While serial models claim that basic syntactic information is processed independently of and prior to semantic input information, interactive and cascaded processing models assume a dependency and early interaction between different linguistic features and nonstructural factors, such as word frequency, semantic plausibility, and syntactic cues (cf. Steinbach, Albert, Girnth, Hohenberger, Kümmerling-Meibauer, Meibauer, Rothweiler and Schwarz-Friesel 2007: 56–75). For the present work, comprehension models that deal with semantic prediction (errors) are of special interest. According to incremental, forward-directed models of language comprehension (see Chapter 2.2), interlocutors establish mental discourse representations which they constantly update in the course of the incoming material. In this process, expectation-based predictions are made about future inputs to facilitate the integration of the incoming material in the discourse representation and a forward-directed parsing (cf. Friston 2010; Bornkessel-Schlesewsky and Schumacher 2016). In humor and art-horror, the recipients receive unpredictable, incongruent input so that their predictions fail. The next section explains to which extent this prediction error leads to additional processing effort and how it can be measured indirectly in experiments that investigate reading times or neuroelectric activity.

3.1 Measuring processing costs

Prediction errors and processing costs

If the recipients' predictions about future input do not match the actual input (like a joke's punchline), it is more difficult for the recipients to process the incoming information. Recipients have to update their discourse representations and adapt it to the unexpected input (internal adaptation), or act with respect to the new input (external adaptation) (cf. Friston 2010: 129) to generate meaning of the interplay of given and new information. Furthermore, incongruity interrupts ongoing top-down processes (such as selecting relevant information out of a myriad of information from the environment) through a bottom-up reorientation (cf. Bornkessel-Schlesewsky and Schumacher 2016: 584): "unexpected, novel, salient and potentially dangerous events take high priority in the brain, and are processed at the expense of ongoing behavior and neural activity" (Corbetta and Shulman 2002: 201). Thus, compared to correctly predicted text segments, incongruent input is computationally demanding and leads to increased processing efforts, so-called *costs*. According to surprisal theory, the processing effort of a word is inverse to a word's probability. So, highly predictable input requires less cognitive processing effort than unpredictable, surprising input (cf. Levy 2008; Levy 2011).

Measuring processing costs

The processing costs for the reanalysis of unexpected input are expressed, for example, in longer processing times (e.g. longer reading times) or a more intense processing (e.g. enhanced neuro-electric activity) and can thus be measured indirectly. By comparing the processing efforts and activation patterns of different, incongruent texts with coherent texts, and the nature of the costs, conclusions can be drawn about underlying cognitive mechanisms, providing information about cognitive language processing. Processing costs have already been investigated for a variety of linguistic phenomena. For example, temporary syntactic ambiguities that the recipients initially analyze according to only one of the potential sentence segmentations require costly revisions when the disambiguating information comes in. They elicit longer reading times at the disambiguating text segment (syntactic garden paths, cf. Frazier and Rayner 1982). Regarding costs for a semantic analysis, lexical ambiguities, such as in homonyms like *bank* with two unrelated meanings, cause enhanced processing effort, for example represented in a delayed word recognition. This additional effort can be explained through a competition between the potential meanings of the ambiguous word (cf. Rodd, Gaskell and Marslen-Wilson 2002). Further, non-topic discourse referents elicit enhanced processing efforts, reflected in enhanced neuro-electric activity compared to the continuation of a given topic (topicality) (cf. Hung and Schumacher 2012). The comprehension of new discourse referents is also more demanding than that of given referents (givenness), leading to longer reading times and enhanced neuroelectric activity (cf. Burkhardt 2006; Brocher, Chiriacescu and Heusinger 2018). Figurative language (such as metaphors or metonymies) also elicits enhanced neuro-electric activity due to the difficulty of interpreting the input in a non-literal way (cf. Weiland 2014).

To find out to what extent prediction errors in humor and art-horror texts are reflected in the activity of the human brain and which underlying cognitive processes are required to comprehend humorous or frightening input, the following sections compare the processing effort for humor with coherent and non-resolvable, incoherent texts and transfer experimental findings on processing phases to an analogous art-horror interpretation.

3.2 Comparing incongruity types experimentally

Incongruity types differ, depending on whether or not the incongruent input can finally be integrated into the recipient's discourse representation through disambiguation and reanalysis. In this book, resolvable semantic incongruities played an important role and were compared with non-resolvable incongruity and coherent control texts. To this end, coherent texts and how they are processed are (first) defined in psycholinguistic terms. Then, incongruent text types are presented that are syntactically coherent but contain semantic inconsistencies. These semantic violations can either be repaired by re-analyzing and re-establishing a meaningful reading or they are discarded by the recipient due to their non-sensical features.

Coherence

Coherence "is a content-based connection between successive phrases, sentences, or utterances, manifest at the level of the text base or situation model. For example, readers might assume co-occurrence in time or space [. . . or] infer a causal relationship" (Zacks and Ferstl 2016: 664) between text elements. Coherent texts only comprise semantic segments that can be connected in a referentially, causally, temporally, locally, and structurally congruent way (cf. Müller 2009: 392). Coherence facilitates the recipients' establishment of a mental model and conversely, a mental model facilitates the online establishment of coherence by "connecting successive sentences via an inference so that a plausible interpretation ensues" (Ferstl, Israel and Putzar 2017: 262). A meaningful proposition is immediately conveyed, and the incoming information can be incorporated quickly into the discourse representation (cf. Gernsbacher 1990). Thus, coherent texts are computationally less demanding than incoherent or incongruent texts and are therefore used as control conditions for experimental investigations of incongruity.

Incoherence

In contrast to coherent texts, incoherent texts (also called nonsensical texts, non sequitur or just nonsense) contain a semantically or syntactically incongruent stimulus, which does not produce any meaningful proposition, e.g. "He spread the warm bread with socks" (Kutas and Hillyard 1980: 203). Even after re-analysis, inferences, or shifts, the stimulus cannot be incorporated into the given or a potential new discourse model. The processing of incoherent texts is therefore computationally demanding and elicits processing costs. Mayerhofer and Schacht (2015) showed that these costs are due to integration problems and are reflected in the recipients' processing patterns. Compared to coherent texts, incoherent stimuli elicited longer reading times in *self-paced reading* (SPR) studies, more enhanced negativities in *Event-Related Brain Potential* (ERP) experiments (cf. Mayerhofer and Schacht 2015: 6,9,11), and longer decision times in behavioral *functional Magnetic Resonance Imaging* (fMRI) experiments (cf. Ferstl 2007: 79).

Incongruity in revision texts

Revision texts contain an incongruent information that can be integrated into a coherent reading after reanalysis, e.g. "Franziska to her husband: 'Gosh, I've put on another two kilos!' Says he: 'Well, our offspring will sure be a great kid!'" (Ferstl, Israel and Putzar 2017: 262). At the disambiguating information, the recipients have to abandon the initially established discourse representation suggested by previous stimuli of the context and establish a new representation (cf. Ferstl, Israel and Putzar 2017). This mechanism is called "frame-shifting" (cf. Coulson 2001) (see Chapter 2.2.1.4) or "global updating" (cf. Kurby and Zacks 2012). Revision texts share this mechanism of reanalysis with humor and art-horror (see below) but are neither humorous nor frightening (cf. Ferstl, Israel and Putzar 2017: 262). Psycholinguistic research has shown that these shifts are computationally demanding which is reflected in stronger brain activation (in the brain regions of the precuneus and posterior cingulate cortex) (cf. Whitney, Huber, Klann, Weis, Krach and Kircher 2009) or longer reading times (cf. Coulson and Kutas 1998; Zacks, Speer and Reynolds 2009). However, shifting costs are still under discussion. For example, Ferstl, Israel and Putzar (2017) did not find evidence for revision costs in eye movement experiments.

Incongruity in humor

Chapter 2.2 has shown that the incongruity in jokes arises between the given discourse representation and the incoming material at the punchline. The recipients initially pursue only one potential analysis of the temporary semantic ambiguity and do not predict the information of the punchline (garden path). Therefore, it is more demanding to integrate the incongruent input into the given discourse representation and requires a shift to a second, unexpected reading. The recipients have to detect the incongruity and resolve it (script switching) to get the joke and (re)act amused (cf. Raskin 1985; Attardo 2017b) (see Chapter 2.2). According to the assumption that discourse representations have to be adapted after failed expectation-based predictions, this detection of the incongruity, the textual reanalysis, and the shift to the new reading are computationally demanding for the recipients and lead to additional processing costs compared to coherent texts (cf. Levy 2008; Levy 2011; Bornkessel-Schlesewsky and Schumacher 2016). Psycholinguistic evidence for the processing phases of detection, resolution, and emotional reaction in humor is reviewed in Chapter 3.3.

Incongruity in art-horror

Chapter 1.1 and 2.3 have shown theoretically that the garden path mechanism also applies to the reception of art-horror. After pursuing only one possible text interpretation, the recipients abandon their first discourse representation, shift to a new one to establish a coherent reading, and react with fear and disgust. Analogously to processing garden paths in humor, art-horror also requires cognitive mechanisms of incongruity detection, resolution, and emotional elaboration to establish a coherent reading. Thus, incongruities in art-horror should also be more difficult to process than coherent texts and should, therefore, also elicit additional processing costs. Psycholinguistic research has not yet investigated whether art-horror's revision and subsequent emotional reaction elicit additional processing costs compared to coherence, humor, incoherence, or revision texts or to what extent the cognitive processing costs of art-horror differ from other incongruities with respect to intensity and time-course. Thus, this book hypothesizes that the processing phases of art-horror comprehension are the same as in humor, which is attested experimentally in Chapter 4.

3.3 Evidence for incongruity detection and resolution

The detection of incongruity and its reanalysis with a corresponding actualization of the established discourse model (resolution, script switching) are hypothesized to elicit processing costs. Psycholinguistic experiments have already assessed established humor models and their particular processing phases of detection and resolution, comparing the processing costs for incongruent, unexpected punchlines of jokes with the cognitive effort needed for texts that do not require the cognitive mechanisms of incongruity detection and resolution (such as in coherent, expected input). Further, cognitive costs for humor have been compared to the cognitive effort needed for texts where these mechanisms were applied without resulting in a humorous reading (such as in revision texts) or where they could not be applied successfully (such as in completely incoherent texts without possible resolution). Experimental evidence for processing costs has been found in increased reading times, enhanced electrophysiological activity, and a particular activation of brain regions for both phases. The next sections review their results. First, evidence for increased processing effort over both comprehension stages is presented. Then, evidence for incongruity detection is depicted in more detail, followed by a review of experimental findings for resolution evidence.

Reading times: Evidence for frame-shifting in humor

Coulson and Kutas (1998) assessed the humor model of frame-shifting through psycholinguistic experiments using the Self-Paced Reading Paradigm (SPR).[18] They compared reading times of humorous, incongruous punchlines with those of unexpected yet coherent endings and found that participants took more time to read the punchlines. They also found that jokes, whose contexts initially suggested a certain coherent ending (high cloze probability,[19] high constraint), elicited longer reading times than jokes whose contexts did not strongly suggest a coherent ending (low cloze probability, low constraint) (cf. Coulson and Kutas 1998: 8–9,12). Coulson and Kutas associated the increased reading times with the additional cognitive costs of frame-shifting, needed to repair the semantic violation triggered through incongruent punchlines.

Using the same conditions, Coulson, Urbach and Kutas (2006) recorded eye movements including gaze durations (here, time for the first reading, from start to end of a stimulus), regressions (eye movements back to the left, previously read material) and total viewing durations on a word. They reproduced the reading time findings from Coulson and Kutas (1998), finding longer total viewing durations in the humor condition. The gaze durations of the first reading did not differ significantly, suggesting that the costs were not caused through word recognition challenges. Thus, the longer total viewing durations were interpreted as costs that were due to higher-level processing. They further found that the joke condition elicited more regressive eye movements than the control condition. These increased regressions were interpreted as the recipient's need to go back to a previous text part and the corresponding processing stage, re-start the semantic analysis of an initial interpretation, shift to another frame, integrate the new meaning into the

---

18 Readers who would like to familiarize themselves with the methods of self-paced reading (SPR) and event-related brain potentials (ERP) may want to read the introductions of Chapters 4.2/4.4 first.

19 *Cloze Probability* is defined as the "proportion of subjects using [a given] word to complete a particular sentence" (Kutas and Hillyard 1984: 161). It signifies the probability of "a successful attempt to reproduce accurately a part deleted from a 'message' (any language product) by deciding, from the context that remains, what the missing part should be" (Taylor 1953: 416).

discourse representation, and thereby comprehend the joke (cf. Coulson, Urbach and Kutas 2006: 246).

Mayerhofer and Schacht (2015) also came to very similar conclusions with their studies on garden path (GP) jokes (cf. Mayerhofer and Schacht 2015: 2). They modeled the punchlines of 48 jokes to generate the three conditions of jokes (resolvable, humorous incongruity), coherence (coherent and not humorous), and incoherence (irresolvable incongruity and not humorous). Their self-paced reading time measurements of the final word per condition confirmed longer reading times for both incoherent and joke stimuli compared to coherent stimulus endings (cf. Mayerhofer and Schacht 2015: 6). This was interpreted as an increased cognitive effort regarding incongruity detection and resolution. However, this experiment did not confirm a significant reading time difference between incongruent and incoherent condition, which raises the question of whether the mere presence of incongruity (resolvable or not) causes the additional processing costs or whether the presence of jokes seduces the participants to also search intensively for a resolution to the incoherent condition (cf. Mayerhofer and Schacht 2015: 6).

Reading times only reflect the sum of all phases that might occur during the punchline comprehension and therefore, a description of sub-processes is not possible. Because of this, further experiments incorporated Event-Related Brain Potentials (ERP) with a better temporal resolution than reading time experiments, or functional Magnetic Resonance Imaging (fMRI),[20] allowing for a neuroanatomical differentiation of processing stages and their associated cognitive mechanisms, needed for humor appreciation. These experiments found evidence of sub-processes and disentangled the comprehension stages of incongruity detection and incongruity resolution. They are depicted in the next section, separated according to processing phases.

---

[20] In an fMRI, the blood flow in the brain is measured and visualized, indirectly providing information about the active brain areas; active brain regions require oxygen which is delivered to the corresponding region via an increased blood supply. "The signal measured in fMRI depends on this change in oxygenation and is referred to as the blood oxygenation level dependent, or BOLD, signal" Poldrack, Mumford and Nichols (2011): 1. The BOLD value is used to measure blood flow, blood volume, oxygen and thus, neuronal activity (cf. Kropotov (2016): 19). Despite the temporal inaccuracy of this approach, an fMRI provides a topographically accurate map of the activated brain regions and make neuroanatomical assumptions possible.

ERP and fMRI: Evidence for incongruity detection in humor

Neuroelectric activity, measured in ERP experiments, has provided insights into when additional costs for humor processing arise. Despite of different conditions and material modifications, the ERP components of N400 and LAN (see below and Chapter 4.4) were interpreted as evidence of incongruity detection and semantic integration problems.

Coulson and Kutas (2001) conducted an ERP experiment and found electrophysiological brain correlates of humor processing. They compared jokes with unexpected yet coherent endings and found differences between the conditions which not only depended on contextual constraints (high vs. low cloze probability of joke endings) but also on the participant's ability to understand the joke (good vs. poor comprehenders with only the former conducting a complete frame-shift; see Chapter 3.5 on individual differences). Both poor and good comprehenders showed a negativity around 400 ms after stimulus onset (N400). This finding was interpreted according to previous research, associating this electric negativity with lexical integration problems and the stage of incongruity detection (cf. Kutas and Hillyard 1984; van Berkum, Hagoort and Brown 1999; Coulson and Kutas 2001: 72–74; Kutas and Federmeier 2011, see also Chapter 4.4). For good comprehenders, they further found a posterior parietal positivity between 500–700 ms post-onset of the critical word in high constraint jokes. This was interpreted as the ERP component P3b, reflecting the high-level cognitive mechanism of detecting an expectation violation or salient content. In low constraint jokes, good comprehenders showed a frontocentral positivity which was interpreted as P3 or P3a, reflecting a high-level mechanism of orientation (cf. Sutton, Tueting, Zubin and John 1967; Coulson and Kutas 2001: 72–74; Gray, Ambady, Lowenthal and Deldin 2004; Roye, Jacobsen and Schröger 2007; Roehm, Dietmar, Bornkessel-Schlesewsky, Rösler and Schleef 2007; Vespignani, Canal, Molinaro, Fonda and Cacciari 2009; Molinaro and Carreiras 2010; Polich 2012).

Comparing jokes to coherent endings, Du, Qin, Tu, Yin, Wang, Yu and Qiu (2013) also found a more pronounced negativity between 300–450 ms post-onset, which they interpreted as N400 and as reflection of incongruity detection. Feng, Chan and Chen (2014) provided similar results through an ERP study comparing jokes with coherent and incoherent stimulus endings, in the format of question/answer combinations. Adaptations were made in the context sentences (called *setup*), so that the punchlines in a set always remained the same (cf. Feng, Chan and Chen 2014: 62). The study showed specificities during incongruity processing at the midline electrodes with a negativity at 400 ms after the onset of the critical word (N400). The highest peak was reached in the nonsensical condition, followed by the joke condition. In line with Coulson and Kutas (2001), they associated the N400 with the detection of an incongruity and difficulties in semantic integration of incoming material into already established knowledge/an initial script.

Mayerhofer and Schacht (2015) conducted an ERP experiment using the same three conditions of jokes, coherence, and incoherence/nonsense. They found an N400 with strongest effects at midline electrodes for the incoherence (with highest peak) and joke conditions, compared to the coherence condition (cf. Mayerhofer and Schacht 2015: 9,11). The authors found no joke-related *late left anterior negativity* (LLAN), which was assumed to be the cost for the working memory's search for a second script. They related the lack of an LLAN to the presence of the incoherent condition, which might have suppressed a script-switch in the humor condition (cf. Mayerhofer and Schacht 2015: 11). However, they did find a sustained N400 for incoherence and jokes. Due to methodological challenges of including the nonsense condition, their subsequent experiment only compared jokes with coherent endings. While the comparison of jokes/coherence weakly indicated an N400 effect for central midline electrodes in jokes (cf. Mayerhofer and Schacht 2015: 16), this experiment did not replicate the sustained N400 found in their previous ERP experiment. The anticipated LLAN was only found in four anterior electrodes between 580–620 ms, with statistically weak results and no late positivity was found (cf. Mayerhofer and Schacht 2015: 12). A subsequent experiment compared only the conditions of coherence and incoherence. Replicating the results of their first ERP experiment, the main effect of the incoherence condition was a long-lasting N400. The strongest results were in the central midline. This result supported a context-independent detection of the semantic violation (cf. Mayerhofer and Schacht 2015: 16).

Canal, Bischetti, Di Paola, Bertini, Ricci and Bambini (2019) also compared jokes to coherent endings in an ERP experiment. They found a more enhanced negativity between 300–500 ms post-onset for jokes, too. However, their negativity had a left-anterior distribution. Complementing the various ERP components of the first processing phase of jokes, the authors interpreted this effect as *left-anterior negativity* (LAN). Nevertheless, the authors eventually associated the LAN with the detection of joke's incongruity and "the search for an alternative funny script to solve the joke" (Canal, Bischetti, Di Paola, Bertini, Ricci and Bambini 2019: 50).

Chan, Chou, Chen and Liang (2012; 2013) aimed to localize the activated brain regions during humor reception through event-related fMRI studies. Comparing a congruous, unfunny condition (coherence) with an irresolvable, unfunny incongruity condition (incoherence) and a resolvable, funny incongruity condition (jokes) in Mandarin Chinese, Chan, Chou, Chen, Yeh, Lavallee, Liang and Chang (2013) found that the brain regions of the *middle temporal gyrus* (MTG) and the *medial frontal gyrus* (MFG) were increasingly activated during the detection of the incongruity (cf. Chan, Chou, Chen, Yeh, Lavallee, Liang and Chang 2013: 173). Previous studies of the MTG and MFG found that they are responsible for storing semantic knowledge (cf. Wiggs, Weisberg and Martin 1999) and detecting semantic violations (cf. Kuperberg, McGuire, Bullmore, Brammer, Rabe-Hesketh, Wright, Lythgoe, Williams and David 2000; Ni, Constable, Mencl, Pugh, Fulbright, Shaywitz, Shaywitz, Gore and Shankweiler 2000; Newman, Pancheva, Ozawa, Neville and Ullman 2011). Chan, Chou, Chen, Yeh, Lavallee, Liang and Chang (2013) also showed that the *temporal lobe* region was additionally activated in more general operations of semantic storage, detection, and categorization – all of which are important tasks during the incongruity detection (cf. Chan, Chou, Chen, Yeh, Lavallee, Liang and Chang 2013: 174).

Evidence for incongruity resolution in humor

The same ERP experiments also found evidence for a second processing phase. Evidence for a reanalysis was mainly seen in the enhanced components of the ERP component of P600 and the activation of the *inferior frontal gyrus* (IFG), *superior frontal gyrus* (SFG), and *inferior parietal lobule* (IPL) brain regions.

The experiments from Feng, Chan and Chen (2014) found evidence for a resolution phase. Following the aforementioned N400, a positivity occurred between 500–700 ms after stimulus onset in the non-joke and joke condition, compared to the nonsense condition. The authors suggested that this finding represented a P600 or a *late positive complex* (LPC). The positivity in the joke condition, which did not differ significantly from the non-joke condition, was considered a repair sequence of the humorous semantic violation during which the recipients reanalyze the text material and (try to) switch to a coherent reading/second script and thereby resolve the incongruity. Even though Du, Qin, Tu, Yin, Wang, Yu and Qiu (2013) also argued for a resolution phase and the "reconstructing and forming of novel associations" (Du, Qin, Tu, Yin, Wang, Yu and Qiu 2013: 156), they related it to their ERP result of a pronounced frontocentral negativity between 600–800 ms post stimulus onset.

Through their fMRI experiments, Chan, Chou, Chen and Liang (2012; 2013) showed that the increased activity of the IFG, SFG and IPL in humor reception can be associated with processes of disambiguation, script switching, and enriching inferences. The SFG was also related to higher executive functions and an integration process during incongruity resolution (cf. Owen 2000; Buxbaum and Saffran 2002; Petrides 2005; Boisgueheneuc, Levy, Volle, Seassau, Duffau, Kinkingnehun, Samson, Zhang and Dubois 2006; Samson, Hempelmann, Huber and Zysset 2009; Bekinschtein, Davis, Rodd and Owen 2011; Chan, Chou, Chen, Yeh, Lavallee, Liang and Chang 2013: 174). Further, the IPL was interpreted as a reflection of associative judgments and the integration of semantic input into a global reading (Samson, Hempelmann, Huber and Zysset 2009; Lee, Booth, Chen and Chou 2011; Binder, Liebenthal, Possing, Medler and Ward 2004; Price, Mummery, Moore, Frackowiak and Friston 1999; Humphries, Binder, Medler and Liebenthal 2006; Humphries, Binder, Medler and Liebenthal 2007; Chan, Chou, Chen and Liang 2012; cf. Chan, Chou, Chen, Yeh, Lavallee, Liang and Chang 2013: 174). The results supported the assumption that incongruity detection and resolution differ, and that the understanding of humorous stimuli can be divided into two phases.

However, the research results are not entirely clear. While Mayerhofer and Schacht (2015) did find evidence for the first processing phase (N400 mentioned above), they did not find a component that could be interpreted as a resolution phase. Other studies, in turn, did not find any evidence for the incongruity detection, but for the resolution. For example, Shibata, Terasawa, Osumi, Masui, Ito, Sato and Umeda (2017) only found a P600 for jokes and interpreted it as reflection of the incongruity resolution.

The processing in separate phases has also not been consistently documented. For example, the processing phases in Coulson et al. (2001) all occurred in the same time window, making "it unlikely that joke processing can be accounted for in terms of a simple two-stage model with surprise and coherence engaged in sequence" (Coulson and Kutas 2001: 74). Further, the second time window in the experiments from Canal, Bischetti, Di Paola, Bertini, Ricci and Bambini (2019), between 500–700 ms after stimulus onset, included two neuronal components for jokes. The authors traced these results back to two parallel cognitive processes in the phase of incongruity resolution: a sustained LAN and a posterior positivity (P600) for the humorous condition compared to congruent endings. While they interpreted the sustained LAN as "the search for an alternative funny script to solve the joke" (Canal, Bischetti, Di Paola, Bertini, Ricci and Bambini 2019: 50), they associated the P600 with resolving the incongruity by finding a second reading through cognitive inferences and with an update of the ongoing discourse (Canal, Bischetti, Di Paola, Bertini, Ricci and Bambini 2019: 49–50). The authors argued against a serial processing of humor because the discovery of the parallel components in the second time window with "the temporal overlap between the sustained LAN and the P600 effect following 500 ms does not support a strictly serial sequence of mechanisms and suggests instead that the resolution step may be associated with a set of ERP correlates (the sustained LAN and the P600), indicative of a (sic!) different undergoing mechanisms with different functions in solving the joke" (Canal, Bischetti, Di Paola, Bertini, Ricci and Bambini 2019: 51–52).

Incongruity detection and resolution in art-horror

For art-horror, it has not yet been examined experimentally, whether the cognitive processing phases of incongruity detection and resolution elicit additional costs, and to what extent they become visible in increased reaction times or enhanced neuroelectric activity. This work hypothesizes that art-horror requires the same cognitive processing mechanisms of incongruity detection and resolution as humor (for theoretical analysis, see Chapter 1.2.3 and 2.3). If this hypothesis holds true, art-horror should elicit the same additional processing costs as humor does, which is examined experimentally in Chapter 4.

Psycholinguistic research on processing phases in humor has already found experimental evidence that positive emotions, such as exhilaration, are reflected in cognitive processing. Humor and art-horror are both associated with an emotional reaction as a third processing phase with differences in the qualia of that phase. Thus, the next section summarizes findings on a third phase of emotional incongruity elaboration and aims to further disentangle humor from art-horror.

3.4 Evidence for emotions after incongruity

The emotions of fear/disgust and exhilaration are the physical reaction following art-horror and humor, respectively. As shown in the definition of emotion (see Chapter 1.2.1), cognition and emotion are intertwined. Further, language and emotion influence each other directly and indirectly (cf. Foolen 2012: 357; Huntsinger 2013: 571; Schwarz-Friesel 2013: 117; Hendricks and Buchanan 2016). Foolen (2012) argues that "emotions are (a) conceptualized in languages by a variety of word forms, with 'literal' and figurative meaning, (b) can be expressed in a more direct way by prosody, morphology, syntactic constructions and by the use of figurative speech, and (c) are foundational for processing language" (Foolen 2012: 371–372).

Cognitive Appraisal Theory claims that emotions provide experiential, embodied information, which interlocutors can recruit for the interpretation and mental representation of a stimulus. According to this reasoning, emotions serve as "sources of value that originate in cognitions" (Oatley and Johnson-Laird 2014: 138) and thereby help the interlocutors to appraise real, abstract, or fictitious stimuli (cf. Oatley and Johnson-Laird 2014: 138). Thus, emotions do not only follow the evaluation of an object but also influence the appraising process.

Schwarz-Friesel (2013) even argues that emotions are an integral part of cognitive schemata (see Chapter 2.2), providing innate or culturally acquired expressive motor information, reactive cues, or abstract concept information that can be recruited in specific situations (cf. Schwarz-Friesel 2013: 112). Schwarz-Friesel assumes that emotions can also have their own cognitive schemata "that consist exclusively of affective body sensations and reaction patterns and are linked to other affective/cognitive schemata" (Schwarz-Friesel 2013: 113).

Thus, the "sentence content is not a purely cognitive content [. . .], the content is automatically loaded with emotion, and this emotion plays a role in the processing of the sentence" (Foolen, Lüdtke, Racine and Zlatev 2012: 370). Neuroimaging studies support this association by showing that the processing of language activates the same neural areas as the processing of emotion. For example, emotional words are processed in the limbic system which is also associated with the processing of emotions, gestures, and prosody (cf. Foolen 2012: 368–369).

Experimental studies have already shown that emotional reactions are also reflected in processing costs and can therefore be measured indirectly. In the following, studies are summarized that have investigated the emotional reaction to humor. They show that after the punchline, exhilaration manifests itself in a third processing phase.

Evidence for a third processing phase in humor

ERP experiments found, in particular, positivities in a third, experimental time-window, which were interpreted as cognitive reflection of an emotional processing phase of humor.

For example, Feng, Chan and Chen (2014) found a centroparietal Late Positive Potential (LPP) in their joke condition between 800–1500 ms after stimulus onset, which was absent in both coherence and incoherence conditions. According to previous research relating the LPP to emotions (cf. Cuthbert, Schupp, Bradley, Birbaumer and Lang 2000; Moratti, Saugar and Strange 2011; Luck 2014), they interpreted it as an amusement phase (cf. Feng, Chan and Chen 2014: 66). Du, Qin, Tu, Yin, Wang, Yu and Qiu (2013) came to similar results, reporting a pronounced positivity between 1250–1400 ms post-onset for jokes compared to coherent texts.

Further, in Mayerhofer and Schacht (2015), a late frontal positivity between 700–1000 ms after stimulus onset was found with significant effects in the joke condition, compared to coherence and incoherence for the left and right regions. The interpretation of this effect was also related to a side study of their first ERP experiment. The authors measured the pupil diameters of the participants and found widened pupils in humorous endings, compared to incoherent and coherent endings. Based on this complementary finding, they suggested that the late frontal positivity of the ERP experiment represented an emotional reaction of mirth (cf. Mayerhofer and Schacht 2015: 10–11).

In the ERP experiment from Canal, Bischetti, Di Paola, Bertini, Ricci and Bambini (2019), the third time window between 700–1100 ms post-onset revealed a Late Positive Complex (LPC) for the humor condition. The authors offered two possible interpretations: Either, this component could represent an ongoing comprehension phase, that includes the participant's elaborative meta-reflections on consequences for the discourse and individual associations with the humorous material. Or, it reflects an emotional reaction of amusement (cf. Canal, Bischetti, Di Paola, Bertini, Ricci and Bambini 2019: 49,51–53).

The spatial differentiation of the activated brain areas and their association with underlying cognitive mechanisms also allowed for the description of a third humor processing phase. For example, Chan, Chou, Chen and Liang (2012; 2013) added a third component to humor models, emphasizing the emotional reaction to humorous stimuli, which had been ignored in linguistic two-stage models so far. During this third phase of humor elaboration, the brain regions of ventromedial prefrontal gyrus (vmPFC), parahippocampal gyrus (PHG), and amygdala (Amg) were activated, which are related to reward (cf. Chan, Chou, Chen and Liang 2012; Chan, Chou, Chen, Yeh, Lavallee, Liang and Chang 2013: 175). The Neural Circuit Model (NCM) of verbal humor (see Figure 12) implements the comprehension stages of incongruity detection and its resolution (consolidated to a comprehension stage, for summary of findings see Chapter 3.3), and the emotional reaction as elaboration phase.

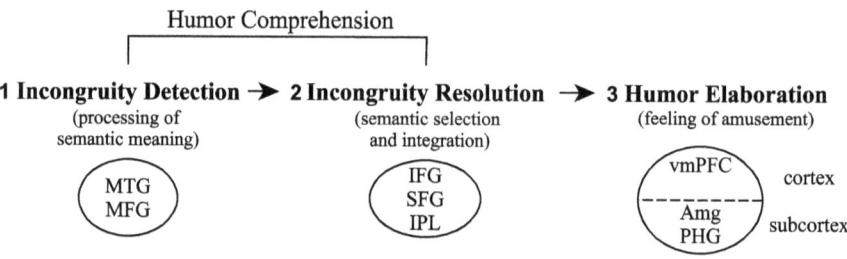

MTG = middle temporal gyrus; MFG = medial frontal gyrus; IFG = inferior frontal gyrus; SFG = superior frontal gyrus; IPL = inferior parietal lobule; vmPFC = ventromedial prefrontal gyrus; PHG = parahippocampal gyrus; Amg = amygdala

Figure 12: Three phases of the neural Circuit Model (NCM) (adapted from Chan, Chou, Chen, Yeh, Lavallee, Liang and Chang 2013: 175).

The *tri-component theory of humor* added an expressive phase of the superficially visible expression of humor, like joyous laughter. It differentiates this phase from NCM's third phase of visceral reactions/invisible appreciation (cf. Chan 2016; Chen, Chan, Dai, Liao and Tu 2017: 284).

While Chan, Chou, Chen, Yeh, Lavallee, Liang and Chang (2013) did not examine the neuronal mechanisms needed for different joke types, Chan and Lavallee (2015) closed this gap by examining jokes with three different LMs of the GTVH and specifying underlying neuronal correlates more accurately. They investigated the LMs of inferring consequences represented in (backward) bridging inference jokes, exaggeration incorporated in exaggeration jokes, and juxtaposition implemented in semantic ambiguity jokes (cf. Chan and Lavallee 2015: 2). Unfortunately, even though a congruent baseline condition was included, a nonsense condition was missing to compare this study successfully with the NCM. Chan and Lavallee found that inference jokes activated the temporo-parietal lobe (temporo-parietal junction) and also the previously identified right middle temporal gyrus (MTG), which Chan and Lavallee related to the inference joke type's requirement of the recipient being able to understand another person's thoughts (Theory of Mind) and interpret the input adequately. During exaggeration jokes as well as ambiguity jokes, the fronto-parietal lobe (the inferior parietal lobule as well as the bilateral inferior frontal gyri) was active, which Chan and Lavallee related to the detection and resolution of new or salient events (cf. Chan and Lavallee 2015: 11–12). Further, they found that the dorsolateral prefrontal cortex and the ventral anterior cingulate cortex were activated in all three joke types; they interpreted this as shared mechanisms that unified the understanding and emotional appreciation of different joke types.

Evidence for a third processing phase in art-horror

In analogy to the third, emotional phase of humor, it is hypothesized that costs related to an emotional reaction should also determine a third processing phase of art-horror. So far, there are no experimental approaches that concretely attest the cognitive art-horror models in real-time. However, experiments using skin conductance tests, body sway measurements, body movement changes, heart rate measurements, or qualitative recipients' evaluations already showed that recipients do experience negative emotions during art-horror consumption (cf. Cantor 2004; Hagenaars, Roelofs and Stins 2013; Zuckerman 2015 [1979]). In line with Zuckerman's research, Pendery (2017) argued that fear is processed in the brain regions of the subcortical limbic system, which is also associated with pleasure and reward. Pendery argues that an explanation for the paradox of horror, Carroll's Compensation Theory, lies in this coincidence of brain regions (cf. Pendery 2017: 151–152). This assumption can also be linked to Gaut's rejection of an analogy between negatively evaluated objects and negative emotions (see Chapter 1.2.3). In more general, the emotions associated with art-horror, fear and disgust, have been investigated from a neurocognitive perspective.

The processing of negative emotions has also been investigated using the method of ERPs. In the same way that the ERP component of the LPP was associated with the emotional response to exhilarating stimuli, it was also shown to reflect the emotional response to unpleasant stimuli (cf. Schupp, Cuthbert, Bradley, Cacioppo, Ito and Lang 2000; Cuthbert, Schupp, Bradley, Birbaumer and Lang 2000; Hajcak, Dunning and Foti 2009; van Berkum, Holleman, Nieuwland, Otten and Murre 2009; Hajcak, Weinberg, MacNamara and Foti 2012; Luck 2014). Comparing the participants' reactions to neutral, pleasant, and unpleasant pictures, Hajcak and Nieuwenhuis (2006) found that an LPP, which has already been associated with the emotional reaction to humor, is also elicited through pictures of threatening scenes. They found that this effect is not distinguishable from the neuroelectric reaction to pleasant stimuli (cf. Hajcak and Nieuwenhuis 2006: 293). This finding indicates that the "LPP is sensitive to the emotional intensity or motivational significance rather than the valence" (Hajcak and Nieuwenhuis 2006: 295). However, Hajcak and Olvet (2008) found that the LPP after unpleasant stimuli (here sad faces and violent images) lasts longer than the LPP after pleasant stimuli (up to 1000 ms), which they associate with a longer-lasting allocation of attention and a negativity bias (cf. Hajcak and Olvet 2008: 254).

Regarding the emotion of fear, Williams, Palmer, Liddell, Le Song and Gordon (2006) found that stimuli of fearful faces effected the neuroelectric activity earlier than happy faces and reported enhanced positivities starting at 120 ms after stimulus onset, compared to enhanced negativities at around 230–350 ms after picture onset of happy faces (cf. Williams, Palmer, Liddell, Le Song and Gordon 2006: 458). They interpreted this finding as processing priority of fear signals, "such that processing of positive signals may be suppressed until vigilance for potential danger is completed" (Williams, Palmer, Liddell, Le Song and Gordon 2006: 458). This result is in line with Hajcak, Weinberg, MacNamara and Foti (2012), who reported an early positivity (P1) with a peak around 120 ms after stimulus onset (at electrode Oz) for fearful compared to neutral faces (cf. Hajcak, Weinberg, MacNamara and Foti 2012: 445). Schupp, Junghöfer, Weike and Hamm (2004; 2004) come to a similar interpretation. Although the effect reported by them for stimuli with threatening faces is an enhanced, early posterior negativity, which is supplemented by a later, enhanced LPP, they also interpret the results as a "more elaborate perceptual analysis" (Schupp, Ohman, Junghöfer, Weike, Stockburger and Hamm 2004: 189) of threatening faces.

ERP correlates were also reported for the emotion of disgust. Luo, Shen, Zhang, Feng, Huang and Li (2013) found that physical (core) and moral disgust can be associated with different phases of processing. While both correlate with stronger, frontal negativities with peaks at around 320 ms and 400 ms, physical disgust also influences an early posterior negativity (EPN) at occipital–temporal electrodes and a more enhanced late positive component (LPC) at left centroparietal electrodes (cf. Xu, Li, Ding, Zhang, Fan, Diao and Yang 2015: 244–245).

Xu, Li, Ding, Zhang, Fan, Diao and Yang (2015) compared neuroelectric activity after frightening and nauseating stimuli and found that "disgusting stimuli elicited a larger P2 than fearful ones, and the difference waves of P3 amplitude under disgusting contexts were smaller than that under fearful contexts" (Xu, Li, Ding, Zhang, Fan, Diao and Yang 2015: 1) (both compared to neutral stimuli). They interpreted this result as an indicator that disgust requires more of the recipients' attention, which impairs inhibitory control more strongly (cf. Xu, Li, Ding, Zhang, Fan, Diao and Yang 2015: 189).

The ERP results on the processing of negative emotions show that some correlates generally reflect emotions (such as the LPP), while the art-horror related emotions of fear and disgust can be additionally associated with early, priority-related effects.

Emotions might also influence incongruity detection and resolution

According to Blanchette and Richards (2010), emotions influence the high level cognitive processes of interpreting, judging, reasoning, and decision making by impairing or promoting the cognitive mechanisms underlying them all. These mechanisms are attention control, priming, reflection, and computational capacity (cf. Blanchette and Richards 2010: 585), which are also important resources in language processing. Thereby, emotions also influence how interlocutors create a "coherent representation of the world, anticipate upon what may be coming next, and make choices about courses of action" (Blanchette and Richards 2010: 562). Emotions affect the underlying mechanisms differently so that the higher level processes of interpreting, judging, reasoning, and decision making are also affected differently with respect to the degree that they depend on each mechanism (cf. Blanchette and Richards 2010: 585). Thus, "not all specific emotions produce the same effects on all cognitive processes" (Blanchette and Richards 2010: 584). Emotions can have both positive, improving, and negative, impairing effects on language processing. For example, negative emotions, such as anxiety, reduce the interlocutor's computational capacity (for cognitive efficiency, also see Chapter 3.5), attention control, and reasoning capacities. Negative emotions also bias more negative interpretations, decrease cognitive control, impair executive control, and are attention demanding (cf. Darke 1988: 145; Channon and Baker 1994; Eysenck, Derakshan, Santos and Calvo 2007: 339; Blanchette and Richards 2010: 585;

Hartikainen, Siiskonen and Ogawa 2012; Blanchette and Caparos 2013: 400; Jasinska, Yasuda, Rhodes, Wang and Polk 2015; Xu, Li, Ding, Zhang, Fan, Diao and Yang 2015). Impaired attention control negatively influences the cognitive mechanisms of predicting, shifting and model updating (cf. Eysenck, Derakshan, Santos and Calvo 2007: 336,347), which have all been identified as important mechanisms in humor and art-horror processing. Being associated with increased creativity and flexibility, positive emotions can also reduce processing capacities by enabling the interlocutors to activate "more mental content than negative moods, thereby reducing the ability of people in positive moods to deploy cognitive resources to meet task demands" (Huntsinger and Schnall 2014: 580). Finally, emotions' influence on language processing has also been discussed in the context of working memory capacity. The (additional) processing of emotions competes with the processing of language, since both processes depend on the limited capacity of the processing working memory (cf. Calvo and Carreiras 1993; Eysenck, Derakshan, Santos and Calvo 2007: 340).

However, Kanske and Kotz (2011) found that negative emotions can also be associated with higher motivation, which activates additional resources and results in faster processing. Thus, cognitive emotion processing is also discussed in the context of stimulus relevance for the interlocutors and their tasks (also see Chapter 2.2.2). While Oatley and Johnson-Laird (2014) claim situations that are relevant to the interlocutors' beliefs or goals evoke emotions, Kanske and Kotz (2011) and Kanske (2015) argue that it is the emotion that makes a stimulus relevant and worth processing with high engagement. Overall, relevance of a stimulus has a positive impact on processing efficiency (cf. Blanchette and Caparos 2013: 412; Kanske 2015: 457).

Against this backdrop, the serial, three-stage processing of humor has been questioned. In line with the experiment design by Coulson and Kutas (1998), Ferstl, Israel and Putzar (2017) compared humorous punchlines with revision texts that included a resolvable yet unfunny incongruity. They aimed not only to prove the cognitive costs of incongruity but also find distinctive features of humor. By recording participants' eye movements, they not only found that revision texts did not elicit additional costs in reading times nor increased regressive eye movements compared to coherent and incoherent endings, but also that the humorous punchlines were read more quickly and caused less regressions than coherent, incoherent, and revision texts. Contrary to the assumptions of the two-stage models and previously described costs for incongruity processing, they even concluded that humor facilitated discourse processing. They considered that this facilitation could be related to humor's positive connotation and positive emotional valence. In line with Appraisal Theory's assumption that emotions contribute to the evaluation of a stimulus, they suggested that the mirthful reaction to humor gives an immediate feedback if the text was interpreted correctly (Ferstl, Israel and Putzar 2017: 277–279; cf. Clore and Palmer 2009). This is in agreement with later work from Canal, Bischetti, Di Paola, Bertini, Ricci and Bambini (2019) and previous doubts from Coulson and Kutas (2001), as the authors argued for parallelly running cognitive processes, questioning the usefulness of a "strictly serial two-stage model [. . .] for understanding the comprehension of verbal humor" (Ferstl, Israel and Putzar 2017: 278).

Unfortunately, the facilitating effect was measured here only for positive emotions, although Schupp, Ohman, Junghöfer, Weike, Stockburger and Hamm (2004) were able to show a facilitating effect for threatening stimuli. This leaves a gap in knowledge about how negative emotions facilitate cognitive processing (see Chapter 4). Another unanswered question relates to the aforementioned findings from Kanske and Kotz (2011) and Kanske (2015). The negative emotions in art-horror could also influence the detection and resolution phase. Since both positive and negative emotions can have both impairing and promoting effects on cognitive processing, experimental research is needed to disentangle the third processing phase of humor and art-horror's emotional elaboration (see Chapter 4).

Finally, recipients' individual features, such as cognitive capacities, emotional sensitivity or character traits, impact reasoning and language comprehension. Therefore, the next section reviews findings on individual differences and their influence on incongruity processing in art-horror and humor.

3.5 Individual differences in incongruity processing

Different people find different texts funny or scary and this has to be considered when analyzing humor and art-horror. Hence, this chapter is dedicated to an overview of the individual differences that influence the processing of incongruity in humor and art-horror.

People differ from each other in many ways and change over their entire lifespan. These individual differences (ID) result from the interaction of a person's physical characteristics, innate or acquired abilities (such as age, sex, intelligence, vocabulary size, world and expert knowledge, attitudes, character traits, or cognitive disorders) and the qualitative and quantitative input of their environment (cf. Daneman 1980; van Berkum, Holleman, Nieuwland, Otten and Murre 2009; Papenberg, Bäckman, Chicherio, Nagel, Heekeren, Lindenberger and Li 2011; Schumacher and Meibauer 2013; Kaufman, Kaufman and Plucker 2014; Kozhevnikov 2014; Bornkessel-Schlesewsky, Philipp, Alday, Kretzschmar, Grewe, Gumpert, Schumacher and Schlesewsky 2015; Antoniou, Cummins and Katsos

2016). Language acquisition and processing are affected by general cognitive functions and subject to interindividual and intraindividual differences. Therefore, the investigation of ID also provides a better understanding of the mechanisms underlying language processing. Determining individual differences ultimately makes it possible to make predictions about language processing (cf. Prat 2011; Kidd, Donnelly and Christiansen 2018) and thus, about (differences in) successful incongruity processing in humor and art-horror.

Individual differences in language comprehension

ID in language comprehension are reflected, for example, in variations in working memory functions, that is in the ability of consciously storing and manipulating discourse representations (cf. Kidd, Donnelly and Christiansen 2018: 156). For example, Just and Carpenter (1992) found that individuals with larger capacities in working memory were better at connecting syntactic and pragmatic input information and pursuing multiple syntactic sentence analyses. Later, Caplan and Waters (1999) also associated the verbal working memory with the allocation of syntactic information. Finally, differences in working memory are also discussed in the context of variations in retrieving lexical elements and corresponding comprehension problems (cf. van Dyke, Johns and Kukona 2014; Kidd, Donnelly and Christiansen 2018: 161).

Further, variations in controlling and regulating discourse representations and responses (executive functions) are influenced by ID (cf. Kidd, Donnelly and Christiansen 2018: 156–162). This implies, for example, updating discourse representations or switching to new representations. Therefore, ID also plays a role in the resolution of incongruities (cf. Novick, Hussey, Teubner-Rhodes, Harbison and Bunting 2013; Vuong and Martin 2014; Nozari, Trueswell and Thompson-Schill 2016; Kidd, Donnelly and Christiansen 2018). Prat (2011) argued that ID influence how strongly executive functions have to be activated to successfully perform a linguistic task. The less activation needed, the "greater available resources for engaging in additional, non-essential, elaborative processes" (Prat 2011: 638–642) and the more efficient a person is (efficiency). She further indicated that the comprehension effectivity is mirrored in a person's neural adaptability to changing tasks, and the synchronization of brain areas (cf. Prat 2011: 638–642).

Individual cognitive capacities for additional processing costs of humor

The previous chapters have shown that incongruity causes additional processing costs. Hence, it is important for the recipients to be able to access free, cognitive capacities of working memory and executive functions in order to cope with the additional effort and solve the incongruity. If recipients are not able to master the additional effort, they may not be able to solve the incongruity and understand the joke, or take more time to do so. In humor research, it has already been shown that joke processing depends on the individual abilities of the recipients. For example, Coulson and Kutas (2001) found that some of their participants did not perform the frame-shift during humor reception. In their ERP experiments, these poor comprehenders (identified through weaker scores in post-hoc comprehension questions) showed different electrophysiological correlates in the time windows of incongruity detection and resolution compared to good comprehenders (reported in Chapter 3.3). Even though poor comprehenders also showed an enhanced negativity between 300–500 ms after high constraint jokes (distributed more frontally), they did not show any correlates reflecting a resolution phase (cf. Coulson and Kutas 2001: 74). Ku, Feng, Chan, Wu and Chen (2017) also separated their participants into good and poor comprehenders. Poor comprehenders showed a less enhanced P600 than good comprehenders, which was interpreted as a less successful resolution of jokes' incongruities (cf. Ku, Feng, Chan, Wu and Chen 2017: 59).

Additionally, the individual cognitive capacity is related to the participants' age, which also influences the processing of humorous punchlines. Uekermann, Channon and Daum (2006) and Shammi and Stuss (2003) showed that older participants have poorer capacities of working memory, verbal abstraction, mentalistic ability, and language comprehension, which was associated with their frequent failure in choosing the correct joke punchline in a set of different conditions. Nevertheless, the elderly still appreciated humor and reacted emotionally.

Sex differences in humor processing

Variability in humor processing is also associated with sex differences. For example, men and women differ in humor preferences. While men preferred aggressive humor and rated sexual jokes (with female victims) as funny, women preferred nonsense humor and rated sexual jokes (with female victims) as less funny (cf. Mundorf, Bhatia, Zillmann, Lester and Robertson 1988; Derks and Arora 1993; Johnson 1992; Herzog 1999). Further, activated brain areas during humor reception differ. Investigating brain regions during humorous cartoon comprehension, Azim, Mobbs, Jo, Menon and Reiss (2005) showed, on one hand, that male and female participants share comprehension strategies in semantic knowledge retrieval and language comprehension (associated with the temporal–posterior junction and temporal pole and the inferior frontal gyrus). On the other hand, they showed that female participants more strongly activated executive functions and language decoding strategies (associated with more strongly activated left prefrontal cortex), higher reward response but lower reward expectation (associated with stronger activity of mesolimbic regions, including the nucleus accumbens) (cf. Azim, Mobbs, Jo, Menon and Reiss 2005: 16496). Kohn, Kellermann, Gur, Schneider and Habel (2011) supported that women activate more emotion-related brain regions than men (associated with the ventral system with amygdala, insula, and anterior cingulate cortex) (cf. Kohn, Kellermann, Gur, Schneider and Habel 2011: 888). In their ERP experiments, Chang, Ku and Chen (2018) observed a gender difference in a late processing phase between 1000 and 1300 ms post-onset, which they interpreted as differences in the integration of cognitive and emotional aspects. While women invested more mental effort to reconcile cognitive and emotional aspects of processing, the male participants showed a higher degree of automatic processes at the transition between comprehension of the incongruity and emotional response. Further, the reading time experiments from Ferstl, Israel and Putzar (2017) not only found a facilitation effect of humor compared to coherent texts (reported in Chapter 3.3) but also that men profited more from this effect than women. They suggested that the feedback of amusement, which indicated immediately that the text was understood correctly, helped men more than women, compensating their disadvantage in processing nonhumorous material and inferencing from verbal stimuli (cf. Ferstl, Israel and Putzar 2017: 280).

Personality differences in humor processing

Beyond linguistic and cognitive abilities, humor processing is also influenced by personality traits such as extroversion and neuroticism, exhilaratability, mood, and the sense of humor. For example, Mobbs, Hagan, Azim, Menon and Reiss (2005) showed that extraversion correlates with the activation of the right orbital frontal cortex, ventrolateral prefrontal cortex, and bilateral temporal cortices during humor reception. In contrast, introversion correlated especially with an enhanced activation of the bilateral amygdala. Further, the authors found that emotionally stable participants showed enhanced activation of brain regions associated with reward (right orbital frontal cortex, caudate, and nucleus accumbens). These results suggest that "personality style plays a fundamental role in the neurobiological systems subserving humor appreciation" (Mobbs, Hagan, Azim, Menon and Reiss 2005: 16502). This finding is also supported by the studies of Ku, Feng, Chan, Wu and Chen (2017), who showed that more amused participants of their ERP experiment showed stronger emotion-related positivities (such as the LPP) (cf. Ku, Feng, Chan, Wu and Chen 2017: 60–61).

Personality features also correlate with the intensity and frequency with which an emotional reaction to humor is expressed in recipients' faces. For example, Ruch, Köhler and van Thriel (1996) and Ruch (2005) found a correlation between participants' cheerfulness and smile intensity. Also, they found the character traits of seriousness and bad mood correlated negatively with the strength and frequency of exhilaration and laughter. The fear of being laughed at, gelotophobia, also correlated negatively with frequency and intensity of shown laughter reactions (cf. Ruch, Köhler and van Thriel 1996; Ruch 2005; Ruch and Proyer 2008a; Proyer 2014) (see Chapter 4.3).

Further, the personality trait of sensation seeking (see Chapter 1.2.3) correlates with the preference for nonsense humor and decreasing enjoyment of resolved incongruities (cf. Forabosco and Ruch 1994; Samson, Hempelmann, Huber and Zysset 2009). The latter also correlates with age differences in intolerance/conservatism (cf. Ruch, McGhee and Hehl 1990).

Extrapolating individual differences to art-horror

Since art-horror reception, like the processing of humorous incongruity, is dependent on the cognitive, linguistic, and emotional abilities of the recipients, it can be assumed that the additional costs of detecting and solving incongruities are also subject to the individual cognitive capacities of the recipients in horror processing. While this has not yet been investigated experimentally, other correlations between ID and horror processing have already been investigated. For example, a recipients' gender has been associated with preferences in the art-horror genre. Lin (2017) reported sex differences in coping strategies in virtual-reality horror games. In her study, women used disengagement and cognitive avoidance strategies (closing one's eyes or saying "This is not real.") more often than men, while men approached the threatening stimulus more often (cf. Lin 2017: 356). Martin (2019) summarized findings on sex differences in art-horror consumption as follows: women visit the horror genre less often and enjoy it less than men. Women show and report higher levels of fear and anxiety during horror reception than men, which is attributed to a generally increased level of disgust sensitivity and empathetic concern in women. In terms of empathy, Martin further summarized that a low level of empathy leads to more art-horror enjoyment and vice versa, that high levels of empathy and personal distress reduce the enjoyment of art-horror. In terms of disgust, Martin (2019) suggested that disgust sensitivity (cf. Rozin, Haidt, McCauley, Dunlop and Ashmore 1999; Schienle, Dietmaier, Ille and Leutgeb 2010) might be a predictor of art-horror enjoyment. In line with cf. Zuckerman; Zuckerman (1994; 2015 [1979]) and Pendery (2017), he also depicted a relationship between art-horror enjoyment, the individual search for sensation and an individual's optimal level of arousal (see also Chapter 1.2.3) (cf. Martin 2019: 17). These experimental findings on ID can be linked to Gaut's conceptual assumption that a negatively evaluated object does not automatically result in negative emotions (see Chapter 1.2.3). On the contrary, especially among the sensation seekers, positive emotions seem to arise during the reception of art-horror.

Just as the personality trait of extraversion is important to predict the reception of humor, it has also been investigated in the reception of art-horror and has been associated with more frequent horror consumption. Furthermore, it has been shown that the trait of neuroticism is associated with higher fear arousal, whereas recipients with high emotional stability are less likely to experience fright (cf. Reynaud, El Khoury-Malhame, Rossier, Blin, Khalfa and García 2012; Martin 2019: 10).

3.6 Intermediate results

In this chapter, work dedicated to an empirical examination of humor and art-horror models was presented. The aim was to continue the theoretical comparison of humor and art-horror from the previous chapters with an empirical perspective. This chapter derived how theoretical assumptions can be transferred, in general, to experimental correlates, and, in particular, to an experimental analysis of humor and art-horror processing.

The notion of incongruity has been embedded in language comprehension models. According to incremental, forward-directed models of language comprehension, interlocutors make expectation-based predictions about incoming material to integrate it more easily into established mental discourse representations (cf. Friston 2010; Bornkessel-Schlesewsky and Schumacher 2016). In humor and art-horror, the interlocutors' predictions fail because they receive an unpredictable, incongruent input. Thus, compared to correctly predicted, coherent texts, humor and art-horror need an effortful update of the mental representation, including a textual reanalysis and shift to the new reading. This is computationally demanding and leads to additional cognitive effort (so-called costs) (cf. Levy 2008; Friston 2010; Levy 2011; Bornkessel-Schlesewsky and Schumacher 2016). These costs are expressed in the reactions of the recipients, for example in longer reading times or enhanced electrophysiological activity. They can be measured indirectly by comparing recipients' reactions to humor and art-horror texts with those to coherent, incoherent and unresolvable, or incongruent and unemotional texts.

Reading time experiments compared the processing of humor and expectation-coherent texts and found prolonged reading times for humor on the critical word and the first spill-over region. These were interpreted as additional costs for frame-shifting and updating the mental representation (cf. Coulson and Kutas 1998; Coulson and Kutas 2001; Mayerhofer and Schacht 2015).

The recipients' neuroelectric activity during humor reception, measured in ERP experiments with a high temporal resolution, delivered psycholinguistic evidence for the processing phases of detection, resolution, and emotional reaction. Evidence for the first humor processing stage of incongruity detection was found in the ERP components of N400, LAN, and P3, which were interpreted as a reflection of semantic integration problems, the detection of an expectation violation or salient content, an orientation mechanism, or the search for an alternative reading (cf. Coulson and Kutas 2001; Feng, Chan and Chen 2014; Mayerhofer and Schacht 2015; Canal, Bischetti, Di Paola, Bertini, Ricci and Bambini 2019). Other methodological approaches (fMRI) also support the fact that problems of semantic integration and incongruity detection occur in humor reception. In event-related fMRI studies, it was found that the brain regions of the middle temporal gyrus, medial frontal gyrus and temporal lobe were increasingly activated during humor reception. They can be associated with the storage of semantic knowledge, the detection of semantic violations, and categorization (cf. Chan, Chou, Chen and Liang 2012; Chan, Chou, Chen, Yeh, Lavallee, Liang and Chang 2013). Evidence was also found for the second humor processing phase of incongruity resolution through the same methodological approaches. ERP experiments found a P600 and it was considered a repair sequence of the humorous semantic violation during which the recipient reanalyzes the text material and switches to a coherent reading/second script (cf. Feng, Chan and Chen 2014; Shibata, Terasawa, Osumi, Masui, Ito, Sato and Umeda 2017; Canal, Bischetti, Di Paola, Bertini, Ricci and Bambini 2019). Again, fMRI experiments supported a second processing stage of resolution, separated from incongruity detection. The increased activation of the inferior frontal gyrus, superior frontal gyrus, and inferior parietal lobule during humor reception were associated with processes of disambiguation, script switching, enriching inferences, executive functions, an integration process during incongruity resolution, associative judgments, and the integration of semantic input into a global reading (cf. Chan, Chou, Chen and Liang 2012; Chan, Chou, Chen, Yeh, Lavallee, Liang and Chang 2013).

Since language, cognition, and emotion influence each other directly and indirectly (cf. Foolen 2012: 357; Huntsinger 2013: 571; Schwarz-Friesel 2013: 117; Hendricks and Buchanan 2016), the emotional reaction of exhilaration is also reflected in processing costs as third phase in humor models. In ERP experiments, LPP, LPC, and a late frontal positivity were associated with amusement (cf. Feng, Chan and Chen 2014; Mayerhofer and Schacht 2015; Canal, Bischetti, Di Paola, Bertini, Ricci and Bambini 2019). Widened pupils in humorous endings also supported the interpretation of an emotional reaction (cf. Mayerhofer and Schacht 2015). FMRI experiments outlined the brain regions activated during emotional reactions to humorous stimuli, ventromedial prefrontal gyrus, parahippocampal gyrus and amygdala, and related them to reward and humorous elaboration (cf. Chan, Chou, Chen and Liang 2012; Chan, Chou, Chen, Yeh, Lavallee, Liang and Chang 2013).

However, experimental research does not consistently support the chronological stages of detection and resolution in humor models: Mayerhofer and Schacht (2015) did not find a component that could be interpreted as a resolution phase. Shibata, Terasawa, Osumi, Masui, Ito, Sato and Umeda (2017), in turn, did not find any evidence for the incongruity detection. Coulson et al. (2001) and Canal, Bischetti, Di Paola, Bertini, Ricci and Bambini (2019) doubt a serial processing because their findings all occurred in the same time window. Additionally, the emotions elicited in humor and art-horror might not only be reflected in their own, third processing phase but also influence the stages of detection and resolution. It has been shown that emotions influence cognitive and language-related processes of interpreting, judging, reasoning, and decision making by impairing or promoting underlying cognitive mechanisms, such as attention control, priming, reflection, and computational capacity (cf. Blanchette and Richards 2010). Both negative and positive emotions can have positive, improving, and negative, impairing effects on language processing. For example, on one hand, negative emotions, such as anxiety, can reduce computational capacity, attention and cognitive control, executive functions and reasoning capacities (cf. Darke 1988: 145; Channon and Baker 1994; Blanchette and Richards 2010: 585; Hartikainen, Siiskonen and Ogawa 2012; Blanchette and Caparos 2013: 400; Xu, Li, Ding, Zhang, Fan, Diao and Yang 2015; Jasinska, Yasuda, Rhodes, Wang and Polk 2015), thereby impairing cognitive mechanisms of predicting, shifting and model updating (cf. Eysenck, Derakshan, Santos and Calvo 2007: 336,347). On the other hand, negative emotions can be associated with higher motivation and stronger relevance of the stimulus so that additional cognitive resources are activated, resulting in faster processing (cf. Kanske and Kotz 2011; Kanske 2015). Analogously, positive emotions can also reduce processing capacities by enabling the interlocutors to be more creative and flexible and activate more content in parallel. However, due to the limited processing capacity of working memory, more processing rapidly leads to the maximum load, so that it takes longer to process the content (cf. Huntsinger and Schnall 2014: 580). This also applies to the parallel processing of emotions and language (cf. Calvo and Carreiras 1993; Eysenck, Derakshan, Santos and Calvo 2007: 340).

Furthermore, variations between and within individuals influence cognitive mechanisms and language processing, which are summarized as individual differences. Factors such as cognitive capacity, intelligence, language skills, age, gender, and personality traits correlate with the efficiency with which a person processes input, controls, regulates and updates discourse representations, adapts to changing tasks, and synchronizes brain areas. They influence how a person masters additional effort for difficult input, and thus how a person resolves incongruities (cf. Prat 2011; Novick, Hussey, Teubner-Rhodes, Harbison and Bunting 2013; Kidd, Donnelly and Christiansen 2018). For example, Coulson and Kutas (2001) were able to show that subjects who scored poorly in post-joke comprehension questions also showed no ERP correlates for the resolution phase. This was interpreted as an incomplete frame-shift due to poor cognitive capacities. Sex differences play a role in genre preferences, active brain areas during humor reception, executive functions, emotional reactions, and feedback mechanisms (cf. Mundorf, Bhatia, Zillmann, Lester and Robertson 1988; Johnson 1992; Derks and Arora 1993; Herzog 1999; Azim, Mobbs, Jo, Menon and Reiss 2005; Kohn, Kellermann, Gur, Schneider and Habel 2011). Further, (the prediction of) humor processing is determined by personality traits such as extraversion, neuroticism, exhilaratability, mood, and sense of humor. They influence the activation of brain areas as well as intensity and frequency of facial expressions following humorous stimuli (cf. Mobbs, Hagan, Azim, Menon and Reiss 2005; Ruch 2005; Ruch and Proyer 2008a; Proyer 2014).

The shortcoming of all humor experiments and, more generally, of all humor theories is that none include a control condition which incorporates a resolvable incongruity, inducing emotions other than exhilaration. Thus, theories that attempt to explain humor on the basis of incongruity face the challenge of describing only those incongruities that actually trigger humor and exhilaration, and of separating humorous incongruity from incongruity that does not cause joy and laughter. Even though humor research often mentions similarities between humor and art-horror, a detailed experimental comparison investigating a shared underlying mechanism is missing. So far, art-horror has been analyzed from a literary science perspective so that experimental results are rare. In order to determine the underlying, higher-level mechanisms of incongruity processing but also phenomena-related peculiarities as distinctive moments between different incongruity phenomena, further experimental comparisons are needed. These experiments now also have to include further emotional reactions to incongruity that go beyond exhilaration. If the incongruity in humor and art-horror is indeed processed by the same cognitive mechanisms, art-horror and humor would have to show the same psycholinguistic results for the detection and resolution of incongruity and differ only in the emotions triggered.

By comparing participants' reading times in the self-paced reading time paradigm (see Chapter 4.2), their facial expressions through FACS (see Chapter 4.3), and their neuro-electric activity through ERPs (see Chapter 4.4) in humor and art-horror, the following chapter attests the three processing stages of incongruity detection, resolution, and emotion.

4 Humor & horror: An experimental comparison

Previous research has compared the processing costs of humor with costs of coherent, incoherent and revision texts. They found that the processing of humorous material lead to additional cognitive costs due to the detection and resolution of incongruities, and an emotional reaction (see Chapter 3). A comparison condition with a resolvable incongruity leading to emotions other than exhilaration has always been missing. This book closes this research gap from a psycholinguistic point of view by being the first to experimentally compare humor and art-horror and address the real-time processing of art-horror.

This chapter investigates the following research questions through three experiments:
1. Does art-horror elicit additional processing costs compared to (in)coherent items?
2. How do the cognitive processing costs of art-horror differ from costs of humorous, incongruent items, with respect to intensity and time-course of the observed costs?
3. Are these processing costs associated with the local incongruity of the stimulus? Can they be correlated with incongruity detection and resolution?
4. Do the recipients react emotionally after incongruity detection and resolution?

The innovative idea of the current book is to broaden humor experiments (see Chapter 3) with art-horror to verify if the incongruity in art-horror texts is cognitively processed, resolved, and elaborated the same way as it is in humorous texts.

Therefore, suitable minimal triplets were created for the three conditions humor, art-horror, and coherence, and later incoherence. They were developed according to the working definitions of art-horror and humor (see Chapters 1.3 and 2.4) as resolvable incongruities that most likely cause additional cognitive costs and result in the emotions of fear/disgust or exhilaration, respectively. To prepare the material for the on-line experiments, the minimal triplets were normed through off-line judgments in two questionnaires (see Chapter 4.1). Assuming that reading behavior and difficulties in reading comprehension indirectly provide information about underlying cognitive processes, the first experiment compared participant's reading times in the SPR paradigm (see Chapter 4.2). The second experiment was run in parallel with the reading time experiment. Using FACS, it was verified whether the emotions associated with art-horror (fear/disgust) and humor (exhilaration) were visibly mirrored in the participants' facial expressions (see Chapter 4.3). Comparing participant's ERPs, the third experiment investigated with a high temporal resolution to what extent cognitive functions necessary to process art-horror and humor (incongruity detection, resolution, and emotion) are reflected in neuro-electric activity of the human brain (see Chapter 4.4).

4.1 Stimuli norming: Questionnaire I and II

In the previous chapters, it was pointed out conceptually and through examples of psycholinguistic experiments that art-horror and humor contain incongruities that are processed by the recipients in a three-step of detection, resolution, and elaboration (e.g. Raskin 1985; Carroll 1999; Grodal 2000; Coulson and Kutas 2001; Coulson, Urbach and Kutas 2006; Chan, Chou, Chen and Liang 2012; Chan, Chou, Chen, Yeh, Lavallee, Liang and Chang 2013; Feng, Chan and Chen 2014; Mayerhofer and Schacht 2015; Canal, Bischetti, Di Paola, Bertini, Ricci and Bambini 2019, see also Chapters 1.2.3, 2.3, 3.3, and 3.4). To make the phenomena experimentally comparable, minimal triplets were generated in the three conditions art-horror, humor, and coherence, which differed only in one segment (punchline):

- Art-horror stimuli contained surprising, semantic incongruities that were resolvable through a script switch leading to a coherent reading and an emotional elaboration to fear or disgust.
- Humor stimuli also contained surprising, semantic incongruities resolved through a script switch and led to a coherent reading and exhilaration.
- Coherence served as control and contained no opposition, so that a coherent reading was immediately recognizable without script switch and emotional elaboration.

A norming study was conducted to collect off-line judgments regarding the perceived humor, art-horror, and surprise of potential test items, and preselect proper stimuli for subsequent on-line experiments. Participants were asked to rate the scariness, funniness, surprise effects, and comprehensibility of the minimal triplets on a 7-point Likert scale. While scariness and funniness questions verified whether a given item triggered the intended effect of being scary or exhilarant, surprise and comprehensibility questions tested for the presence and strength of incongruities and their resolvability.

It was predicted that art-horror stimuli reached high values on the Likert scale in surprise questions because the incongruities included were unexpectable. High scores in scariness were predicted for art-horror items because the incongruities were intended to be fearsome. At the same time, incongruities were resolvable so that good comprehensibility was predicted. Humor items were predicted to reach high scores in surprise and funniness due to unexpected incongruities that are resolved to an exhilarant second script. Good comprehensibility in humor items assessed, again, if the incongruity was resolvable to a coherent reading. For the control condition low values in scariness, funniness, and surprise were predicted along with high comprehensibility due to missing incongruities.

4.1.1 Questionnaire I

4.1.1.1 Methods

Participants
Overall, 55 participants (36 male, 19 female) ranging from 18 to 48 years of age (mean 29.4) took part. Most participants (43) were monolingual German native speakers and eleven were bilingual native German speakers. One non-native speaker with a C2 German level participated. The majority of the participants had completed a college entrance exam or higher.

Material
This questionnaire comprised the three conditions art-horror, humor, and coherence. Minimal triplets were created by replacing the punchlines of humorous items with endings that elicit scary or coherent readings (cf. Meimberg 2011; Mayerhofer and Schacht 2015; 140signs 2015; all items adapted). The minimal triplets exploited the same SO and LM of the GTVH, and mostly contained global incongruities. A total of 42 minimal triplets (126 items) were rated. The triplets had a length of two to five sentences varying with regard to sentence complexity and direct speech. Critical words appeared at the last position in a sentence. They had the same word category within a triplet (except for one adjective). The majority of critical words were nominal phrases (104), followed by verbal phrases (18), or predicative adjectives (4). They were normalized with respect to number of syllables and characters, for all conditions; a one-factorial ANOVA revealed no significant differences between the three conditions with $F(2,120) = 1.68$ ($p = 0.191$) and $F(2,123) = 0.429$ ($p = 0.653$) for the number of syllables and characters, respectively. The critical words were not yet normalized to Leipziger Wortschatz word frequency (cf. Universität Leipzig 2021), because priority was given to comprehensibility, surprise, and scariness/funniness of the stimuli (see Table 3); a one-factorial ANOVA revealed differences between the three conditions with $F(2,123) = 3.6$ ($p = 0.03$).

Table 3: Word frequency of critical segments (means and standard deviations (sd) per condition (cf. Universität Leipzig 2021).

	Mean	Sd
Art-horror	13.29	3.34
Humor	14.21	4.76
Coherence	11.81	4.21

Table 4 exemplifies the triplet structure (English translations in italics):

Table 4: Minimal triplet example for the three conditions art-horror, humor, and coherence.

Condition		Context	Critical word
1a	Art-horror	Behutsam steckte er ihr den Trauring an den Finger. Der Moment war perfekt. Er berührte ihre Wange. Sie setzte gerade richtig ein: die	Leichenstarre. *rigor mortis.*
1b	Humor		Viagra. *Viagra.*
1c	Control group: coherence	*He carefully put the wedding ring on her finger. The moment was perfect. He touched her cheek. She/It just started kicking in: the*	Liebe. *love.*

Items were complemented by 36 fillers (Garcia Rosas 2010; Pohl 2010; Webfail Entertainment GmbH 2012; Dewi 2014; Quadrasophics 2015; 140signs 2015; Componeo 2016a; Componeo 2016b; Componeo 2016c; Hormann 2018; Ullrich 2018; Webfail Entertainment GmbH 2020; Betzold 2021; Componeo 2021; Made My Day GmbH 2021, all items adapted) of two to three sentences in length and had typical scary or humorous content, which was easily recognized because of a richer context.

Items were split into four lists according to the Latin squares design so that each subject saw each target only once and only art-horror targets and fillers or humor targets and fillers. The latter split was conducted to avoid that the participants' emotional reaction to art-horror and humor items would influence each other with regard to participant's different emotional reactions. All lists were pseudorandomized and rated by (nearly) the same number of participants (13–15 each). After every item, the following closed questions had to be answered on a 7-point Likert scale with verbal anchor (with 1 = not at all and 7 = absolutely); the final question required a yes/no/undecided response.

The two art-horror lists included the following four questions (English translations in italics):

1. Der Text hat das Potential jemanden zu gruseln.
The text has the potential to scare somebody.

The participants were asked to rate the frightening potential of a given item. We did not ask directly if the text was scary to receive a more distanced rating. This was due to participant's reports and internal feedback of pilot examples. People subjectively said they were in general never afraid or watched the scariest movies without goose bumps, but in the end, they admitted that (some of) the sentences were scary. Thus, there was a need to facilitate a more objective rating and avoid dishonesty in a genre that is often instrumentalized as a test case for courage. With respect to item selection, scary items had to reach a mean value of 4 or above to count as art-horror in subsequent reading time studies and ERP experiments.

2. Das Ende des Textes hat mich überrascht.
The end of the text surprised me.

The second rating asked how greatly a given item surprised the participants. It checked the predictability/unexpectedness of the critical segment. Surprise had to reach a mean value of 4 or above to count as sufficiently incongruent in subsequent reading time studies and ERP experiments.

3. Der Text ist lustig.
The text is funny.

The third question asked whether participants found the item funny. Since the structure of the short art-horror sentences resembled stereotypical jokes rather than stereotypical art-horror, there was a risk that the participants laughed about the art-horror items. Thus, to control for the effects of funniness these (dark) humor/art-horror items were later excluded from subsequent comprehension studies.

4. Ich habe den Text verstanden.
I understood the text.

This question asked whether participants understood the text. It assessed whether the incongruity in art-horror items confused participants and if participants interpreted the incongruity as nonsense without a resolution phase. Three answers were possible: "Ja/*yes*" (= 1), "Nein/*no*" (= 2) and "Ich weiß nicht/*I do not know*" (= 3).

The two humor lists included the following three questions (English translations in italics):

1. **Der Text ist lustig.**
   The text is funny.

Participants were asked to rate how funny the text was and only the best working humorous items were included in later experiments. We did not expect the same risk of dishonesty with the first question on the art-horror lists and, therefore, directly asked about the participant's subjective impression. We did not ask for an emotional experience (as in the art-horror lists). We revised this question in Questionnaire II (see below). Humorous items had to reach a mean value of 4 or above to count as humor in subsequent reading time studies and ERP experiments.

2. **Das Ende des Textes hat mich überrascht.**
   The end of the text surprised me.

Identical to question two on the art-horror list, this question asked to what extent a given item surprised the participants to check for predictability/ unexpectedness. Again, surprise had to reach a mean value of 4 or above to count as incongruent in subsequent reading time studies and ERP experiments.

3. **Ich habe den Text verstanden.**
   I understood the text.

The third question of the horror list probing if the items were alternatively interpreted (here as potentially being scary) was not included in the humorous lists. We did not anticipate humorous items being interpreted as scary. Thus, the last question tested for confusing nonsense effects of the incongruity by asking whether participants understood the text. "Ja/*Yes* (1)", "Nein/*No*(2)" and "Ich weiß nicht/*I do not know* (3)" were possible answer option. Values had to approach 1 to be included into later experiments.

Procedure

The survey was conducted on-line through the platform *Qualtrics* (Qualtrics 2005). The participants received a link to the survey via email or through the platform *prolific* (Prolific 2014). *Prolific* only activated those participants for the study who had previously stated in a self-disclosure that German was their native language. After clicking on the link, the survey started immediately with an introduction of general information and formal questions. After a welcoming address, participants were informed about their voluntary and anonymous participation and had to provide informed consent to participate. Next, participants randomly received one of the four lists. After reading and rating every item on the given scale, the participants saw a thank-you page stating that the study was completed. Participation took around 20 minutes.

Data analysis

Means and standard deviations (sd) were computed for the surprise, funniness, and scariness questions. One-way, repeated measures ANOVA calculations tested for significant differences between surprise, scariness, and funniness means. To counter problems of multiple comparisons, pairwise comparisons between surprise and funniness means were calculated with an adjusted significance level set to $p < .0375$ based on a modified Bonferroni procedure (cf. Keppel and Wickens 2004). To test whether there was a significant difference between the three possible answers of the comprehension question (nominal scale: Yes/No/I do not know), Pearson's X^2 was computed and the answer scores were computed in percent.

4.1.1.2 Results

Art-horror items reached elevated scariness values with a mean of 4.41 (sd = 1.04), elevated surprise values with a mean of 4.79 (sd = 0.79), and a low funniness mean of 2.18 (sd = 0.68) compared to coherence. The coherent items in art-horror lists reached a slightly elevated scariness mean of 2.89 (sd = 1.12), and slightly elevated surprise mean of 3.42 (sd = 0.91), low funniness means of 2.16 (sd = 0.7). Humor items showed elevated surprise values with a mean of 4.27 (sd = 0.47), but only slightly elevated mean funniness values, 2.85 (sd = 0.73). Coherence items in humor lists also showed a slightly elevated surprise mean of 3.52 (sd = 0.73) and low funniness values (mean of 2.18, sd = 0.6) (see Figure 13).

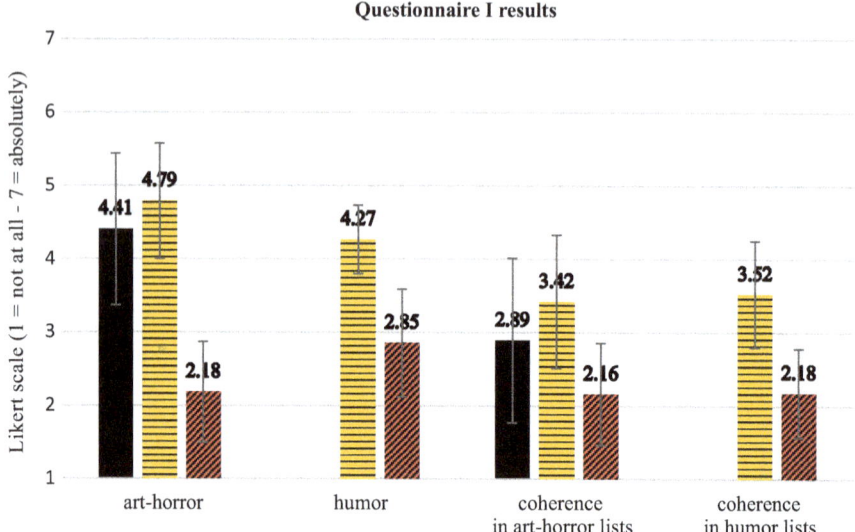

Figure 13: Results of Questionnaire I regarding means per condition and question. Scariness, surprise, and funniness were rated on a 7-point Likert scale (1 = not at all; 7 = absolutely), error bars = sd.

The differences between scariness in art-horror and coherence[21] were significant with $F(1,82) = 41.315$ ($p < .0001$). The differences between surprise in art-horror, humor, coherence in art-horror, and coherence in humor were significant with $F(3,164) = 32.233$ ($p < .0001$).

Pairwise comparisons of surprise effects (adjusted significance level set to $p < .0375$) revealed the following results: Differences between art-horror and humor were significant with $F(1,82) = 13.81$ ($p = .0004$). Differences between art-horror and coherence in art-horror lists were significant with $F(1,82) = 54.66$ ($p < .0001$). Differences between humor and coherence in humor lists were significant with $F(1,82) = 31.11$ ($p < .0001$). Differences between coherence in art-horror lists and coherence in humor lists were not significant with $F(1,82) = 0.33$ ($p = .57$) (see Table 5).

---

[21] Since there are no significant differences between the coherence values of the art-horror and humor lists, I assume that there are no between-subject differences in the other comparisons either.

Table 5: Pairwise comparisons of surprise; n.s. = not significant.

surprise	Art-horror		Humor		Coherence (in art-horror)		Coherence (in humor)	
	F	p	F	p	F	p	F	p
Art-horror	/		13.81	.0004	54.66	<.0001	/	
Humor	/		/		/		31.11	<.0001
Coherence (in art-horror)	/		/		/		.33	n.s.

The differences between exhilaration means in art-horror, humor, coherence in art-horror lists, and coherence in humor lists were significant with F (3,164) = 10.55 (p < .0001). Pairwise comparisons (adjusted significance level set to p < .0375) revealed significant differences both between art-horror and humor with F (1,82) = 18.82 (p < .0001) and between humor and coherence in humor lists with F (1,82) = 21.44 (p < .0001). Differences between art-horror and coherence (F (1,82) = .03 (p = .88)) and between the coherence conditions (F (1,82) = .01 (p = .91)) failed significance (see Table 6).

Table 6: Pairwise comparisons of exhilaration; n.s. = not significant).

exhilaration	Art-horror		Humor		Coherence (in art-horror)		Coherence (in humor)	
	F	p	F	p	F	p	F	p
Art-horror	/		18.82	<.0001	n.s.		/	
Humor	/		/		/		21.44	<.0001
Coherence (in art-horror)	/		/		/		.01	n.s.

Comprehensibility scores (percentual and X^2) for the last question of each item (*I understood the text. Yes/No/I do not know*) are summarized in Table 7 per condition.

Table 7: Percentual comprehensibility values and Pearson's X^2 for the three answer possibilities of yes/no/I do not know.

	Yes (%)	No (%)	I do not know (%)	X^2
Art-horror	94.14	1.83	4.03	912.3
Humor	82.27	8.21	9.52	656.4
Coherence (in art-horror)	91.03	3.66	5.31	828.3
Coherence (in humor)	83.74	7.22	9.04	696.7

4.1.1.3 Discussion

Art-horror items reached elevated means in scaring and surprising potential, while the scores in art-horror's funniness remained low. Art-horror items were highly understandable. Humor items also matched expectations with elevated surprise means. Thus, both art-horror and humor surprised the participants, which can be interpreted as participant's detection of incongruity. The difference between surprise in art-horror and humor (significantly lower) shows that art-horror's incongruity was experienced more intensely; this might be an early hint, in line with Rothbart (2017 [1976]), at why art-horror triggers fear instead of exhilaration. The higher scores in art-horror surprise could also relate to the fact that participants are more used to reading humorous stimuli and are, therefore, less surprised. Art-horror's and humor's comprehensibility reflects that the surprise/incongruity was resolved to a coherent reading and did not confuse the participants.

Humor's funniness values were significantly higher than coherence and art-horror but did not show the expected values above 4. On one hand, this finding could relate to the different question formats concerning scariness and funniness; while the scariness question asked for the potential of an emotional reaction, the funniness question did not include an emotion-related word, nor did it ask for the potential to exhilarate. On the other hand, this finding indicates that the material was simply not funny enough and needed improvements.

There were no surprise and funniness differences in the coherent items, and as such the influence of distribution on art-horror and humor lists can be excluded. The elevated surprise scores in the coherence conditions could relate to the short, unusual text format which would also explain the slightly elevated comprehension scores in humor lists.

Overall, even though art-horror items reached good scores in scariness, surprise, and comprehensibility, humor items needed improvements concerning funniness. The format of the funniness question also needed adaptations. This was addressed in a second questionnaire.

4.1.2 Questionnaire II

To deal with challenges from the preceding ratings and improve the material, the second norming questionnaire adapted given triplets according to individual scores and changed the format concerning the funniness question. This questionnaire included more items to generate enough functioning triplets for later experiments.

4.1.2.1 Methods

Participants
Ratings of 75 participants (35 female, 39 male, 1 missing specification) ranging from 18 to 60 years of age (mean 29.65) were recorded. Most participants (60) were monolingual native German speakers and 15 were bilingual native German speakers. The majority of the participants had obtained a college entrance exam or higher. One participant (male, 29 years old, monolingual German native speaker) was excluded because he skipped most questions. Thus, a total of 74 participants were included in this analysis.

Material
Questionnaire II included the same conditions as the preceding one with art-horror, humor, and coherence. Minimal triplets of the preceding study were adapted, and supplementary triplets were added (taken and adapted from the same items sources as in questionnaire I, see 4.1.1.1) so that this questionnaire included a total of 67 triplets. The triplets fulfilled the same criteria concerning length (two to five sentences varying with regard to sentence complexity, and direct speech), critical word position (last triplet position), and word category within a triplet (except for one adjective, one verb and one preposition phrase). The majority of critical words were nominal phrases (141), followed by verbal phrases (38), and predicative adjectives (7) and prepositional phrases (1). They were normalized with respect to number of syllables and characters for all conditions; a one-factorial ANOVA revealed no significant differences between the three conditions with $F(2,198) = 0.23$ ($p = 0.79$) and $F(2,198) = 0.29$ ($p = 0.75$)

for syllables and characters, respectively. Words were not yet normalized to *Leipziger Wortschatz* (cf. Universität Leipzig 2021) word frequency (see Table 8); a one-factorial ANOVA revealed differences between the three conditions with F (2,198) = 3.91 (p = 0.02).

Table 8: Word frequency of critical segments (means and standard deviation (sd) per condition (cf. Universität Leipzig 2021).

	Mean	Sd
Art-horror	13.16	4.09
Humor	14.09	4.46
Coherence	12.08	3.92

To limit participation time, items were split into six lists by applying the Latin Square Design with three lists focusing on art-horror and coherence and three lists with humor and coherence items. As in questionnaire I, art-horror and humor items never appeared in the same list so as to not blur art-horror and humor reactions. All lists were pseudorandomized and rated by (nearly) the same number of participants (13–14 each).

Fillers were adapted to reduce the art-horror influence, and supplemented by other emotion texts like grief, love, and fury as well as nonsensical fillers.

In total, this questionnaire included 211 items with 67 triplets and 40 fillers (supplementary fillers were taken and adapted from the same articles and websites as in questionnaire I, see 4.1.1.1).

The questions after each item remained the same as in Questionnaire I (see Chapter 4.1.1.1), except for the funniness question. Similar to the idea that art-horror items challenge the honesty of the participants, humor could also be perceived as a test concerning participants' comprehension capacity or personality traits, and therefore might cause honesty problems to the participants. Furthermore, since we asked for an emotional reaction in the scariness question (to scare somebody), we adapted the adjective funny in the funniness question to the emotionally related verb exhilarate. Both adaptations contributed to a more homogenic question pool. Thus, the funniness question asked about the exhilaration potential:

1. Der Text hat das Potential jemanden zu erheitern.
The text has the potential to exhilarate someone.

The questions after every item also had to be rated on a 7-point Likert scale (with 1 = not at all and 7 = absolutely) except for the comprehensibility question with the answer options "Ja/*Yes*" (= 1), "Nein/*No*" (= 2), "Ich weiß nicht/*I do not know*" (= 3).

Procedure
The same procedures as in Questionnaire I were applied. Participation took around 40 minutes.

Data analysis
Means and standard deviations were computed per condition for the surprise, scariness, and funniness questions. In preparation for the SPR experiment (see next chapter), triplets were reduced to the 36 with highest values for both scaring potential in art-horror and exhilaration potential in humor. One-way, repeated measures ANOVA calculations tested for significant differences between surprise, scariness, and funniness means. Pairwise comparisons between surprise and funniness means were calculated with an adjusted significance level set to p < .0375 based on a modified Bonferroni procedure (cf. Keppel and Wickens 2004). To test whether there was a significant difference between the three possible answers of the comprehension question (nominal scale: Yes/No/I do not know), Pearson's X^2 was computed and the answer scores were computed in percent.

4.1.2.2 Results
Overall, art-horror items reached higher scariness scores than in questionnaire I with a mean of 4.92 (sd = 1.70). Surprise values were also more elevated with a mean of 5.49 (sd = 1.94). Funniness reached a slightly elevated mean of 2.79 (sd = 1.09). Comprehensibility showed a mean of 1.09 (sd = 0.38). Coherent items in art-horror lists showed slightly elevated means in scariness (3.10, sd = 1.94), surprise (3.70, sd = 1.89) and funniness (2.74, sd = 1.79). Humor items also showed a high surprise mean of 5.10 (sd = 1.53) and approached elevated funniness values with a mean of 3.91 (sd = 1.88). Surprise and funniness means of coherence items in humor lists were slightly elevated (surprise 3.44, sd = 1.87 and funniness 2.57, sd= 1.66) (see Figure 14).

Comprehensibility scores per condition (percentual and X^2) (*I understood the text. Yes/No/I do not know.*) are summarized in Table 9.

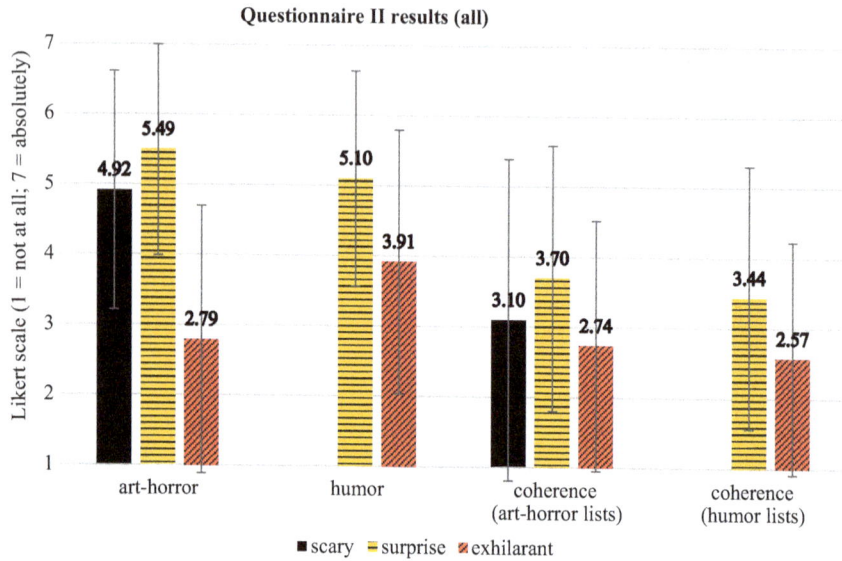

Figure 14: Results of Questionnaire II for all 67 triplets. Means per condition and questions. Scariness, funniness and surprise were rated on a 7-point Likert scale (1 = not at all; 7 = absolutely), error bars = sd.

Table 9: Percentual comprehensibility values and Pearson's X^2 for the three answer possibilities of yes/no/I do not know.

	Yes (%)	No (%)	I do not know (%)	X^2
Art-horror	94.20	2.66	3.14	1340.9
Humor	91.40	3.39	5.21	1254.0
Coherence (in art-horror)	88.38	4.00	7.62	1127.9
Coherence (in humor)	85.75	3.44	10.81	1013.0

This norming study prepared the material for the subsequent experiments so that the 36 best working triplets with highest scores in scariness and exhilaration were selected. After this selection, the art-horror items reached a scariness mean of 4.97 (sd = 1.68), surprise values 5.62 (sd = 1.48) and funniness remained at 2.79 (sd = 1.97).

Humor items showed a higher surprise mean of 5.22 (sd = 1.39) and a higher funniness mean of 4.39 (sd = 1.74). Scores in art-horror lists for coherence slightly decreased to a scariness mean of 2.89 (sd = 2.87) and a surprise mean of 3.64 (sd = 1.88). The funniness mean was slightly higher (2.88, sd = 1.84). In humor lists, coherence ratings decreased in surprise to 3.46 (sd = 1.89). The funniness mean was slightly higher (2.66, sd = 1.67) (see Figure 15).

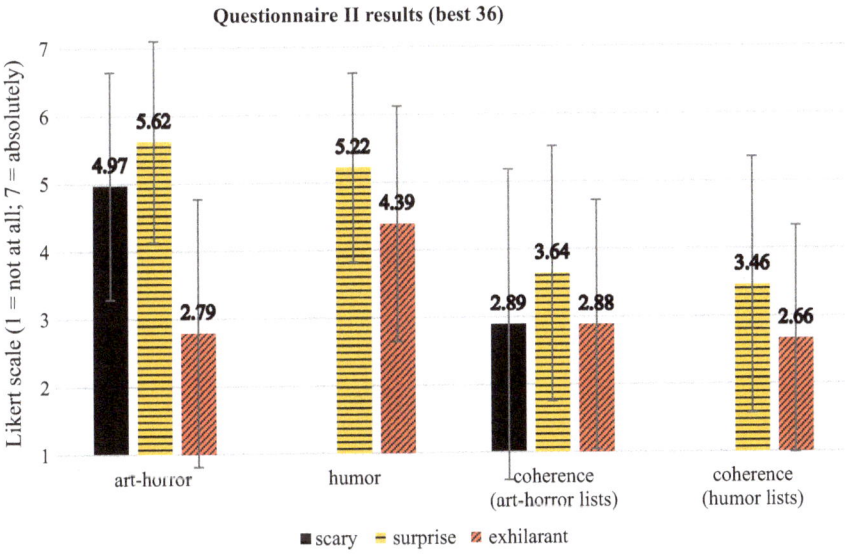

Figure 15: Results of Questionnaire II for the 36 triplets. Means per condition and questions. Scariness, funniness, and surprise were rated on a 7-point Likert scale (1 = not at all; 7 = absolutely), error bars = sd.

The differences between scariness in art-horror and coherence were significant with $F (1,70) = 86.61$ ($p < .0001$). The differences between surprise in art-horror, humor, coherence in art-horror, and coherence in humor were significant with $F (3,140) = 72.446$ ($p < .0001$).

Pairwise comparisons (adjusted significance level set to $p < .0375$) revealed significant differences between art-horror and humor ($F (1,70) = 7.08$ ($p < .001$)), art-horror and coherence ($F (1,70) = 103.4$ ($p < .0001$)), and humor and coherence

($F (1,70) = 109.77$ ($p < .0001$)). The differences between coherence in art-horror lists and coherence in humor lists was not significant ($F (1,70) = 0.756$ ($p = .388$)) (see Table 10).

Table 10: Pairwise comparisons of surprise; n.s. = not significant.

surprise	Art-horror		Humor		Coherence in art-horror		Coherence in humor	
	F	p	F	p	F	p	F	p
Art-horror	/		7.08	<.0001	103.4	<.0001	/	
Humor	/		/		/		109.77	<.0001
Coherence (in art-horror)	/		/		/		.756	n.s.

The differences between exhilaration means in art-horror, humor, and coherence in art-horror lists, as well as coherence in humor lists were significant with $F (3,140) = 52.135$ ($p < .0001$). Pairwise comparisons (adjusted significance level set to $p < .0375$) revealed significant differences between both art-horror and humor with $F (1,70) = 117.18$ ($p < .0001$) and humor and coherence in humor lists with $F (1,70) = 132.37$ ($p < .0001$). Differences between art-horror and coherence and between the coherence conditions failed significance (see Table 11).

Table 11: Pairwise comparisons of exhilaration; n.s. = not significant.

exhilaration	Art-horror		Humor		Coherence in art-horror		Coherence in humor	
	F	p	F	p	F	p	F	p
Art-horror	/		117.18	<.0001	.3	n.s.	/	
Humor	/		/		/		132.37	<.0001
Coherence (in art-horror)	/		/		/		1.71	n.s.

Comprehensibility scores per condition (absolute, percentual, and X^2) (*I understood the text. Yes/No/I do not know*) are summarized in Table 12.

Table 12: Percentual comprehensibility values and Pearson's X^2 for the three answer possibilities of yes/no/I do not know.

	Yes (%)	No (%)	I do not know (%)	X^2
Art-horror	95.91	1.82	2.27	775.3
Humor	93.96	2.91	3.31	739.3
Coherence (in art-horror)	89.44	2.70	7.86	632.2
Coherence (in humor)	89.09	3.64	7.27	616.4

4.1.2.3 Discussion

The questionnaire material was improved in art-horror and humor conditions compared to questionnaire I by adjusting given items, expanding triplets, and selecting the 36 best triplets (those with high values in both scariness and exhilaration). Art-horror items, again, met expectations and reached high means in scaring and surprising potential. Art-horror's exhilaration potential showed slightly increased scores but remained at coherence's exhilaration level. Humor items were also improved, reaching scores above 4 in surprise and exhilaration potential (the latter with significantly higher scores compared to both art-horror and coherence).

Both art-horror and humor surprised the participants, reflecting their detection of incongruities. Compared to humor's surprise potential, surprise in art-horror remained significantly higher supporting the previous hypotheses that art-horror's incongruity was experienced more intensely (and, in line with Rothbart (2017 [1976]), more fearsomely). Alternatively, lower surprise potential in humor could also reflect the aforementioned participants' familiarity with humorous punchlines.

Comprehensibility reached good scores in art-horror and humor, supporting the interpretation that surprise/incongruity was resolved to a coherent reading and did not confuse the participants; incongruity did not lead to an irresolvable nonsense reading. Comprehensibility showed even better values in art-horror and humor than coherence conditions. In line with Ferstl, Israel and Putzar (2017), this could be due to the immediate feedback of fear or exhilaration after a resolved art-horror or humor incongruity.

Even though (slightly) elevated, coherence conditions did not differ significantly concerning surprise and funniness, and an influence of distribution on art-horror and humor lists can, again, be excluded. The elevated surprise scores in coherence conditions (in combination with slightly increased comprehensibility scores in art-horror and humor lists) could again relate to the unusual text format.

The selection of the 36 best triplets, on one hand, successfully prepared material for later experiments. On the other hand, it had the shortcoming that many items had to be excluded even though they reached (very) high scores in one condition. These exclusions might explain why the overall scores did not improve to the maximum. In addition, the standard deviations in the selected 36 triplets were higher than in the previous questionnaire. This might be explained as follows: Some triplets worked well in the art-horror condition, while others worked better in the humor condition. While the overall scores of the triplet matched the selection conditions, the values for funniness and scariness within a triplet were mostly not exactly the same but showed (sometimes big) differences. This raises the critical question whether there was another underlying factor that made some triplets more suitable for an art-horror reading and others more suitable for a humor reading. Since the participants only saw an art-horror or humor list, this effect cannot be attributed to individual genre preferences (see Chapter 3.5 on individual differences).

4.2 Reading times: Experiment I

Assuming that readers immediately try to interpret the segments they have read (immediacy assumption) and fixate on each word for as long as they need to understand it (eye-mind assumption), reading behavior indirectly provides information about underlying cognitive processes. To understand the given text, readers subconsciously decide for themselves which words they want to fixate on and where they need breaks. Thus, difficulties in reading comprehension lead to longer reading times (RT), or in other words, the longer a person needs to read a critical segment, the more cognitive costs are elicited (cf. Just and Carpenter 1980: 329–330). An investigation of reading behaviors using incongruent texts provided insights into the cognitive processes that are activated for understanding incongruities. To attest whether art-horror's incongruity elicits the same prolonged reading times (interpreted as additional processing costs) as reported for humorous texts (cf. Mayerhofer and Schacht 2015: 6, see Chapter 2.3) and whether these costs are stronger or weaker in art-horror or humor, an on-line reading experiment was conducted.

Cognitive processing costs of art-horror were compared to those of humorous and coherent texts, using the normed minimal triplets (see Chapter 3.1.1) in the self-paced reading paradigm (SPR). For this purpose, the stimuli were split into segments so that reading times were recorded of each segment through a computer. Recording times started with the appearance of a segment on the screen and ended with the participant pressing a button, which activated the next sentence segment. Readers controlled how long they wanted to fixate on a segment and when the next segment of a sentence should appear on the monitor, hence the name *self-paced* (cf. Just, Carpenter and Woolley 1982: 230; Jegerski 2014: 22). To untangle reading times of the critical segments from wrap-up effects (cf. Rayner, Kambe and Duffy 2000) and investigate whether reading time effects reached into regions after the critical segment (punchline), this experiment prolonged the minimal triplets. Three additional segments (spill-over region 1–3) were introduced so the stimuli did not end at the punchline. Thus, in total, the participants clicked successively through three context segments, two introductory segments of the target sentence, one critical segment with the punchline, and three spill-over regions. This paradigm made it possible to compare the reading times (dependent variable) of the minimal triplets and draw conclusions about different processing mechanisms (see Figure 16 and description in the material section of this chapter).

In line with reading time findings from Coulson and Kutas (1998), Coulson, Urbach and Kutas (2006), and Mayerhofer and Schacht (2015), it was predicted that incongruity (the detection and subsequent resolution thereof) elicited comprehension difficulties. These difficulties were expected to cause longer reading times at the critical segment in the humorous condition relative to the coherent control condition. Longer reading times were also predicted for art-horror stimuli at the critical segment relative to the control condition, due to a shared mechanism of incongruity and subsequent resolution mechanisms. Both humor and art-horror would show incongruity effects that expand into spill-over region 1 but the reading times of humor and art-horror would be similar to those of the coherent conditions in spill-over region 2. Spill over region 3 was the final sentence segment, for which increased reading times were predicted for all three conditions due to sentence wrap-up effects (see Figure 16).

Since art-horror and humor elicit emotions, the influence of both positive and negative emotions (exhilaration vs. fear/disgust) on the processing speed had to be considered. Considering that both positive and negative emotions can prohibit or improve incongruity processing (see Chapter 3.4), the extent to which art-horror and humor processing differ was investigated in an exploratory way.

The procedure of this reading time study was closely linked to a parallelly running experiment, which used the paradigm of the *Facial Action Coding System* (FACS) (see Chapter 4.3). Participants' faces were recorded during the SPR tasks and analyzed to disentangle which facial movements and correlated emotions were activated. To correlate the FACS analysis with individual character

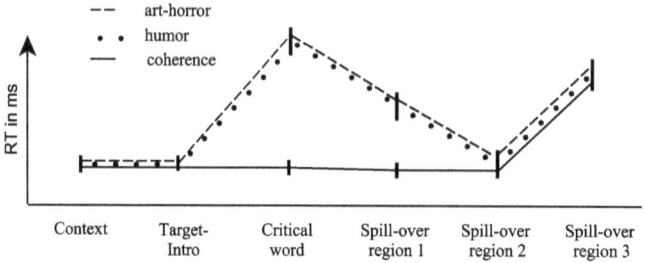

Figure 16: Schematic illustration of predictions of reading times (RT) for the three conditions art-horror, humor, and coherence.

traits, four questionnaires asked for the participants' disgust sensitivity, cheerfulness, seriousness, bad mood, and gelotophobia scores. This section therefore includes information on overlapping procedures.

4.2.1 Methods

Participants

Overall, 48 participants (10 male) ranging from 18 to 52 years of age (mean = 21.1, median = 22, sd = 5.73) took part. They were German native speakers and mostly students at the University of Cologne.[22] One participant (male, 33 years old) had to be excluded due to technical problems during the experiment so that a total of 47 participants (9 males), 18–52 years old (mean = 23.92; median = 22, sd = 5.7) went into the analysis. All participants had normal or corrected-to-normal visual acuity. The participants received credit points for their university courses or 9 € / hour. Their data was collected and analyzed according to the ethical standards of the XLinC lab.

---

[22] Research by Platt, Hofmann, Ruch and Proyer (2020) showed that gelotophobia influences the participant's facial reaction to "laughter-eliciting enjoyable emotions" (Platt, Hofmann, Ruch and Proyer 2020: 500). These reaction patterns may be a reason to exclude gelotophobes from humor studies (see exclusion rules in the FACS study). Although six participants reached high values in the gelotophobia questionnaire Geloph<15> (values above the cut-off point of ≥ 37,5; here ranging between 38–47), they were not excluded in this SPR experiment since we were still in an exploratory phase. They did not show significant reaction time differences compared to participants without this fear (ANOVA-styled sum-coded contrasts to test for main effects of group for the critical regions and the regions of spillover 1 and 2 in every condition). This led us to the assumption that there are no on-line effects due to gelotophobia concerning the reading and reaction time to verbal, humorous stimuli.

Material

The 36 best rated minimal triplets from Questionnaire II were improved according to individual scores and adapted to the following structure: 1) context, 2) target (with introduction, critical segment, and spill-over regions). The context contained three segments. The target sentence was split in two introductory segments, the critical word (one segment including a noun and its determiner or an inflected verb) and a spill-over region. The spill-over segments were introduced by a non-coordinating "und"/"*and*" or by a preposition in cases where non-coordination through the "und"/"*and*" was not possible. The three conditions of art-horror, humor and coherence again only differed in the critical segment.

Table 13 illustrates the structure of the minimal triplets (translations to English in italics; slashes indicate the segment split):

Table 13: Example of minimal triplets of the SPR material in the three conditions art-horror, humor, and coherence.

Condition	Context (3 segments)	Target sentence		
		Intro (2 segments)	Critical segment (1 segment)	Spill-over (3 segments)
1a Art-horror	Dreißig Jahre lang / waren meine Frau und ich / glücklich und zufrieden.	Dann / kam	unsere Vergiftung *our poisoning*	und / wir / bereuen es.
1b Humor			unser Treffen *our encounter*	
1c Control group: coherence	*For thirty years, / my wife and I / have been happy and content.*	*Then / came*	unsere Trennung *our separation*	*and / we / regret it.*

The critical segments were balanced over all conditions concerning word frequency, word length and number of syllables. The mean word frequency in the *Wortschatz Leipzig* (cf. Universität Leipzig 2021) was 13.47 for the art-horror condition, 14.28 for the humor condition and 12.39 for the coherence condition. A one-factorial ANOVA revealed no significant differences between the three conditions with $F(2,105) = 1.821$ ($p = 0.167$). The mean word length in characters was 13.25 for the art-horror condition, 14.78 in the humor condition and 13.22 in the coherence condition. A one-factor ANOVA revealed no significant differences between the three conditions with $F(2,105) = 0.179$ ($p = 0.837$). The mean of syllables was 4.06 in the art-horror condition, 4.3 in the humor condition and 4.06 in the coherence condition. A one-factor ANOVA also did not reveal significant differences between the three conditions with F (2,105) = 0.366 (p = 0.695).

The triplets were split into three lists following the Latin Square Design, so that each participant received 12 art-horror items, 12 humor items, and 12 coherent items without redundancies in addition to 20 fillers. Thus, participants never saw more than one item of a minimal triplet. The fillers included stereotypical humor, stereotypical horror and texts treating the emotions of love, sadness, and anger, all to distract from the structure of the minimal triplets and the intended emotions of art-horror and humor. Every list was pseudorandomized.

To ensure that the participants read attentively, binary, factual comprehension questions were constructed for 33 of the 56 target and filler items. The questions focused on the context sentences of the target items or on any segment of the filler items and clearly asked for a "yes" or "no" response, e.g. if the context sentence was "Karl was free. After 47 years in prison, he walked through the gate into the open air.", the comprehension question requiring a "no" answer was "Is Karl still in prison?". The rest of the filler and target items was followed by the question "Weiter?"/"*Next?*".

Procedure
The participants received a sheet with information about the self-paced reading method and the experiment procedure. Then they received a sheet with the participant's consent on data and personality protection. Participants read and signed it and took a copy home. Afterwards, the participants answered questions (in)dependently of their daily fitness concerning visual acuity, medication and drug consumption that might influence the experiment. Due to the parallelly running FACS experiment (see next chapter), the participants answered the questionnaires on gelotophobia (GELOPH<15>), disgust sensitivity (in German: *Fragebogen zu Erfassung der Ekelempfindlichkeit*, FEE), state cheerfulness (State-Trait-Cheerfulness-Inventory with 18 questions on state cheerfulness, STCI-S18) and trait cheerfulness (State-Trait-Cheerfulness-Inventory with 30 questions on trait cheerfulness, STCI-T30). Eventually, the participant was led to the study room and sat in front of a desktop computer. The software OpenSesame (cf. Mathôt, Schreij and Theeuwes 2012) was used to present the experiment digitally. After a digital repetition of the experiment procedure, a test run with three test items made the participants familiar with the keyboard and the clicking procedure. Finally, the experiment started.

The context segments were presented segment-by-segment and noncumulatively at the speed of the participant's button pressing. Next, the target sentence was presented in the moving-window paradigm: Initially, the sentence was represented through underscores and spaces. Then, each consecutive segment was revealed word-by-word, linearly, and non-cumulatively through the participants' self-paced button pressing (cf. Just, Carpenter and Woolley 1982: 230). After every item, a comprehension question, or the question "Weiter?" ["Next?"] had to be answered by pressing keyboard keys marked with "Ja" ["Yes"] or "Nein" ["No"]. The first word of the items and the following questions always started at the same location in the middle of the left side of the screen. Two short breaks interrupted the presentation. In order to facilitate the correlation of this SPR experiment with the FACS videos (see Chapter 4.3), each item and filler began with a beep-tone. After the 36 items, the 20 fillers and the last keypress, an information window appeared on the screen to indicate that the experiment was finished. As a debriefing, the participants were informed about the experiment's content. Study participation took between 10–20 minutes.

Data analysis
Trials with extreme reaction times of less than 200 ms or more than 4000 ms comprised 0.3 % of the data, including targets and fillers from all participants, and were removed from the data set. Five items (three coherent, two humorous) had to be excluded due to technical problems. We calculated the accuracy with which the participants responded to the comprehension question. Trials with false responses were not excluded for three reasons: First, the questions were only meant to maintain the participant's attention. Second, the comprehension questions concerning the content (not "Weiter?" ["Next?"]) only covered 33 of the 56 items and never asked for details about the critical region. Third, the participants could have detected the incongruity and could have been afraid or amused without answering correctly.

Residual reading times were computed for each participant (cf. Ferreira and Clifton 1986; Trueswell and Tanenhaus 1994). The entire data set was taken into account with both targets and fillers. Residual reading times were used without further trimming and account for the differences in: a) word length (since there is no linear relationship between the word length and the reading time), b) word position within a sentence (since it also does not affect reading times linearly), c) experiment type, d) the log-transformed trial number (readers accelerate with the experiment progress), and e) individual reading pace differences of the participants.

As a second step, a mixed-effects regression model of residualized reading times was fit in R version 3.5.0 (R Core Team 2019) using the lme4 package version 1.1–17 (Bates, Maechler, Bolker, Walker, Christensen, Singmann, Dai,

Scheipl, Grothendieck, Green and Fox 2019) for the three types of the predictor variable condition (coherence, humor, art-horror). Such a two-step model of reading time data analysis was used in Jaeger (2008a), Hofmeister, Jaeger, Arnon, Sag and Snider (2013) and in Hofmeister (2011) (for the implementation in R see Jaeger 2008b). We included random intercepts and slopes for participants and items where supported by the data (Barr, Levy, Scheepers and Tily 2013). In cases of convergence failures or of zero/perfectly correlated random terms with very low standard deviations, the random effects structure was simplified following Baayen, Davidson, Doug, J. and Bates (2008). ANOVA-style sum-coded contrasts were used to test for main effects, using the mixed model functionality of the package afex version 0.21–2 implemented in the function 'mixed' (Singmann, Bolker, Westfall, Aust and Ben-Shachar 2019). P-values were obtained using the Satterthwaite approximation implemented in the R lmerTest package version 3.0–1 (Kuznetsova, Brockhoff and Christensen 2017).

Even though the questionnaires on gelotophobia (GELOPH<15>), disgust sensitivity (FEE), state cheerfulness (STCI-S18) and trait cheerfulness (STCI-T30) were conducted in relation to the facial expressions of the participants (for descriptions and results, see next chapter), we verified whether reading times were also affected by participants' individual states/traits of cheerfulness, seriousness, and bad mood. Using the R package ggpubr (R Core Team 2019), correlation tests (cor.test) and scatter plots (ggscatter) were conducted for every character aspect and the z scores of art-horror (as difference score of art-horror minus coherence) and humor (as difference score of humor minus coherence) on the critical segment and the first spill-over region.

4.2.2 Results

Participants responded to the 33 content-related comprehension questions (excluding "Weiter?" ["Next?"]) with a mean accuracy of 0.89 ranging between 0.667 and 1. The log residual reading times of the critical region and the first and second spill-over segment in every condition and across all participants in a reduced model without random slopes for the subject – due to convergence problems in the maximal model with correlations of "not a number" or 1 for both in subjects and items – revealed the following effects (see Figure 17).

For the critical region, the main effect of condition is significant with $\chi2(2) = 6.89$, $p = 0.03$. The humorous condition takes longer to read than the coherent condition ($\beta = 0.075$, se = 0.029, t = 2.589, p = 0.0143) and the art-horror condition (β = 0.06, se = 0.0267, t = 2.275, p = 0.0297). There is no difference between the humorous and the art-horror conditions (β = −0.014, se = 0.026, t = −0.546, p = 0.5887).

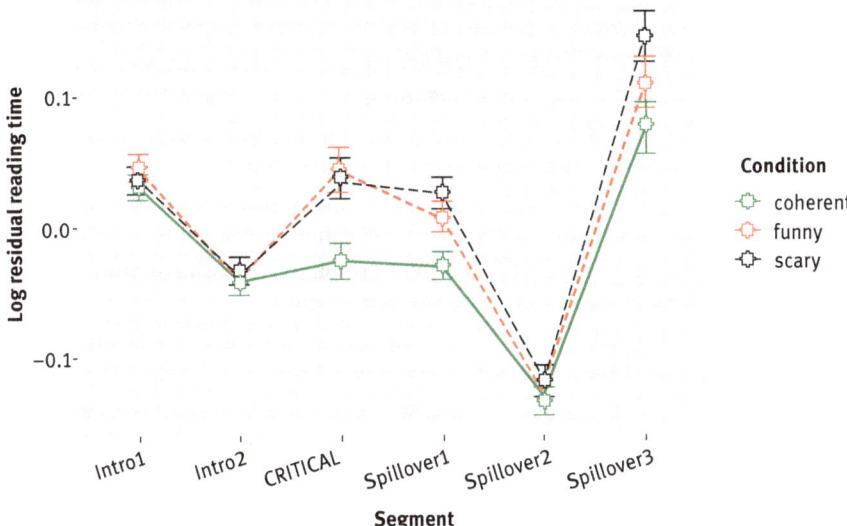

Figure 17: Log residual reaction times for the six target segments over all conditions, error bars = sd.

For the region after the critical segment, called spill-over 1, the main effect of condition is significant χ2(2) = 13.67, p = 0.001. The humorous condition was read more slowly than the coherent condition (β = 0.04, se = 0.015, t = 2.710, p = 0.0071). The art-horror condition was also read more slowly than the coherent condition (β = 0.057, se = 0.015, t = 3.861, p = 0.0004). Again, there is no significant difference between the humor and the art-horror conditions (β = 0.017, se = 0.015, t = 1.168, p = 0.243).

The spill-over region 2 did not show a main effect with χ2(2) = 1.04, p = 0.6. The humor condition was read at the same speed as the coherent condition (β = 0.011, se = 0.0155, t = 0.688, p = 0.496). The art-horror condition was also read at the same speed as the coherent condition (β = 0.019, se = 0.0202, t = 0.926, p = 0.0361). No significant differences between the humor and the art-horror condition were observed (β = 0.0254, se = 0.0195, t = 1.306, p = 0.201).

Correlations with questionnaires revealed no reliable effects.

4.2.3 Discussion

This experiment tested whether art-horror evokes the same incongruity as humor, whether this incongruity elicits additional processing costs compared to coherent items and how the cognitive processing costs of art-horror differ from costs of humor with respect to intensity and time-course. Assuming that increased reading times reflect processing costs, an experiment was conducted in the self-paced reading paradigm. Reading times were recorded for minimal triplets in the three conditions art-horror, humor and coherence, whose structure only differed in the critical segment of the punchline.

Overall, the SPR experiment supported the hypothesis: both art-horror and humor elicited longer reading times than the coherent condition at the critical segment. The increased reading times were prolonged in both conditions to the first spill-over region relative to the coherence condition.

The increased reading times in the humor condition replicate findings from Coulson and Kutas (1998), Coulson, Urbach and Kutas (2006), and Mayerhofer and Schacht (2015). Emotional facilitation effects for the humor condition relative to coherence (cf. Ferstl, Israel and Putzar 2017) were not found. Thus, the experimental results support the assumption that the increased reading times can be traced back to costs for the cognitive mechanisms of detecting and resolving the incongruity and/or to a costly emotional elaboration phase.

The longer reading times in art-horror on the critical segment and the subsequent spill-over region 1, compared to coherent stimuli, clearly indicate that the inherent incongruity elicits additional processing costs. Even though the results of the SPR experiment are methodologically not fine-grained enough to differentiate the three stages of incongruity detection, resolution, and elaboration, they support this work's hypothesis that the incongruities in humor and art-horror provoke comparable processing costs, which might arise from the same underlying cognitive mechanisms. This challenges the assumption of previous research that the interplay of detection, resolution and elaboration of an incongruity is a distinctive feature of humor (cf. Coulson and Kutas 1998; Coulson 2001; Coulson, Urbach and Kutas 2006; Chan, Chou, Chen and Liang 2012; Chan, Chou, Chen, Yeh, Lavallee, Liang and Chang 2013; Feng, Chan and Chen 2014; Mayerhofer and Schacht 2015; Ferstl, Israel and Putzar 2017; Canal, Bischetti, Di Paola, Bertini, Ricci and Bambini 2019).

In the second spill-over region, reading times of art-horror and humor were the same as those of the coherent conditions so that the conclusion can be drawn that the incongruities in humor and art-horror were already resolved at this stage into a coherent reading.

The integration of the sentence-final position elicited the predicted increased reading times for all conditions at the third spill-over region, which supports the decision to remove critical segments from the sentence-final position to separate incongruity effects and wrap-up effects.

Interestingly, art-horror reading times did not differ significantly from humor. On one hand, this missing differentiation may support the hypothesis that the processing mechanisms of humor and art-horror (including potential facilitating or inhibiting effects of an emotional reaction) are indeed exactly the same. On the other hand, the reading paradigm might not be fine-grained enough to find differences between underlying cognitive processes and emotions of art-horror and humor. Moreover, future experiments could compare reading times of art-horror and humor to a nonresolvable, incoherent condition or revision texts to determine whether emotions facilitate incongruity resolution relative to unemotional incongruities, as reported by Ferstl, Israel and Putzar (2017).

The simultaneous analysis of facial expressions, described in the next chapter, tried to differentiate between different emotional reactions to art-horror and humor stimuli.

4.3 Facial expressions: Experiment II

To ascertain that humor and art-horror elicited the intended emotional reactions of exhilaration (with a positive valence) and fear/disgust (with a negative valence) during humor and art-horror reception, respectively, a second experiment was conducted in parallel to the prior reading time experiment. Assuming that during the reading experiment, emotions were visible in the participants' facial movements, this experiment analyzed participants' facial expressions as a mirror to their emotions through the Facial Action Coding System (FACS).

FACS (cf. Ekman, Friesen and Hager 2002a; Ekman, Friesen and Hager 2002b) is a comprehensive description system of facial nonverbal communication. Through FACS, it is possible to notate facial, muscular activity and resulting facial expressions unitarily in an internationally accepted and interdisciplinary way. Based on the anatomy of the human face, FACS describes visible facial movements and their intensity in action units (AU). These movements are generated through muscular contractions or relaxations and lead to facial expressions, and head and eye movements. An AU can correlate with one single muscle (e.g. AU 1: inner brow raiser) or summarizes a group of muscles and their visible movements (e.g. AU 4: brow lowerer) (cf. Ekman, Friesen and Hager 2002a: 2–3,5; Ekman, Friesen and Hager 2002b: 17,20). Due to the anatomical symmetry of the face, most AUs exist symmetrically on the right and left face side. In total, 44 AUs are defined and categorized into the three groups: upper face (eyebrows, eyelids, forehead), lower face (with the directions up/down, horizontal, oblique, orbital, miscellaneous) and head and eye positions. AUs' intensity is notated in five degrees from A (trace) to E (maximum) (cf. Ekman, Friesen and Hager 2002b: 1,4–5). Figure 18[23] compares the description of the facial anatomy to the encoding of facial movements through AUs with a start and an end point:

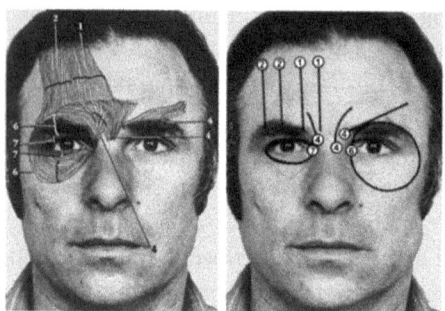

Figure 18: Comparison of the muscular anatomy of the human face (left picture) and its notation in action units (AU), here AU 1, 2, 4, 6, and 7 (right picture). The encircled number indicates the ending point of a movement (Ekman, Friesen, and Hager 2002b: 15.

Participants' facial expressions are assumed to correlate with their experienced emotions, so that facial expressions can be used to measure emotions indirectly. This approach is supported by experimental research from, amongst others, Ekman, Friesen and Ancoli (1980) and Rosenberg and Ekman (2020), who found evidence not only for a coherent relation between participant's facial expressions and their self-reported emotion across time episodes but also in distinct, event-related situations. Even though evidence for an emotion is influenced by cross-cultural, developmental, contextual, individual, psychophysiological, and behavioral factors of participants and coders, prototypic AU combinations are translated to six underlying basic emotions, including happiness, disgust, and fear (cf. Ekman, Friesen and Hager 2002a: 173–174).

In the current book, it was expected that the participants would show facial movements at critical words and spill-over regions of the humor and art-horror conditions, associated with the emotion of exhilaration (as a facet of happiness [cf.

---

[23] Figures 18–25 are reproduced with the permission from the Paul Ekman Group.

Ruch 2005: 90]), fear and disgust, respectively. Table 14 shows which emotion was associated with which AU. Then, the corresponding AUs are defined successively.

Table 14: Association of emotions and facial movements (in Action Units).

Emotion	Action Units
Exhilaration	12 (+6)
Disgust	10 and/or 9
Fear	1+2+(4/5)

AU 12

Exhilaration correlates, amongst other expressions, with smiling, which occurs in the lower face where the lip corners are pulled back and upwards in an oblique movement (AU 12: lip corner puller, see Figure 19). During AU 12, the deepening of the nasiolabial furrow (between nose and mouth) and infraorbital furrow (underneath the eyes) are visible. AU 12 raises the skin next to the nasolabial furrow and the infraorbital triangle upwards (under the eyes). In strong AU12s, further changes are visible, such as narrowed eyes, crow's feet at eyes' corners and widened nostrils (cf. Ekman, Friesen and Hager 2002b: 178).

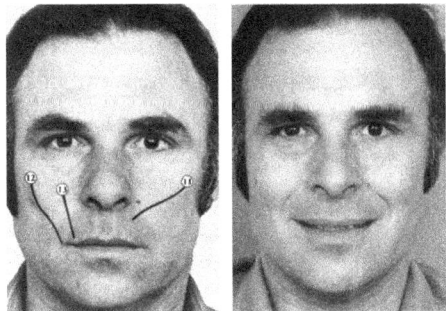

Figure 19: Comparison of AU 12 (lip corner puller) as a schema of the oblique movement (left picture) and its facial expression (right picture) (Ekman et al. 2002b: 175,484).
Side note: the facial expression on the right side also includes AU 25 (open mouth).

AU 6

Additionally, AU 12 can be combined with AU 6 (cheek raiser and lid compressor, see Figure 20), corresponding to a muscle that surrounds the eye. During this movement, the skin of temples and cheeks are pulled towards the eyes and the infraorbital triangle is pushed upwards. Further, the skin around the eyes is moved in the direction of the eye sockets, narrowing the eyes, and the lateral eyebrows may be pull downwards. Below the eyes, the skin may wrinkle or bag, and the lower eyelid furrow is deepened. The eye cover fold may change. Crow's feet may be visible. In strong AU 6s, further changes are visible, such as deeper nasolabial and infraorbital furrows, raised upper lip (outer parts) (cf. Ekman, Friesen and Hager 2002b: 31).

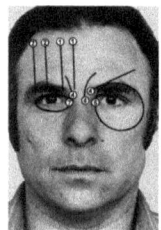

Figure 20: Comparison of AU 6 (cheek raiser and lid compressor) as schema (left) and facial expression (middle). Combination of AU 6 and AU 12 (right) (Ekman et al. 2002b: 15,468,485).

AU 10

The emotion of disgust is expressed, in part, through AU 10 (upper lip raiser, see Figure 21). This AU describes the raising of the upper lip (center is raised more than outer parts), which opens the mouth if expressed with high intensity. The infraorbital triangle is pushed upwards, which can cause wrinkles under the eyes. While deepening the nasolabial furrow, AU 10 also lifts its upper region. Nostril wings become widened and raised (cf. Ekman, Friesen and Hager 2002b: 95).

AU 9

Additionally to AU 10, AU 9 (nose wrinkler, see Figure 21) expresses disgust. During this movement, the skin close to both sides of the nose is raised, resulting in wrinkles at both nose sides and at the root of the nose. The upper lip and the infraorbital triangle move upwards, resulting in a wrinkled or deepened infraorbital furrow, bunched skin below the lower eyelid, narrowed eye aperture. During AU 9, the eyebrows (especially the middle part)

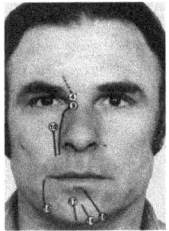  

Figure 21: Comparison of AU 10 (upper lip raiser) and AU 9 (nose wrinkle) as schema (left picture) and facial expressions (middle: AU 10, right: AU 9) (Ekman et al. 2002b: 91,95). Side note: Middle picture also shows AU 25 (opened mouth).

are lowered. Further changes might be visible, such as widened nostrils or a deepened nasolabial furrow (cf. Ekman, Friesen and Hager 2002b: 93).

The emotion of fear is correlated, amongst others, with raised inner and outer brows (AU 1, inner brow raiser, and AU 2, outer brow raiser, see Figure 22). AU 1 and 2 are combined with lowered brows (AU 4, brow lowerer, see Figure 23) or raised upper lids (AU 5, see Figure 24).

AU 1

The facial changes that are due to the inner brow raiser concern the inner eyebrow parts, which are pulled upwards to an oblique form. The skin in the middle of the forehead wrinkles horizontally (cf. Ekman, Friesen and Hager 2002b: 20).

AU 2

Complementary to AU 1, the outer brow raiser pulls the outer corners of the eyebrows upwards, changing them to an arch form. This movement stretches the lateral eye cover fold upwards. Horizontal wrinkles above the outer eyebrows or in the forehead's center may appear (cf. Ekman, Friesen and Hager 2002b: 22).

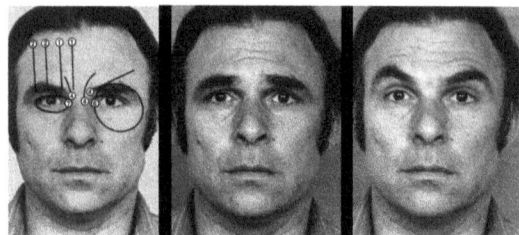

Figure 22: Comparison of AU 1 and 2 as schema (left) and facial expression (middle: AU 1, right: AU 2) (cf. Ekman et al. 2002b: 15,466).

AU 4

Fear can be expressed through a combination of AU 1 and 2 with AU 4 (see Figure 23). The brow lowerer pushes the inner (and lateral) eyebrows and the eye cover fold downwards and pulls the right and left brow together. This movement can minimize the eye aperture and produce vertical or oblique wrinkles between the brows as well as horizontal wrinkles at the root of the nose (cf. Ekman et al. 2002b: 17).

Figure 23: Facial expressions of AU 4 (brow lowerer, left) and its combination with AU 1 and AU 2 (right) (cf. Ekman et al. 2002b: 466, 472).

AU 5

To express fear, AU 1 and 2 are also combined with AU 5 (see Figure 24). During this facial movement, the eye aperture is widened. The upper eye lids raise and may vanish, which makes the upper eyeball more visible (protrusion). This movement may also uncover the sclera above the iris more strongly. In a strong AU 5, the skin around the eyes is pulled upwards so strongly that the lower eyelids are also raised (cf. Ekman et al. 2002b: 24).

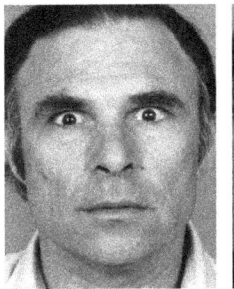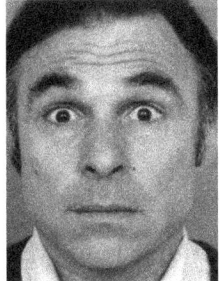

Figure 24: Facial expressions of AU 5 (upper lid raiser, left) and its combination with AU 1 and AU 2 (right) (cf. Ekman et al 2002b: 467,472).

Figure 25 visually summarizes the predicted AUs for the humor condition (exhilaration with AU 12 [+6]) and the art-horror condition (fear with AU 1+2+4/5; disgust with AU 10 and/or 9).

1 2 3 4 5

Figure 25: Visual summary of predicted facial expressions. 1: happiness (AU 6,12). 2: disgust (AU 9), 3: disgust (AU 10), 4: fear (AU 1,2,4); 5: fear (AU 1,2 5) (Ekman et al. 2002b: 472–4/4,485) . Side note: In 3, AU 25 (open mouth) is activated additionally.

To identify whether the predicted facial movements (= dependent variable) and their correlating emotions were activated during art-horror and humor reception, the participants' faces were filmed concurrently with the SPR experiment and analyzed through FACS.

Participants' individual personality traits can correlate with the type of the facial expressions, their frequency and intensity. Ruch (2005) showed that the degree of participants' cheerfulness correlated with the intensity of their facial expressivity. Increased cheerfulness led to hyper-expressivity of AU 12, low cheerfulness correlated with hypo-expressivity of AU 12 (cf. Ruch 2005: 104). Therefore, this experiment tested for participants' personality traits of cheerfulness, seriousness, bad mood, disgust sensitivity, and gelotophobia, which all potentially influence AUs' intensity, frequency, and duration in the art-horror and humor conditions.

The German short versions of the two State-Trait-Cheerfulness-Inventory (STCI) questionnaires were conducted (cf. Ruch, Köhler and van Thriel 1996; Ruch, Köhler and van Thriel 1997; Ruch 2017). They asked for the participants' disposition to cheerfulness, seriousness, and a bad mood both as a momentary state (questionnaire STCI-S18 measured state-cheerfulness, state-seriousness, and state-bad mood) and an enduring trait (STCI-T30 measured trait-cheerfulness, trait-seriousness, and trait-bad mood). This survey served the purpose to correlate the results with the participants' exhilaratability and facial movements in the experimental humor condition (cf. Ruch, Köhler and van Thriel 1996). Contrary to short, hilarious incidents, state-cheerfulness is a mood "which facilitates the induction of exhilaration; it represents a state of enhanced preparedness to respond to an appropriate stimulus with smiling and laughter" (cf. Ruch, Köhler and van Thriel 1996: 304–305). State-cheerfulness lasts longer than the reaction to one stimulus, fluctuates less in intensity and is less dependent on the stimulus itself. It comprises the five facets: a prevalent cheerful mood, a low-threshold of smiling, a calm management of adversities, an active repertoire of cheerfulness triggers, and a generally cheerful way of interactivity (cf. Ruch, Köhler and van Thriel 1996: 308). Exhilaration, in turn, is understood here as a momentary increase in this cheerful state (cf. Ruch, Köhler and van Thriel 1996: 305). Trait-cheerfulness is the participant's exhilaratability as a long-term disposition with individual differences in frequency, intensity, duration, and ease of being exhilarated (cf. Ruch 2005: 305). Exhilaration is also influenced by participants' individual degree of seriousness and bad mood both as a state and trait. Seriousness is understood as a dominance of participants' serious states, their thorough, intense, and reasonable consideration and planning of events and goals, rational communication, and distanced perspective on humorous stimuli of any kind. Bad mood is defined as the prevalence of a general bad mood, sadness, and humorlessness (cf. Ruch, Köhler and van Thriel 1996: 308). It was predicted that participants with high scores in cheerfulness and low scores in both seriousness and bad mood would show the expected AUs of happiness more frequently and more intensely than participants with low cheerfulness, and high seriousness and bad mood. Participants with high scores in seriousness and bad mood were expected to show the AUs of fear more often and more intensely.

It is not only the personality traits of seriousness and bad mood which show that humorous stimuli are occasionally not recognized nor appreciated as cheerful or positive. Humorous instances can even cause fears. Gelotophobia is the fear of being laughed at and being ridiculous, which is associated with shame, low joy, and consequences like "social withdrawal to avoid being laughed at / ridiculed, appear 'cold as ice' / humorless, low self-esteem, low social competences, psychosomatic disturbances, [. . .] lack of liveliness, spontaneity, [. . . and] humor/laughter are not relaxing & joyful social experiences" (Ruch and Proyer 2008a: 50, cited from graph). Further, the facial activity of gelotophobic participants differs from participants without gelotophobia (cf. Proyer 2014: 257). Gelotophobes show a "congeal, clumsy, 'agelotic' face", called "Pinocchio syndrome" due to the facial appearance of a "wooden puppet" (Ruch and Proyer 2008a: 50, cited from graph). Thus, including gelotophobes in experiments on humor and joyful facial expressions can cause artefacts in the data. To assess gelotophobia and exclude (extreme) gelotophobes from this experiment, the questionnaire GELOPH<15> was conducted. GELOPH<15> examines on the basis of 15 questions to what extent laughter frightens, paralyses, or embarrasses the participants and indicates the participants' gelotophobia with the degrees of slight, pronounced or extreme (cf. Ruch and Proyer 2008b: 23). Participants with extreme gelotophobia (cut-off value at 37.5 of 60) were excluded from this experiment.

Personality traits also influence other emotions and their relation to facial expressions (cf. Ruch 2005: 107). Since disgust played a role in the emotional reaction to art-horror stimuli, the German version of Haidt's disgust scale for the assessment of the participants' disgust sensitivity, in German *Fragebogen zur Erfassung der Ekelempfindlichkeit* (FEE) (cf. Schienle, Walter, Stark and Vaitl 2002), was conducted. It comprised the factors death/deformation, body excretions, spoilage, oral defense, and hygiene. Participants' individual sensitivity to disgust was correlated with the frequency and intensity of the AUs shown during art-horror reception. It was predicted that higher values in disgust sensitivity would correlate with more frequent and more intense AUs in the art-horror condition.

Finally, FACS is established in psychological emotion studies, robotics, and the creation of animation movies. It is rarely used in psycholinguistic research. So, this book not only contributes fundamental research on humor and art-horror processing but also explores to what extent FACS is methodologically useful for experimental linguistics.

4.3.1 Methods

Participants
Results of the SPR participants (see Chapter 4.2) who agreed to video recordings of their faces (six exclusions) and who were not gelotophobic (five exclusions with a cut-off value of 37.5 in the GELOPH<15> questionnaire, see below) went into the analysis. In total, 36 native German speakers (7 male) with normal or

corrected to normal visual acuity ranging from 18 to 52 years of age (mean = 23.92, median = 22, sd = 6.12) were analyzed.

Material
Since this experiment was run in parallel to the reading time study, the test items remained the same as in the SPR experiment (see Chapter 4.2).

The short German version of the STCI-S18 (cf. Ruch, Köhler and van Thriel 1996; Ruch, Köhler and van Thriel 1997; Ruch 2017) examined the participants' degree of cheerfulness, seriousness, and bad mood as a momentary state. It comprised 18 statements scored on a Likert scale from 1 (not applicable to me at all) to 4 (absolutely applicable to me).

The short German version of the STCI-T30 (cf. Ruch, Köhler and van Thriel 1996; Ruch, Köhler and van Thriel 1997; Ruch 2017) comprised 30 statements on the cheerfulness, seriousness, and bad mood as personality traits, which had to be scored on a Likert scale from 1 (not applicable to me at all) to 4 (absolutely applicable to me).

The questionnaire FEE (cf. Schienle, Walter, Stark and Vaitl 2002) examined the participant's disgust sensitivity. It comprised 37 statements on potentially disgusting instances that had to be rated on a 5-point Likert scale (1 = not disgusting; 5 = disgusting).

GELOPH<15> (cf. Ruch and Proyer 2008b) examined to what extent the laughter of other people frightens, paralyses, or embarrasses the participants. It comprised 15 questions, which had to be scored on a Likert scale from 1 (not applicable to me at all) to 4 (absolutely applicable to me).

Procedure
In parallel to the reading experiment (see procedure descriptions in Chapter 4.2), participants' faces were filmed secretly with a digital camera. In the debriefing, participants were informed about the experiment's content. Participants either provided informed consent or the recordings were immediately erased. Next, they received the four German questionnaires of GELOPH<15>, FEE, STCI-S<18>, and STCI-T<30>. Participation time ranged between 10–20 minutes for reading the stimuli and around 15 minutes to answer the questionnaires.

Data analysis
The (videos of the) participants' faces were analyzed manually in the Software *ELAN* (The Language Archive 2018). As a certified FACS rater, I examined whether the participants' faces showed the predicted AU 12 and 6 for exhilaration, and AU

1, 2, and 5 for fear or AU 10 for disgust in the corresponding conditions. A second rater (interrater reliability) was not consulted due to quantitatively insufficient AU results. Total occurrence scores, mean frequencies, and standard deviations were computed per condition.

One-way, repeated measures ANOVA calculations tested for significant differences between art-horror, humor, and coherence at and after the critical segment for the predicted AU (combinations) 1+2+4 and/or +5, AU 9, AU 10, AU 12, and AU 12+6. Pairwise comparisons between AU 12s in all conditions after the critical segments and between AU 12s at and after the critical humor segment were calculated with an adjusted significance level set to $p < .033$ based on a modified Bonferroni procedure (cf. Keppel and Wickens 2004).

Mean scores from STCI-S<18> were calculated for the three state dimensions of cheerfulness (questions 2, 6, 8, 12, 13, and 16), seriousness (questions 3, 5, 7, 10, 15, 17), and bad mood (questions 1, 4, 9, 11, 14, and 18).

Mean scores from STCI-T<30> were computed for the three trait dimensions of cheerfulness (questions 2, 8, 11, 12, 15, 17, 19, 23, 28, and 30), seriousness (questions 1, 5, 7, 9, 13, 16, 18, 21, 25, and 27), and bad mood (questions 3, 4, 6, 10, 14, 20, 22, 24, 26, and 29).

Mean scores from FEE were calculated according to the five categories death/deformation (questions 6, 13, 16, 21, 24, 26, and 32), body excretions (questions 5, 11, 17, 22, 25, 31, and 35), spoilage (questions 4, 10, 18, 20, 27, 28, 29, and 30), oral defense (comprising questions 2, 3, 7, 8, 12, 37) and hygiene (comprising questions 1, 9, 14, 15, 19, 23, 33, and 36).

Correlations of AUs' frequency with the participants' individual states, traits, and sensitivities were computed qualitatively due to quantitatively insufficient AU results.

The values in the questionnaire GELOPH<15> were summed up to a total score for each participant. Participants who reached scores above 37.5 were excluded. The mean was conducted before and after the exclusions.

4.3.2 Results

Questionnaire results
In the GELOPH<15> questionnaire, 48 participants responded with total values between 16 and 47 resulting in a mean of 27 (median = 27; sd = 8). Five of the participants reached values above the gelotophobia cut-off value of 37.5 (Ruch and Proyer 2008b: 23) with values between 38 and 47 and a mean of 42 (median = 42; sd = 3.39). They were excluded from the FACS and the further questionnaire analyses. This brought the adjusted mean to 26 (median = 28; sd = 7).

The results of the STCI-S18 were split into the subcategories of state-cheerfulness, state-seriousness, and state-bad mood with 6 questions each, on a 4-point Likert scale. Cheerfulness reached a mean of 16 (median = 17; sd = 4; min = 6; max = 22); seriousness showed a mean of 15 (median = 15; sd = 3; min = 8; max = 22); bad mood had a mean of 8 (median = 6; sd = 4; min = 6; max = 24).

The results of the STCI-T30 were split into the three subcategories of trait-cheerfulness, trait-seriousness, and trait-bad mood with 10 questions each, on a 4-point Likert scale. Cheerfulness reached a mean of 32 (median = 34; sd = 5; min = 19; max = 40); seriousness showed a mean of 26 (median = 26; sd = 4; min = 18; max = 35); bad mood had a mean of 19 (median = 20; sd = 6; min = 10; max = 31).

The results of the disgust sensitivity questionnaire (FEE) show a mean of 123 ranging between 84 and 170 (with a maximum possible value of 185; median = 122; sd = 23). The FEE included five subcategories with the following results: The category death had a mean of 18 (median = 18; sd = 7; min = 7; max = 34), body secretion showed a mean of 28 (median = 30; sd = 6; min = 16; max = 34), spoilage resulted in a mean of 28 (median = 29; sd = 6; min = 16; max = 39), hygiene showed a mean of 30 (median = 31; sd = 6; min = 17; max = 40), and oral rejection had a mean of 22 (median = 22; sd = 6; min = 10; max = 30).

FACS results

Overall, participants had facial reactions in only 148 cases (11.42 % of the 1296 potential reactions) at or after the critical segment. There were significantly more AUs after the critical segment than at it (6 to 142) with $F(1,28) = 11.77$, $p = .002$. The AU combination 1+2+4 and/or 5 appeared only three times in total (2 % of the 148 AUs shown), once on the critical art-horror segment and twice immediately after it. AU 9 and 10, both disgust predictors, appeared ten (9 %) and twenty-one times (30%), respectively, after the critical art-horror segment. They were shown three and sixteen times, respectively, after the critical humor segment and once and eight times, respectively, after the critical coherent segment. The exhilaration predictor, AU 12, was shown most frequently (48 %) and appeared five times on, thirty-six times after, and thereof nine times together with AU 6 (10 %). AU 12 was also seen twenty times after the critical art-horror segment (in six cases together with AU 6) and ten times after the critical coherence segment. Mean frequency for these facial expressions per condition on and after the critical segment ranged between 0 and .08 (sd between 0 and .12) as depicted in Figure 26.

One-factorial ANOVAs revealed that there were no significant differences between the three conditions on the critical segment of AU combination 1+2+4/5, 9, 10, and 12+6. Only AU 12 differed significantly between conditions since it only appeared at the critical segment of the humor condition with F (2,105) = 3.86, p = .024

One-factorial ANOVAs revealed that, after the critical segment, AU 12 and 12+6 differed significantly between the conditions with F (2,105) = 4.4, p = .015 and F (2,105) = 3.45, p = .035, respectively. Pairwise comparisons (adjusted significance level set to p < .033) revealed significant differences for AU 12 between humor and coherence with F (1,70) = 7.54, p = .008, but not between art-horror/humor or art-horror/coherence. A pairwise comparison for AU combination 12+6 revealed significant differences between humor and coherence with F (1,70) = 7.33, p = .009 and between art-horror and coherence with F (1,70) = 5, p = .029. Differences between humor and art-horror were not significant. AU 12 at the critical segment also differed significantly from its appearance after the critical segment with F (1,70) = 12.57, p = .0007. The other AUs did not differ significantly between conditions or at/after critical segments.

Participants were separated in reacting and non-reacting groups per condition to verify whether participants' individual states, traits, and sensitivities showed correlation patterns with the AU frequencies. The non-reacting group constituted four participants who did not show any of the predicted facial reactions neither at the critical segment nor after it (see Table 15).

Mean questionnaire results of (non-)reacting participants over all conditions

The four participants who made up the non-reacting group had a gelotophobia mean of 27 (median = 30, SD = 7.44, min = 16, max = 32), which is in agreement with the overall gelotophobia mean of 26. These participants were also in agreement with the FEE means with scores of 19 in the category death, 28 in body secretion, 31 in spoilage, 31 in hygiene, and 23 in oral rejection. They matched the overall means of the STCI-T30 with a cheerfulness score of 33, a seriousness score of 27, and a bad mood score of 20. In the STCI-S18, those participants showed scores, that were again close to the overall mean, with a cheerfulness score of 18, a seriousness score of 11, and a bad mood score of 6 (see Table 15).

Additionally, seven participants did not show facial reactions in the art-horror condition. They had a gelotophobia mean of 28 (median = 30, sd = 8.19). Their FEE means approximated the overall mean with scores of 18 in the category death, 23 in body secretion, 26 in spoilage, 25 in hygiene, and 20 in oral rejection. Their mean scores in the STCI-T30 and STCI-S18 were close to the overall means with 34 and 17 in cheerfulness, 26 and 14 in seriousness, 17 and 7 in bad mood (see Table 16).

The 25 participants, who did show art-horror reactions, had a (slightly) lower gelotophobia mean (25, median = 23, sd = 6.3) than the non-reacting participants

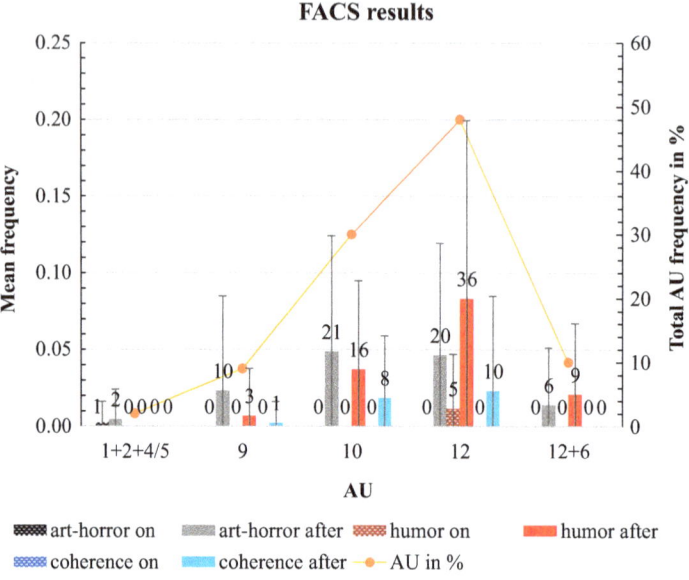

Figure 26: FACS results – mean frequency of action units (AU) per condition on and after the critical segment, and percentage of AU of 148 AU shown across conditions and locations.
error bars = sd numbers above bars = absolute numbers of AU shown
AU 12+6 = shows how many of the AU 12 were shown with AU 6

Table 15: FEE, STCI, STHI and Geloph<15> – Mean results of non-reacting participants compared to reacting participants and overall means over all conditions.

Questionnaire / participant group	Overall (36)	Non-reacting (4)	Reacting (32)
FEE: death	18	19	18
FEE: body secretion	25	28	25
FEE: spoilage	28	31	28
FEE: hygiene	30	31	29
FEE: oral rejection	22	23	22
STCI-T30: cheerfulness	32	33	32
STCI-T30: seriousness	26	27	26
STCI-T30: bad mood	19	20	19
STCI-S18: cheerfulness	16	18	15

4.3 Facial expressions: Experiment II — 153

Table 15 (continued)

Questionnaire / participant group	Overall (36)	Non-reacting (4)	Reacting (32)
STCI-S18: seriousness	15	11	15
STHI-S18: bad mood	8	6	9
GELOPH<15>	26	27	27

Table 16: FEE, STCI, STHI and Geloph<15> – Mean questionnaire results of non-reacting participants compared to reacting participants in the three conditions art-horror, humor, and coherence.

Questionnaire / participant group per condition	Art-horror		Humor		Coherence	
	Non-reacting (7)	Reacting (25)	Non-reacting (7)	Reacting (25)	Non-reacting (19)	Reacting (13)
FEE: death	18	18	16	19	19	17
FEE: body secretion	23	26	24	25	25	26
FEE: spoilage	26	28	26	28	28	27
FEE: hygiene	25	31	32	29	29	30
FEE: oral rejection	20	22	22	22	22	22
STCI-T30: cheerfulness	34	32	35	32	33	32
STCI-T30: seriousness	26	26	25	26	27	24
STCI-T30: bad mood	17	20	16	20	18	22
STCI-S18: cheerfulness	17	15	15	16	16	14
STCI-S18: seriousness	14	15	17	15	15	15
STHI-S18: bad mood	7	9	9	9	7	10
GELOPH<15>	28	25	23	27	25	26

and (slightly) higher FEE means with scores of 18 in the category death, 26 in body secretion, 28 in spoilage, 31 in hygiene, and 22 in oral rejection. Matching overall means, their STCI-T30 scores were 32 in cheerfulness, 26 in seriousness, and 20 in bad mood (the latter slightly higher than in non-reacting participants). Their scores STCI-S18 were 15 in cheerfulness, 15 in seriousness, and 9 in bad mood, which was again close to the overall means but higher or equal to the non-reacting participants.

Seven participants (only one overlap with the art-horror non-reacting participants) did not show the predicted AUs in the humor condition. They had a gelotophobia mean of 23 (median = 22, sd = 3.09). Their FEE means also approached the overall means with scores of 16 in death, 24 in body secretion, 26 in spoilage, 32 in hygiene, and 22 in oral rejection. The scores in the STCI-T30 were close to the overall means with values of 35 in cheerfulness, 25 in seriousness, and 16 in bad mood. Their STCI-S18 also approached the overall means with scores of 15 in cheerfulness, 17 in seriousness, and 9 in bad mood.

Twenty-five participants showed the predicted facial activity in the humor condition and had an unexpectedly higher gelotophobia score compared to the non-reactors in this condition (mean = 27, median = 26). Their FEE scores were also higher or equal (except for the lower category of hygiene, which was also lower compared to all other reacting groups) and reached 19 in the category of death, 25 in body secretion, 28 in spoilage, 29 in hygiene, and 22 in oral rejection. The scores in the STCI-T30 remained the same compared to the reacting group of art-horror. Compared to the non-reacting humor group, they had unexpectedly lower cheerfulness scores and higher bad mood values with values of 32 in cheerfulness, 26 in seriousness, and 20 in bad mood. Their STCI-S18 matched the means of the non-reacting participants in the humor condition as well as the overall means (except for a lower state-seriousness score) with scores of 16 in cheerfulness, 15 in seriousness, and 9 in bad mood.

Since it was predicted that the coherence condition would not elicit facial activity, it was surprising that 13 participants did show some of the AUs related to fear or exhilaration. Those participants had a gelotophobia score of 26 (median = 26, sd = 7.07) and FEE means of 17 in the death category, 26 in body secretion, 27 in spoilage, 30 in hygiene, and 22 in oral rejection. While the cheerfulness scores (32) of the STCI-T30 matched the overall mean, seriousness (24) was (slightly) lower than the overall mean compared to all other participant groups. Bad mood was the highest with a score of 22 compared to all other participant groups. While the STCI-S18 score in seriousness (15) matched the overall mean, the cheerfulness mean was the lowest (14) compared to all other participant groups. The bad mood scores were highest (10) compared to all other participant groups.

Finally, the 19 participants did not show facial movement in the coherence condition and had a gelotophobia mean of 25 (median = 23, sd = 5.64) and FEE means of 17 in death, 26 in body secretion, 27 in spoilage, 30 in hygiene, and 22 in oral rejection. The STCI-T30 and the STCI-S18 scores of this group matched the overall means with 33 and 16 in cheerfulness, 27 and 15 in seriousness, 18 and 7 in bad mood. Trait-seriousness was higher in non-reacting than in reacting participants in the coherence condition.

4.3.3 Discussion

In order to investigate participants' facial expressions as a window into their emotions during humor and art-horror reception, a FACS experiment was conducted simultaneously to the reading time experiment (see previous section). FACS is a unified notation system that describes facial, muscular activity and resulting facial expressions, in action units (AU), enabling them to be correlated with emotions. This experiment predicted that the emotions associated with humor (exhilaration represented by AU 12 or 12+6) and art-horror (fear represented by AU 1+2+4/5 and disgust represented by AU 9 and/or 10) were evoked in the participants and visible on their faces. Further, this experiment tested whether the participants' personality traits of cheerfulness, seriousness, bad mood, and disgust sensitivity influenced the facial expressions.

First, the elicited AUs appeared in only 11.42 % of the 1296 potential reactions. Compared to FACS studies investigating the Duchenne Display during the elicitation of positive emotions (cf. Hofmann, Platt and Ruch 2017: 5), facial expressions in this study were few in number. This might be due to the setting of the experiment and the missing of supporting pictures or movies during item presentation (see my evaluation of FACS for experimental linguistics at the end of this chapter).

However, trends were recognizable. The predicted AU combinations did emerge in the expected condition: The exhilaration AUs (12 and 12+6) appeared with highest absolute numbers in the humor condition. AU 12 appeared significantly more often in the humor condition than in the coherence condition. Disgust AUs (9 and/or 10) were seen with highest absolute numbers in the art-horror condition. Fear AUs (1+2+4/5) generally had the poorest scores but were only seen, as expected, in the art-horror condition.

The FACS analysis indicated the subjectivity of the reaction and interpretation of art-horror and humor stimuli. It showed that the participants reacted differently to art-horror and humor with variances between and within participants. On one hand, some participants laughed during the art-horror condition. Despite art-horror's cruelty, the resolution of the incongruity seemed to be enough to make the participants laugh. The difference between AU 12 frequency in humor and art-horror was therefore not significant. In this context, however, it should be noted that humor and laughter can be used as coping strategies to deal with difficult situations (cf. Trouvain and Truong 2017). AU 12 can further serve as a socially regulating smile in communication. The question whether only the Duchenne Display as a combination of AU 12+6 reflects joy accurately is still under discussion (cf. Ekman, Davidson and Friesen 1990; Girard, Shandar, Liu, Cohn, Yin and Morency 2019). On the other hand, some participants showed horror-related reactions in the humor condition. By splitting the participants into reacting and non-reacting groups per condition, it became apparent that some participants reacted only in one condition. The increased standard deviations also indicated the differences between and within participants.

Qualitative correlations with questionnaire results revealed trends for each condition. In the art-horror condition, reacting participants had equal or higher scores in all questionnaire categories except for trait and state cheerfulness and the gelotophobia score. These results support our hypotheses since high scores in both trait and state seriousness and bad mood as well as high FEE scores were predictors for a higher fear reaction (more often, more intense). Future research has to investigate the relationship between seriousness, bad mood, the participant's sensitivity to disgust and the frequency/intensity of the AUs shown during art-horror reception with quantitatively stronger results to verify – in analogy to cheerfulness as a disposition for exhilaration (cf. Ruch 1997: 333) – whether these traits and sensitivities are a disposition to facial expressions of fear and disgust and to predict facial fear reactions more precisely .

Regarding results of the questionnaires, qualitative trends in the humor condition do not support our hypotheses. In particular the gelotophobia score, which was a non-reacting predictor in the humor condition, had slightly higher scores in reacting participants. This trend might support the hypothesis that gelotophobia scores below the cut-off value do not influence the FACS results, for example through symptoms of the Pinocchio syndrome (cf. Ruch and Proyer 2008b; Ruch, Hofmann, Platt and Proyer 2014). Furthermore, the gelotophobia scores were lower for the non-reacting participants in the art-horror condition which is also contrary to predictions (cf. Platt, Hofmann, Ruch and Proyer 2020: 492). Even though trait cheerfulness scores were slightly higher for the non-reacting group (contrary to predictions), state cheerfulness for non-reacting participants was slightly lower in the humor condition compared to the reacting participants. Therefore, (lower) state cheerfulness might have dominated the influence on the (missing) facial expressions and outbalanced the general disposition to being cheerful (trait) (cf. Ruch, Köhler and van Thriel 1997: 7). This result is also in conflict with López-Benítez, Acosta, Lupiáñez and Carretero-Dios (2018) who found that people with high trait cheerfulness are generally more sensitive to an emotional environment and show more intense changes of state cheerfulness due to their better understanding and management of that situation (cf. López-Benítez, Acosta, Lupiáñez and Carretero-Dios 2018: 1589).

Finally, the most interesting observation appears to be that significantly more AUs were seen *after* the critical segment compared to *at* the segment, thus relatively late. This tendency supports three-stage humor models which claim that the participants' emotional reactions appear only after detecting and resolving the incongruity. This observation also supports the tri-component model of humor. The latter added a phase of emotional expression to the more cognitive appreciation. Analogously, this tendency also supports a three-stage model of art-horror. However, in line with Ferstl, Israel and Putzar (2017) and compared to the art-horror condition, some humor reactions already appeared at the critical word. This might be a hint that humor facilitates the incongruity resolution so that emotional reactions appear earlier and are, thus, visible earlier.

This experiment also served to explore the extent to which FACS is methodologically useful for experimental linguistics. Even though the aforementioned trends support results of known three-stage humor and analogous art-horror models, findings were quantitatively poor. Thus, the question of whether FACS is helpful in psycholinguistic research is linked to the shortcomings of this experiment. The reasons for the limited results could lay in the unnatural lab situation, which is a shortcoming of nearly all controlled FACS studies. Visibly expressed emotions, and in particular laughter, are highly linked to social contexts and interactive communication (cf. Trouvain and Truong 2017: 399), which are not present in a laboratory setting. Further, time limitation may have had an influence. Even though the items were read at the participants' individual speed (self-paced reading paradigm, see previous chapter), it was occasionally observed that participants clicked to the next item faster than they could react emotionally. Thus, in future experiments, FACS could help to verify whether some reactions might have fallen into the context sentences of the next item, which was not tested for in this experiment. Due to the temporal latency of the emotional reaction, it was also not possible in this experiment to correlate the reaction with one of the three spill-over regions. It also has to be recognized that the stimuli were kept short and were not accompanied by pictures or movies (cf. Gross and Levenson 1995), which might have hindered the participants to immerse themselves into the context's situation and fully enjoy it.

With regard to the individual differences within and between participants, which play an important role in highly subjective and emotion-related language phenomena, FACS can be a tool for checking the participants' emotional interpretations. In this experiment, despite the preceding stimulus norming, the FACS analysis suggested that some of the extended reading times in the SPR experiment might not have been interpreted as humorous or scary. Overall, the decision to use FACS must consider the high amount of work required to become a FACS coder and large time investment in the FACS analysis.

4.4 Neuro-electric activity: Experiment III

To compare the processing functions and phases of humor and art-horror with a high temporal resolution, this chapter investigates to what extent cognitive functions required to process art-horror and humor are reflected in neuro-electric activity of the human brain. To this end, the method of electroencephalography and essential findings for language processing are explained. Then, the findings of humor processing (see Chapter 3) are made fruitful for this work's neuro-electric research of art-horror processing.

Using the method of *electroencephalography* (from Greek *enképhalos* = brain and *gráphein* = to write), it is possible to measure electrophysiological brain activity on the cranial surface non-invasively and continuously (cf. Luck 2014: 25, 32). The neurons of the human brain generate postsynaptic potentials, whose sums are recorded through electrodes placed on the scalp and visualized by an *electroencephalogram* (EEG)) with a high temporal resolution in milliseconds. This method was developed by Berger (1929), who was the first to measure and plot the voltage fluctuations of the human brain over time. The postsynaptic potentials react to incoming material so that the measurements of their activity in relation to that event, called *Event-Related Brain Potentials* (ERP), provide time-locked and averaged information about the processing of the input (cf. Luck 2014: 12,39–40). While the first unambiguous, sensory ERPs of humans were published by Davis (1939) and Davis, Davis, Loomis, Harvey and Hobart (1939), the first computer-averaged ERPs were recorded by Galambos and Sheatz (1962). The ERP approach assumes that a certain event, like a critical stimulus of an experiment, entails relatively different amplitudes, latencies, or topographies of the postsynaptic, electrical signal compared to a control condition. Linking processing costs directly (on-line) to neuro-electric activity in the human brain, ERPs facilitate a time-sensitive search for different cognitive components and related functions needed to process the input.

In an ERP setup (see Figure 27), participants look at a computer screen, which presents the experimental items. Electrodes placed on the participants' heads are connected to an amplifier to intensify the electric signal and are filtered to reduce noise. The continuous signal, measured in milliseconds (EEG), is sent to a digitization computer with event codes. With a time-lock to the onset of the critical segment, the signals are extracted from the EEG, aligned, and averaged point-by-point per participant (and later across all participants) across items of a condition resulting in averaged ERP fluctuations. Thus, fluctuations that occur randomly are canceled out and only experimentally elicited waves remain. Finally, averaged deflections are plotted (cf. Luck 2014: 7; Rommer and Federmeier 2018: 248).

4.4 Neuro-electric activity: Experiment III — 159

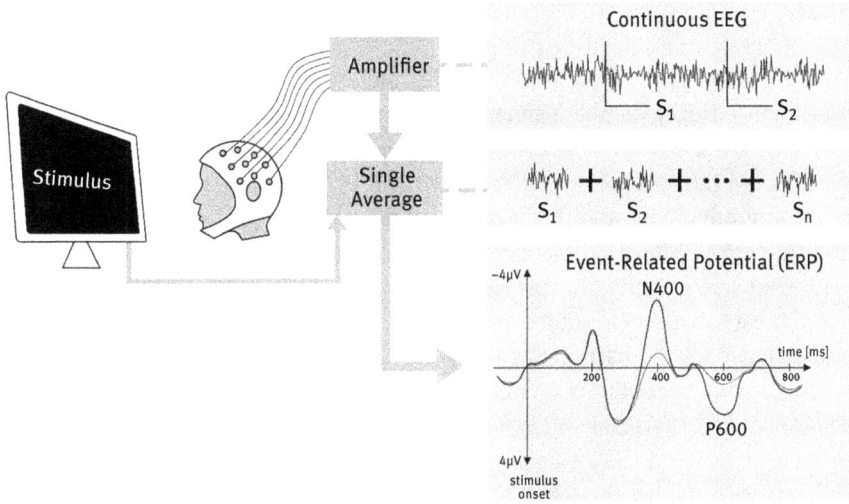

Figure 27: Schema of recording procedure (adapted from Hung 2011: 46).

The scalp-recorded signals can be modulated experimentally to systematically extract variations between computational operations of a target and a control condition: "a set of voltage changes that are consistent with a single neural generator site and that systematically vary in amplitude across conditions [. . .]" (Luck 2014: 68) is called ERP *component*. Describing the *contingent negative variation* as a reflection of the participant's preparation for expected upcoming targets, Walter, Cooper, Aldridge, McCallum and Winter (1964) discovered the first cognitively induced component. ERPs are helpful for a more detailed characterization and visualization of the underlying brain processes, even though it is not possible to relate a measured component to a specific underlying cognitive process. This is due to the measurement of stimulus processing over time with the potential of activating several brain areas and functions simultaneously (superposition and inverse problem) (cf. Luck 2014: 44,47–48).

Based on the research questions of whether art-horror causes cognitive costs and to which extent these costs differ from humor costs, language-related ERP components that reflect the detection, resolution and elaboration of incongruities are important for this work. Thus, the components of the N400, LAN, P600, and LPP are explained in the following.

N400

The ERP component of the N400 is a neuro-electric wave with negative polarity (negativity). Negativities are generally assumed to be produced through prediction errors (cf. Bornkessel-Schlesewsky and Schumacher 2016: 597–598). The N400 has a latency period between 250 and 600 ms after stimulus onset that peaks around 400 ms and that has largest effects at centroparietal regions. Kutas and Hillyard (1980) first discovered increased N400 amplitudes in sentences that contained semantically unexpected, incongruous words, such as "He spread the warm bread with socks" (Kutas and Hillyard 1980: 203). They interpreted this result as costs for the participant's search for meaning in nonsense relative to a coherent control condition. While Kutas and Hillyard (1984) specified that the N400 depended inversely on word expectancy (cloze probability) and semantic priming of a word, Federmeier and Kutas (1999) and Friederici, Pfeifer and Hahne (1993) related the N400 to the (mis)match of a word with semantic features of the preceding context and the costs for integrating the (in)congruent word into the discourse. The N400 component is dependent on word frequency with higher amplitudes for infrequent stimuli (cf. Allen, Badecker and Osterhout 2003). The N400 depends on the givenness/newness of the input within a discourse with stronger amplitudes for new input, reflecting integration difficulties (cf. Burkhardt 2006) and is sensitive to violations of the participants' world knowledge (cf. Hagoort, Hald, Bastiaansen and Petersson 2004). Hung and Schumacher (2012) also suggested that the amplitude of the N400 is inversely proportional to a stimulus' predictability. Further factors that influence the amplitude of the N400 are word repetition; neighboring lexemes of the mental lexicon; word position in the sentence and the discourse; and orthographic, phonological, and morphological features of the compared conditions (cf. van Petten, Kutas, Mitchinger and McIsaac 1991; van Berkum, Hagoort and Brown 1999; Kutas and Federmeier 2018: 387). The N400 has also been associated with processing costs of figurative language use. For example, Weiland (2014) and Weiland–Breckle and Schumacher (2018) found N400 effects for the computation of metonymies and metaphors. They argue that "the enhanced cost for metaphors reflects the activation process of two unrelated domains via mapping or extended predication" (Weiland-Breckle and Schumacher 2018: 443) while the marginally reduced negativity during metonymy processing reflects a "mapping operation [. . .] within a domain" (Weiland-Breckle and Schumacher 2018: 464).

Research has already found that the N400 plays an important role in the processing of humor. In Chapter 3.3, it has been shown that the N400 is widely associated with the participants' detection of the incongruity in the humorous punchline, which violates the semantic expectations of the incoming material (cf. Coulson and Kutas 2001; Feng, Chan and Chen 2014; Mayerhofer and Schacht 2015).

LAN

Another neuro-electric wave with negative polarity is the *Left-Anterior Negativity* (LAN). It appears in the same time window as the N400 but is topographically visible in the left-anterior part of the head (instead of a centroparietal distribution of the N400). The LAN is attributed to enhanced demands on working memory (cf. King and Kutas 1995) and morphosyntactic violations (cf. Friederici, Pfeifer and Hahne 1993; Molinaro, Barber and Carreiras 2011). In humor research, the LAN has been associated with the detection of the incongruity at the punchline and with frame-shifting. For example, Canal, Bischetti, Di Paola, Bertini, Ricci and Bambini (2019) found a LAN for jokes, compared to the coherent control condition, and interpreted it as the recipients' search for a new script. For art-horror, there are no ERP findings of its cognitive processing so far and thus, no results on incongruity detection and the N400 or LAN component.

P600

A further language-related ERP component is the P600, a positivity starting at around 500 ms after stimulus onset, with a peak at around 600 ms, and with largest effects at posterior scalp regions. Initially, the P600 was only related to syntactic processing costs: Osterhout and Holcomb (1992) found that syntactic anomalies, that are inconsistent with a first preferred interpretation, elicit an enhanced P600. For example, in the syntactic garden path sentence "The broker persuaded to sell the stock was sent to jail" (Osterhout and Holcomb 1992: 787), the P600 appears at the first *to*, which challenges the first interpretation of *persuaded* and requires a reanalysis and disambiguation to arrive at the passivized verb interpretation. Hagoort, Brown and Groothusen (1993) found the P600 (here called *syntactic positive shift*) in subject-verb mismatches reflecting syntactic computation costs. Furthermore, the P600 is sensitive to agreement violations of number, case, gender, or verb tense, which they interpreted as reflection of the parser's syntactic reanalysis and repair mechanisms (cf. Swaab, Ledoux, Camblin and Boudewyn 2012: 420–421).

However, studies by Kuperberg, Sitnikova, Caplan and Holcomb (2003), Kuperberg, Caplan, Sitnikova, Eddy and Holcomb (2006), and Burkhardt (2007) showed that the P600 is not limited to syntactic reanalysis but can also reflect semantic anomalies (such as animacy violations requiring thematic role reassignments) or parsing costs related to discourse memory (such as the evaluation of new input, the drawing of inferences for a previously established mental model and updating it). It has also been associated with the processing of newly introduced referents and indirect anaphors (cf. Burkhardt 2006; Schumacher 2009). Furthermore, late positivities have also been associated with processing costs of figurative language use. For example, Weiland (2014) found late positivities in metaphors processing which she interpreted as costs for pragmatic processes such as an implicature based interpretation (cf. Weiland 2014: 185). Likewise, Schumacher (2019) found late positivities for the processing of metonymy types whose "lexical representation does not provide immediate access to the intended interpretation. The comprehender shifts the meaning at the expense of the core representation being no longer accessible" (Schumacher 2019: 326). Schumacher interpreted the late positivities as a "reflection of a meaning extension and the updating of the representation during the referential shift" (Schumacher 2019: 326). Bambini, Bertini, Schaeken, Stella and Di Russo (2016) even found these effects in natural communication situations with a supportive context and interpreted them as "truly pragmatic interpretative processes needed to make sense of a metaphor and derive the speaker's meaning, also in the presence of contextual cues" (Bambini, Bertini, Schaeken, Stella and Di Russo 2016: 1).

In the context of humor research (see Chapter 3.3), the time window of the P600 (500 – 700 ms) has been widely associated with a semantic reanalysis and resolution of the incongruity towards a coherent reading, but with inconsistent components. While Feng, Chan and Chen (2014) and Canal, Bischetti, Di Paola, Bertini, Ricci and Bambini (2019) indeed detected a P600, Coulson and Kutas (2001) found a P3b (which is discussed to belong to the same family as the P600 [cf. Swaab, Ledoux, Camblin and Boudewyn 2012: 424–427]) for good comprehenders. Mayerhofer and Schacht (2015) also looked at this time window, searching for a reanalysis effect in the joke condition, but they only found a P600 for the comparison of their nonsense condition relative to the coherent control condition (experiment IV). No art-horror ERP evidence exists thus far concerning the P600.

LPP

Apart from the elicited cognitive load to detect and solve incongruities, art-horror and humor intentionally try to elicit emotional reactions in the recipients. Thus, it is important for the comparison of art-horror and humor to also verify how far art-horror and humor emotions are (differently) reflected in ERPs. The aforementioned humor research reported that the participants indeed reacted emotionally to jokes, which was reflected in late ERP positivities between 700 – 1100 ms post-onset. Feng, Chan and Chen (2014) found a *late positive potential* (LPP) between 770 – 1100 ms, which is known to start at around 300 ms post-onset with a duration of several hundred milliseconds. It is commonly interpreted as reflection of emotional reactions to both pleasant and unpleasant stimuli, and to be strongest at centroparietal regions (cf. Cuthbert, Schupp, Bradley, Birbaumer and Lang 2000; Schupp, Cuthbert, Bradley, Cacioppo, Ito and Lang 2000; Hajcak, Dunning and Foti 2009; van Berkum, Holleman, Nieuwland, Otten and Murre 2009; Hajcak, Weinberg, MacNamara and Foti 2012; Luck 2014). Both Canal, Bischetti, Di Paola, Bertini, Ricci and Bambini (2019) and Mayerhofer and Schacht (2015) also reported late positivities between 700 – 1000 ms post-onset for jokes compared to coherent stimuli and also suggested that this reflects the participant's emotional reaction. Concerning art-horror's emotional processing, there is no linguistic evidence so far proving emotional or elaborative effects through ERPs. However, neuroelectric research on negative emotions reported early effects, including the positivity of the P1 and negativities, such as the N1, supplementing late emotion-related positivities (see Chapter 3.4).

A shortcoming of the preceding SPR experiment was that art-horror and humor were not compared to unemotional, non-resolvable incongruity as a second control condition. To verify whether different incongruities are processed differently and thus elicit different electric signals, an incoherent condition was added to the already existing material of the SPR experiment.

In this ERP experiment, it was expected that the incongruity in the humor, art-horror, and incoherence conditions engendered prediction mismatches. Both N400 and LAN have been associated with the detection of this mismatch and the search for a new reading. Thus, an N400 or a LAN were predicted for the art-horror, humor, and incoherence condition compared to the coherence condition due to the interpretation subprocess of detecting the incongruity as a semantic violation. The higher the degree of incongruity, surprise, or unexpectedness, the more cognitive costs are elicited and thus, the higher or longer the LAN/N400 amplitude is: it was expected that the incoherence items elicited the strongest scores, followed by art-horror and humor, and lastly by the coherence stimuli. Representing the function of rescanning, reanalyzing, and resolving the incongruity by creating an appropriate interpretation, a P600 was predicted for art-horror and humor. According to the 3-stage humor model from Chan, Chou, Chen, Yeh, Lavallee, Liang and Chang (2013), an emotional reaction follows the interpretation of the humorous condition. This model was here broadened to include art-horror and an emotional elaboration was expected also for the art-horror items. So, in comparison to incoherent and coherent items, a third ERP component was expected (LPP).

Although Rothbart's (2017 [1976]) arousal model of incongruity (see Figure 11) would predict increased cognitive costs due to the recipients' engagement in problem-solving strategies, both positive and negative emotions can accelerate cognitive processing (cf. Kanske and Kotz 2011; Ferstl, Israel and Putzar 2017). Since our preceding SPR experiment did not show significant differences between the art-horror and humor conditions, the extent to which the ERP components differed in humor and art-horror processing were again investigated exploratorily.

4.4.1 Methods

Participants
Twenty-nine Participants (8 males) between 19–29 years of age (mean = 23.73, median = 24, sd = 3.06) took part in this study. They were German native speakers and mostly students from the University of Cologne. One participant (female, 25 years old) had to be excluded due to gelotophobia (with a value of 53 in the GELOPH<15> questionnaire) such that 28 participants at the age of 19–29 (mean = 23.68; median = 24, sd = 3.1) were analyzed. All participants had normal or corrected-to-normal visual acuity. The study participation took around 2.5 hours with 60 minutes for the actual experiment. The participants received credit points for their university courses or 9 € / hour. Their data was collected and analyzed according to the ethical standards of the XLinC lab.

Material
The 36 triplets of the preceding SPR study (with some minimal improvements) were complemented by a fourth condition, called incoherence. For this condition, it was not possible to integrate the (syntactically correct) critical word into a semantically meaningful reading within the given context.

In this study, the context sentence was presented as one segment. The introductory words, the critical word, and the spill-over region were presented with the same segment splits as in the SPR study. Table 17 illustrates the structure of the minimal quadruplets with the following conditions: a) incongruent, scary, b) incongruent, humorous, c) incoherent, and d) coherent (translations to English in italics; Slashes indicate the segment split).

Table 17: Example of minimal quadruplets of the ERP material in the four conditions art-horror, humor, incoherence, and coherence.

Condition	Context (1 segment)	Target sentence		
		Intro (2 segments)	Critical word (1 segment)	Spill-Over (3 segments)
1 a Art-horror	Dreißig Jahre lang waren meine Frau und ich glücklich und zufrieden.	Dann / kam	unsere Vergiftung [our poisoning]	und / wir / bereuen es.
1b Humor			unsere Begegnung [our encounter]	
1c Control group: incoherence	[For thirty years, my wife and I have been happy and content.]	[Then / came]	unsere Lieferung [our delivery]	[and / we / regret it.]
1d Control group: coherence			unsere Trennung [our separation]	

The critical words were again balanced over all conditions in terms of word frequency, word length in characters and word length in syllables. Table 18 shows the means per condition for word frequency in the Wortschatz Leipzig, word length and syllable length.

Table 18: Means of critical segment per condition for word frequency (cf. Universität Leipzig 2021), word length and syllable length.

Condition	Frequency	Word length	Syllable length
Art-horror	13.61	12.86	3.86
Humor	14.58	13.25	4.03
Incoherence	14.11	12.17	3.81
Coherence	12.33	12.83	3.89

A one-factorial ANOVA for word frequency revealed no significant differences between the four conditions with $F(3,140) = 2.03$ ($p = 0.113$). The one-factorial ANOVA for word length revealed no significant differences between the four conditions with $F(3,140) = 0.37$ ($p = 0.78$). Again, the ANOVA for syllable length did not reveal significant differences between the four conditions with $F(3,140) = 0.16$ ($p = 0.928$).

Ninety-six filler items were presented including the fillers of the SPR study (with stereotypical humor, stereotypical horror, texts treating the emotions of love, sadness, and anger) as well as coherent stories and completely nonsensical sentences.

Each participant saw the 240 items in one of two pseudorandomized lists including all items and fillers. The lists were separated into six blocks following the Latin squares design with six items per condition and 16 fillers. The blocks were pseudorandomized individually.

Again, binary, factual comprehension questions were included to ensure the participants' attentive reading. The 168 comprehension questions focused on the context sentences of the target items or on any segment of the filler items and clearly asked for a "yes" or "no" response. The rest of the filler and target items (72 items) was followed by the question "Weiter?"["Next?"].

A cloze probability test was not conducted since the norming questionnaires already asked for the factor of surprise. The conditions humor and art-horror both had high surprise scores above five in the rating questionnaires (see Chapter 4.1.1.3).

EEG procedure

We placed an elastic cap (Easycap GmbH, Herrsching-Breitbrunn, Germany) on the head of the participants. Twenty-six Ag/AgCl scalp electrodes were fixed onto the cap according to the 10/20 system (cf. Jasper 1958; American Encephalographic Society 1994), placing the electrodes at 10 % and 20 % points along lines of latitude and longitude (cf. Luck 2014: 166–167). Bipolar pairs of electrodes were placed at the outer canthi of the eyes as well as above and below the right eye to measure the electrooculogram (EOG) horizontally and vertically. Impedances were kept ≤ 4 kΩ. The EEG was amplified by a Brain Vision Brain-Amp amplifier (Brain Products GmbH, Gilching, Germany) and digitized at a sampling rate of 500 Hz.

We recorded six midline positions (frontal [Fz], fronto-central [FCz], central [Cz], centro-parietal [CPz], parietal [Pz] and parietal-posterior [Poz]), sites at the frontal scalp region (F3 / F4 / F7 / F8), fronto-central (FC1 / FC2 / FC5 / FC6), central (C3 / C4), temporal (T7 /T8), centro-parietal (CP1 / CP2 / CP5 / CP6) and parietal (P3 / P4 / P7 / P8) areas. Electrodes were referenced online to one mastoid and re-referenced to linked left and right mastoids offline (ground: AFz). Figure 28 shows the positioning of the electrodes over the scalp (cf. Luck 2014: 167):

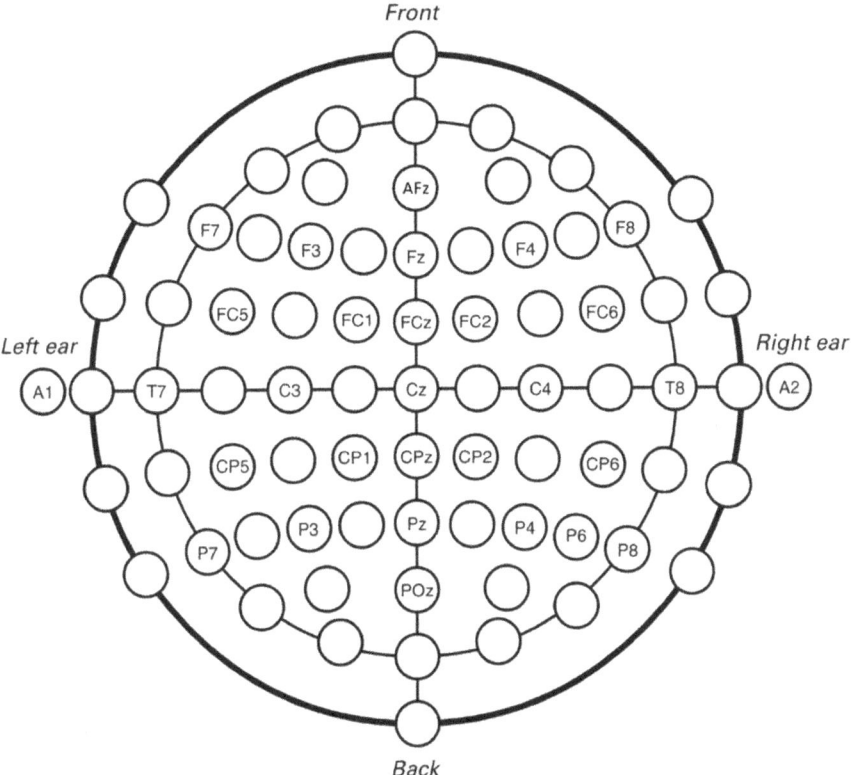

Figure 28: Illustration of electrode cap (extended version) according to 10/20 system (adapted to recorded electrode positions from Luck 2014: 167).

Procedure

The experiment took place in a sound-attenuated cabin where the participants were seated comfortably in front of a computer screen. The participants were told to read the sentences attentively and answer the comprehension questions with the "Yes" or "No" button. Resting-state EEGs were recorded for two minutes with eyes open and for two minutes with eyes closed.

The items were presented in the Software *Presentation* as follows: The background screen was light grey (rgb 170170170) and the text color was dark grey (rgb 515151). After a fixation asterisk in the center of the screen appeared for 500 ms, a complete context sentence appeared until the participant pressed a button. Then, the target sentence including two intro segments, the critical segment and three spillover regions was presented automatically and segment-by-segment without the participants' need to press a button. A one-word segment was presented for 450 ms; a two-word segment was shown for 550 ms. The interstimulus interval was 150 ms. After every item, question marks appeared in the middle of the screen as a prime for the following comprehension question. A binary, factual comprehension question or the question "Weiter?" ["Next?"] followed, which had to be answered by pressing controller keys marked with "Ja" ["yes"] or "Nein" ["no"] within 1000 ms. After three practice sentences, the actual experiment started with its six blocks. After every block, a short break of a few minutes was included depending on the participant's needs. For half of the sessions, the "yes"-button was on the left side of the controller and for the other half, it was on the right side.

At the end, resting-state EEGs were recorded again for two minutes with eyes open and for two minutes with eyes closed.

After the EEG experiment, the participants received the same, four questionnaires like after the SPR experiment: GELOPH<15> (to exclude participants suffering from gelotophobia), STCI-S<18>, STCI-T<30>, and FEE (for descriptions see Chapter 4.3).

Data analysis

A band-pass filter of 0.3–20 Hz removed potential slow signal drifts. To remove artifacts, raw data were scanned automatically and manually. The automatic scanning removed epochs of the EOG channels with amplitudes above the threshold of 40 µV within a 200 ms sliding window. Additionally, artifacts due to eye and muscle movements, signal drifts, or amplifier saturation were marked manually. The ERPs were time-locked to the presentation onset of the critical word. Only artifact-free trials entered into the final data analysis. This resulted in the exclusion of 1.65 % of the critical data (9 rejections in art-horror, 6 rejections in humor, 5 rejections in incoherence, and 12 rejections in coherence).

Time-windows were defined by significance verification for main effects of condition by visual inspection. As a topographical factor for the analyses, the following regions of interest (ROI) were defined for the midline and lateral electrode sides.

Midline:
- ROI 1 (midline-frontal) including the electrodes Fz, FCz and Cz
- ROI 2 (midline-posterior) including the electrodes Pz, POz and CPz

Lateral:
- ROI 1 (left-frontal) including the electrodes F7, F3, FC5, FC1, T7
- ROI 2 (right-frontal) including the electrodes F4, F8, FC2, FC6, T8
- ROI 3 (left-posterior) including the electrodes P7, P3, CP5, CP1, C3
- ROI 4 (right-posterior) including the electrodes P8, P4, CP6, CP2, C4

Potential type I errors due to violations of sphericity were taken care of by adjusting the data according to the Huynh-Feldt procedure (cf. Huynh and Feldt 1970). Pairwise comparisons were computed with an adjusted significance level set to p < .025 based on a modified Bonferroni procedure (cf. Keppel and Wickens 2004).

Trials with false responses to the comprehension question were not excluded for the same three reasons as in the SPR experiment: The questions were only meant to keep the participants' attention up. Furthermore, the content-related questions only covered 168 of the 240 questions and never asked for details about the critical region of the targets. Moreover, it was assumed that the participants could have detected the incongruity and could have been afraid or amused without answering correctly.

Participants with scores above 37.5 in the GELOPH<15> questionnaire were excluded. Since the correlations of the questionnaires STCI-T30, STCI-S18 and FEE with the SPR data did not reveal significant interactions, correlations for the ERP results were not computed.

4.4.2 Results

Behavioral results
Participants responded to the 168 content-related comprehension questions (excluding "Weiter?" ["Next?"]) with a mean accuracy of 0.94 ranging between 0.79 and 0.99.

Electrophysiological results
The visual inspection of the grand-averaged ERPs for the four conditions revealed differences for the time windows between a) 300 – 450 ms, b) 600 – 700 ms, and c) 950 – 1050 ms (see Figure 29).

For the window of interest between 300 – 450 ms, the wave forms showed stronger negativities for the incoherence condition and the two incongruity conditions (humor and art-horror) compared to the coherence condition. The negativity of the incoherence condition was more pronounced than the negativity of the humor and art-horror condition. For the 600 – 700 ms window, the figure indicates more pronounced positivities for the humor, art-horror, and coherence condition compared to the incoherence condition. The third window of interest between 950 – 1050 ms revealed a more positive deflection for the art-horror condition compared to the coherence and the humor condition. There was also a difference between the humor and incoherence condition.

Electrophysiological results

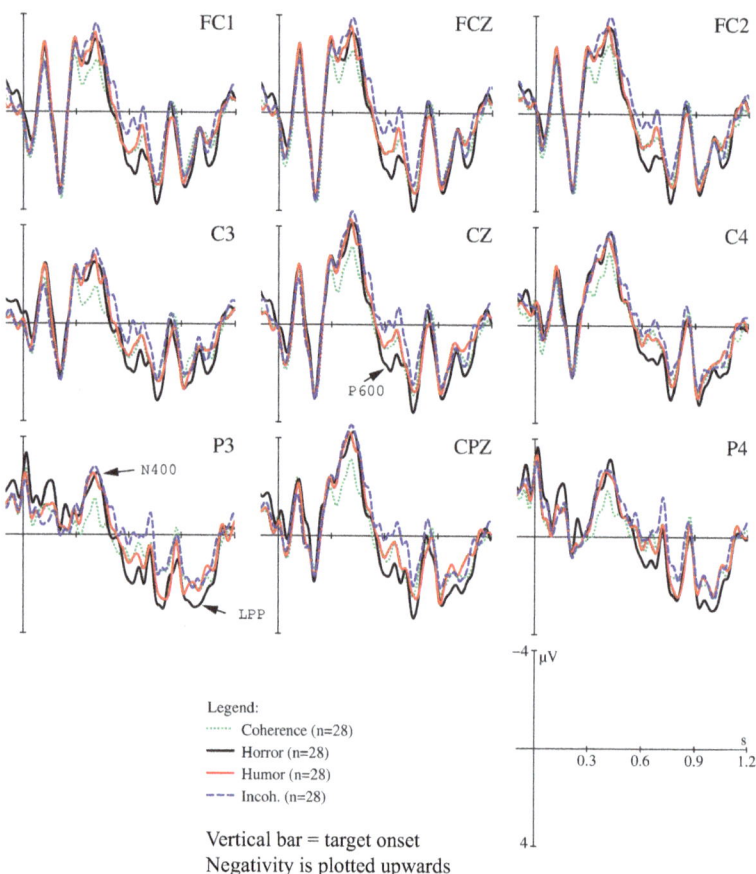

Figure 29: Electrophysiological results of the grand-averaged ERPs for 9 selected electrode sides for the conditions coherence, horror, humor, and incoherence.

Separate ANOVAs were computed for the three time windows of interest (300 – 450 ms; 600 – 700 ms; 950 – 1050 ms) to control for the hypothesized N400/LAN, P600, and LPP.

The lateral analysis showed main effects for the first time window ($F (3,81) = .61$, $p = .005$) and a COND x ROI interaction ($F (3,81) = .8$, $p = .011$). Resolution of this interaction registered effects in ROI 1 ($F (3,81) = 0.78$, $p = .025$) and ROI 3 ($F (3,81) = 0.72$, $p = .0007$). In the second time window, the lateral electrodes

(F (3,81) = 1.07, p = .015) and the midline channels (F (3,81) = 1.013, p = .0057) showed main effects. In the third time window, lateral electrodes showed main effects (F (3,81) = 0.91, p = .0265).

Pairwise comparisons (contrasting humor/coherence, horror/coherence, humor/horror, humor/incoherence, horror/incoherence, and coherence/incoherence, see Tables 19–21) were subsequently carried out to follow up the main effects and interactions.

For the time window between 300 – 450 ms, effects were observed for the comparisons of art-horror to coherence (ROI 3: F (1,27) = 6.14, p = .02), humor to incoherence (ROI 3: F (1,27) = 7.07, p = .013), and incoherence to coherence (ROI 1: F (1,27) = 7.8, p = .0095; ROI 3: F (1,27) = 17.41, p = .0003). The comparison between humor and coherence only approaches significance in ROI 3 (F (1,27) = 5.5, p = .0266). The other contrasts registered not significant effects (see P-values marked by a * only approach significance. "n.s." stands for "no significance", Table 19).

Table 19: Analysis of ROIs in first time window (300–450 ms) for main effects of midline electrodes and lateral electrodes per region of interest for six pairwise comparisons.

	time window 300 –450 ms											
	humor/ coherence		horror/ coherence		humor/ horror		humor/ incoh.		horror/ incoh.		coherence/ incoh.	
	F	p	F	p	F	p	F	p	F	p	F	p
Midline Main effects					.71 / n.s.							
Lat. ROI 1 (left-front.)	2.49	n.s.	1.64	n.s.	.3	n.s.	3.59	n.s.	4.3	n.s.	7.8	.01
Lat. ROI 3 (left-post.)	5.5	*.027	6.14	.02	.32	n.s.	7.07	.013	4.54	n.s.	17.41	<.02

P-values marked by a * only approach significance. "n.s." stands for "no significance".

The second time window (600 –700 ms) revealed significant differences for the lateral analysis between art-horror and incoherence with (F (1,27) = 8.99, p = .006). The comparison between coherence and incoherence laterally only approached our threshold for statistical significance (F (1,27) = 5.51, p = 0.026). The central electrodes also revealed significant differences between humor and incoherence (F (1,27) = 6.53, p = .02), art-horror and incoherence (F (1,27) = 9.03, p = .006), and coherence and incoherence (F (1,27) = 6.07, p = .02). The other contrasts registered not significant effects (see Table 20).

Table 20: Analysis of ROIs in second time window (600–700 ms) for main effects of midline electrodes and lateral electrodes per region of interest for six pairwise comparisons.

	time window 600 –700 ms											
	humor/ coherence		horror/ coherence		humor/ horror		humor/ incoh.		horror/ incoh.		coherence/ incoh.	
	F	p	F	p	F	p	F	p	F	p	F	p
Midline Main effects	.21	n.s.	.69	n.s.	2.04	n.s.	6.53	.017	9.03	.01	6.07	.02
Lateral Main effects	.14	n.s.	1.8	n.s.	2.22	n.s.	2.7	n.s.	8.99	.01	5.51	*.026

P-values marked by a * only approach significance. "n.s." stands for "no significance".

The third time window (950 –1050 ms) revealed significant differences for the lateral analysis between art-horror and coherence (F (1,27) = 6.63, p = .016), and art-horror and humor (F (1,27) = 9.45, p = .005). The other contrasts registered not significant effects (see Table 21).

Table 21: Analysis of ROIs in third time window (950–1050 ms) for main effects of midline electrodes and lateral electrodes per region of interest for six pairwise comparisons.

	time window 950 –1050 ms											
	humor/ coherence		horror/ coherence		humor/ horror		humor/ incoh.		horror/ incoh.		coherence/ incoh.	
	F	p	F	p	F	p	F	p	F	p	F	p
Midline Main effects					.904 / n.s.							
Lateral Main effects	.002	n.s.	6.63	.02	9.45	.005	3.49	n.s.	2.21	n.s.	1.23	n.s.

"n.s." stands for "no significance"

Questionnaire results

Twenty-nine participants responded to the GELOPH<15> with a mean of 26 ranging between 17 and 37 (median = 24; sd = 6.23). One participant reached a value of 53 and was excluded from the analysis.

4.4.3 Discussion

This ERP experiment compared the participant's electrophysiological reactions of the four conditions art-horror, humor, coherence, and incoherence. The aim was to verify whether art-horror evokes additional neuroelectric processing costs, how far these costs reflect cognitive processing functions and phases, and to what extent they differ from other incongruity phenomena, like humor or irresolvable incongruities.

The behavioral data showed that the participants were highly attentive. The electrophysiological results revealed three time windows, in which the four conditions differed significantly. The first time window was set between 300 – 450 ms after the onset of the critical segment, the second between 600 – 700 ms post-onset, and the third between 950 – 1050 ms post-onset.

In the first time window, incoherence and art-horror elicited more enhanced negativities compared to coherence in left-posterior regions (ROI 3). Incoherence also demonstrated this effect in the left-anterior region (ROI 1). In ROI 3, incoherence also differed significantly from humor and showed a more pronounced negativity. Differences between humor and coherence approached significance over left-posterior electrode sites.

The enhanced negativities in this first window of interest met the predictions: compared to the coherence condition, art-horror did elicit enhanced neuro-electric activity in this time window. These costs were functionally related to the detection of the semantic violation, which showed that art-horror shares cognitive mechanisms with the two other incongruity conditions with pronounced negativities (incoherence and humor [the latter only approaches significance]). The negativities in all three incongruity conditions showed stronger distributions at the left posterior region. In line with previous research on semantic violations and prediction errors in humor and the distribution of the negativity, they were here interpreted as N400 effects (cf. Coulson and Kutas 2001; Feng, Chan and Chen 2014; Mayerhofer and Schacht 2015). The stronger effects in incoherence compared to coherence and humor could be explained through incoherence's stronger incongruity due to its non-resolvability. Even though art-horror and humor (nearly) showed enhanced negativities in this time window, they replicated findings from the preceding SPR experiment and did not differ from each other significantly. The missing significance between incoherence and art-horror fit Rotbarth's model, claiming that incongruity needs to range on a high arousal level to elicit fear and that problem-solving strategies, like resolving the incongruity, are activated in later processing phases. The slightly lower scores in humor's negativity reflected the norming study's lower scores in surprise (as expression of incongruity degree) compared to art-horror. Humor seems to be less surprising than art-horror which might be due to humor's higher cultural acceptance and frequency.

In the second window of interest, humor, art-horror, and coherence showed more pronounced positivities when compared to incoherence. While the differences between art-horror and incoherence were significant in lateral and central regions, humor differed significantly to incoherence only at central electrodes. The differences between coherence and incoherence laterally only approached significance, but in midline, they were significant.

While participants seemed to stop processing the incoherence condition in this time-window, the results indicate that they invested in the processing of the three other conditions. Since the positivities of this time window did not show concentrated distributions on one region, they were here interpreted as P600 components and as a reflection of a mental model update and the integration of the incoming input (cf. Bornkessel-Schlesewsky and Schumacher 2016).

Humor research has already shown that these positivities can be attributed to semantic repair mechanisms to solve incongruities (cf. Feng, Chan and Chen 2014; Shibata, Terasawa, Osumi, Masui, Ito, Sato and Umeda 2017; Canal, Bischetti, Di Paola, Bertini, Ricci and Bambini 2019). The finding of the P600 is also in line with research on pragmatic interpretation processes necessary for the computation of figurative language, such as script switches in metaphor processing (cf. Weiland 2014) or meaning extension and discourse updating during referential shifts in metonymy processing (cf. Schumacher 2019; Bambini, Bertini, Schaeken, Stella and Di Russo 2016). Nevertheless, humor and art-horror did not engender additional costs when compared to coherence which replicates results from Feng, Chan and Chen (2014) and Tu, Cao, Yun, Wang, Zhao and Qiu (2014). This finding might indicate that the pragmatic processes, such as the search for a second script and the resolution of the incongruity, were already finished at this stage.

In the third time window, a more positive deflection appeared laterally in art-horror compared to coherence and humor, which answered the predictions partly: While humor did not replicate findings on emotional humor reactions from Feng, Chan and Chen (2014), Mayerhofer and Schacht (2015), and Canal, Bischetti, Di Paola, Bertini, Ricci and Bambini (2019), art-horror did show pronounced lateral positivities. These late positivities in art-horror were interpreted as LPP, reflecting either an ongoing elaboration of the art-horror stimuli or an emotional reaction. Although an emotional response was also expected for humor, this result showed that the processing of humor and art-horror began to differ at this late stage.

Overall, the findings supported two interpretations: first, the results suggested that art-horror and humor shared cognitive resources to handle incongruity (reflected in the N400 and P600 effects) and only differed in the emotional last phase (mirrored in the LPP). While the non-significant difference between humor and coherence conditions, especially in the second and third time window, actually did not fit three-step humor processing models, such as the NCM (cf. Chan, Chou, Chen and Liang 2012; Chan, Chou, Chen, Yeh, Lavallee, Liang and Chang 2013), art-horror results did suggest three phases of incongruity detection, resolution, and elaboration/emotion.

5 Discussion & conclusion

Conceptually and experimentally contrasting the genre of art-horror with the phenomenon of humor, this book gained insights into their common, underlying mechanisms and their cognitive processing. The aim was to both incorporate art-horror for the first time in a model of incongruity detection and pragmatic resolution and refine existing humor models. The following research questions were addressed: Does art-horror evoke the same kind of incongruity as humor? Does art-horror elicit additional processing costs compared to humor and (in)coherent items and do they differ with respect to intensity and time-course? Are these processing costs associated with the local incongruity of the stimulus, its detection, resolution, and emotional elaboration?

This final chapter answers these research questions in a condensed review of the conceptual and experimental results, framing them as a small piece of the puzzle into the general research context. Identifying incongruity as a crucial conceptual mechanism in art-horror and applying existing incongruity models of humor research analogously to art-horror conception and processing, Chapter 5.1 summarizes the conceptual comparison of humor and art-horror. Subsequently, Chapter 5.2 reviews the experimental comparison of humor and art-horror in terms of reading times, facial expressions, and neuroelectric activity (the norming studies from Chapter 3.1 are excluded here to focus on the results relevant to the research questions). Based on these findings, Chapter 5.3 develops a model of incongruity processing for humor and art-horror (IPM). Finally, Chapter 5.4 indicates desiderata for future research.

5.1 Summary of conceptual findings

Incongruity in art-horror

First, this book conceptually pointed out that the phenomenon of incongruity is a mechanism underlying art-horror, which serves to evoke the emotions of fear and disgust. Since its beginnings as Gothic fiction during the 18th and early 19th century, the genre of art-horror uses a broad yet repetitive repertoire of characters (supernatural forces, (human) monsters), settings (dark, mystical geography and architecture), themes (conspiracies, violent sexuality, cannibalism) and narrative strategies (garden path, complex discovery, overreacher plots) based on cultural disruptions and the union of contradictions. These unified oppositions can be, for example, the simultaneity of life and death, reality and unreality, normality and abnormality, health and sickness, or good and evil, making the characters, places, and actions impure and interstitial (Chapter 1.1). This book explored the genre of art-horror with regard to these incongruities and worked out a taxonomy of incongruity that defines the unified contradictions as the trigger of the negative emotions of fear and disgust. While the art-horror genre has been extensively investigated from a literary studies perspective as well as from a psychoanalytical angle, there are few conceptual approaches that grasp art-horror through cognitive incongruity. Carroll's concept of impurity and categorical interstitialty (1999) as well as Grodal's idea of a cognitive dissonance between mental representations (2000) define art-horror as broken categories, united oppositions, and the impossibility to create cognitive consistency between colliding opposite models (see Chapter 1.2.3). According to their approaches, this impurity or dissonance causes cognitive effort and leads to the negative emotions of fear and disgust.

A cognitive art-horror model, which explains and predicts phases of art-horror processing supported by empirical data, does not yet exist. However, there are empirically attested processing models for the phenomenon of humor, which shares crucial content, narrative strategies, and cognitive mechanisms with art-horror.

Transferring insights from humorous incongruity to art-horror

This work builds on theories which highlight humor's cognitive mechanisms in a superordinate model of language comprehension. Being a communication mode, individual ability, and source for laughter and exhilaration, humor was defined here according to the idea of opposing yet overlapping scripts, script-switching, the seven knowledge resources of the GTVH (cf. Raskin 1985; Attardo 1994; Attardo, Hempelmann and Di Maio 2002; Hempelmann and Attardo 2011; Attardo 2017b), and its extensions (cf. Canestrari 2010; Canestrari 2012; Tsakona 2013; Chovanec and Tsakona 2018) (Chapter 2.2). Humor unites incongruous, cognitive concepts. These oppositions can, in line with art-horror's oppositions, be alive/dead, real/unreal, normal/abnormal, and possible/impossible. The opposing scripts are linked through different logical mechanisms in a diegetic situation with agents and victims, following a narrative structure as information distribution, and linguistic aspects. The humorous opposition is further situated in a socio-cultural context of the recipients who also apply pragmatic, meta-communicative strategies. Finally, humor was summarized in a three-step comprehension model, incorporating the detection of the incongruity, its resolution through switching to an alternative reading, and the final positive emotional reaction of exhilaration.

Incongruity was highlighted as the common denominator between humor and art-horror. Terminology and conceptual findings were transferred from humor to art-horror and the three-step incongruity model was applied analogously to art-horror garden paths. Thereby, findings and methodological achievements of humor research were made fruitful for a cognitive art-horror understanding with a focus on the common, cognitive mechanism of incongruity processing (Chapter 2.3). The KRs of the GTVH and its extensions were completely transferable to the analysis of short art-horror instances. Thus, art-horror was also defined as the union of two incongruous yet overlapping scripts, which the recipients understand and appreciate via a resolution mechanism, such as script-switching. This model transfer resulted in a three-step art-horror model, comprised of incongruity detection, its resolution, and an emotional response. Contrary to the assumption of SSTH/GTVH, that two oppositional, overlapping scripts and the script-switching mechanism trigger exhilaration, the current book revealed that the oppositions and script-switching mechanism also applies to art-horror. This shows that the GTVH lacks an element, which tackles differences between humor and other emotions triggered by incongruity resolution.

To test whether pragmatic requirements or the dangerousness of the incongruity account for the distinction between humor and horror, both the seven humor implicatures (cf. Canestrari 2012) and the dangerousness of the context (cf. Rothbart 2017 [1976]) were examined for art-horror:

The seven humor implicatures were applicable to art-horror, which led to the assumption that the necessary pragmatics for enjoying art-horror is not the distinguishing criterion between art-horror and humor. In both humor and art-horror, implicatures sufficient for a successful reception are recognition, understanding, and appreciation. Implicatures that reinforce the success are agreement, intention, playful reply.

Trying to separate humor from incongruities eliciting fear, Rothbart (2017 [1976]) emphasized the influence of arousal level and the dangerousness of the input on the processing of incongruity. Nevertheless, it did not account for art-horror's incongruity resolution. Her humor model suggests that incongruent stimuli are processed according to the elicited arousal (in three levels: low, medium, and high [minimal arousal stimuli are ignored]). While low arousal stimuli are approached immediately with problem-solving strategies, medium and high arousal stimuli are first compared with the dangerousness of the context. If the context is dangerous, fear is generated, the examination is interrupted, and the stimulus is avoided. If it is not dangerous, the recipients invest in problem-solving strategies, which, if successful, lead to a smile or laughter depending on the arousal level. This model helps only partially to differentiate humor and art-horror reactions to incongruity. While the (fictitious) context's dangerousness might indeed influence the reaction to the incongruity and thus separate art-horror from humor, the model does not consider that fear can also arise after or through problem-solving. Further, according to the paradox of painful-art, the fear trigger does not have to be avoided. Thus, in addition to smiles and laughter, the fear reaction has to be integrated into the end of Rothbart's section on problem-solving reactions to incongruity. This does not, however, deny the potential influence of the context's dangerousness, but rather shows that dangerousness does not seem to block incongruity processing. The dangerousness, then, has to be verified, again, after the incongruity resolution within the second script and its new relation to the (fictitious) context.

Incongruity in humor and art-horror

The current chapter conceptually answered the first research question: Humor and art-horror are both based on the union of incongruent yet overlapping scripts. The incongruity between a first script (context, setup, initial mental representation) and the humorous or frightening punchline of garden paths is resolved through the mechanism of switching to a second script and a discourse update. This can lead not only to the positive emotion of exhilaration in humor, but also negative emotions of fear and disgust in art-horror.

To attest empirically whether art-horror and humor are processed equally across the three phases of incongruity detection, resolution, and emotion, three experiments were developed that compared art-horror, humor, coherent and incoherent texts on the basis of reading times, facial expressions, and neuroelectric activity.

5.2 Summary of experimental findings

To answer the research questions on processing art-horror garden paths, incongruities were regarded as prediction errors. These errors interrupt ongoing cognitive processes and require an update of the recipients' discourse representation to give the input meaning (Chapter 3.1). Compared to correctly predicted, coherent texts, this reanalysis and update are computationally demanding, which is associated with additional cognitive effort (costs) (cf. Levy 2008; Friston 2010; Levy 2011; Bornkessel-Schlesewsky and Schumacher 2016). This effort is indirectly reflected, for example, in longer reading times and enhanced electrophysiological activity (Chapter 3.2).

Reviewing humor's experimental research: Processing phases and influencing factors

The current work reviewed experimental results on processing costs of humor research (Chapter 3.3 to 3.6) to deduce hypotheses for an analogous investigation of art-horror processing. While some experiments delivered psycholinguistic evidence for the processing phases of detection, resolution, and emotional reaction, others suggested facilitation effects for the humor condition due to emotional feedback of exhilaration, or several parallel cognitive processes.

Reading-time experiments found prolonged reading times for humor, associated with costs for frame-shifting and updating mental representations (cf. Coulson and Kutas 1998; Coulson and Kutas 2001; Mayerhofer and Schacht 2015).

In ERP experiments, evidence for the processing stage of incongruity detection was seen in the components of N400, LAN, and P3, and interpreted as prediction error, semantic integration problems, the detection of an expectation violation or a salient content, an orientation mechanism, or the search for an alternative reading (cf. Coulson and Kutas 2001; Feng, Chan and Chen 2014; Mayerhofer and Schacht 2015; Canal, Bischetti, Di Paola, Bertini, Ricci and Bambini 2019). Further evidence for this processing stage was found through fMRI experiments, which associated the enhanced activity of the middle temporal gyrus, medial frontal gyrus and temporal lobe during humor reception with the storage of semantic knowledge, the detection of semantic violations, and categorization (cf. Chan, Chou, Chen and Liang 2012; Chan, Chou, Chen, Yeh, Lavallee, Liang and Chang 2013).

Evidence for the second processing stage of incongruity resolution was seen in the ERP component of the P600, and interpreted as semantic reparation, reanalysis, and script-switching (cf. Feng, Chan and Chen 2014; Shibata, Terasawa, Osumi, Masui, Ito, Sato and Umeda 2017; Canal, Bischetti, Di Paola, Bertini, Ricci and Bambini 2019). These findings were not confirmed by Mayerhofer and Schacht (2015). FMRI experiments found increased activation of the inferior frontal gyrus, superior frontal gyrus, and inferior parietal lobule during humor reception, which was associated with disambiguation, script switching, enriching inferences, executive functions, integration processes, incongruity resolution, and associative judgments (cf. Chan, Chou, Chen and Liang 2012; Chan, Chou, Chen, Yeh, Lavallee, Liang and Chang 2013).

The third, emotional processing stage was influenced by the ERP components of LPP, LPC, and a late frontal positivity. They were associated with amusement (cf. Feng, Chan and Chen 2014; Mayerhofer and Schacht 2015; Canal, Bischetti, Di Paola, Bertini, Ricci and Bambini 2019). In fMRI experiments, the brain areas of ventromedial prefrontal gyrus, parahippocampal gyrus and amygdala during humor reception were activated more strongly. This activation pattern was interpreted as reward and elaboration (cf. Chan, Chou, Chen and Liang 2012; Chan, Chou, Chen, Yeh, Lavallee, Liang and Chang 2013).

Several authors doubt this three-stage processing. For example, the ERP findings from Coulson et al. (2001) and Canal, Bischetti, Di Paola, Bertini, Ricci and Bambini (2019) all occurred in the same time window as parallelly running processes, challenging a sequential model. Further criticism came from Ferstl et al. (2017), who suggested that the exhilaration in humor causes a facilitation due to its feedback mechanism. Since emotions can influence cognitive and language-related processes of interpreting, judging, reasoning, and decision making by impairing or promoting underlying cognitive mechanisms such as attention control, cognitive control, priming, reflection, and computational capacity (cf. Blanchette and Richards 2010), they can also influence humor processing. Both positive and negative emotions can influence all three stages both positively (higher cognitive capacity, faster processing) and negatively (prohibited capacity, slower processing) (cf. Darke 1988; Channon and Baker 1994; Blanchette and Richards 2010; Kanske and Kotz 2011; Hartikainen, Siiskonen and Ogawa 2012; Blanchette and Caparos 2013; Kanske 2015; Jasinska, Yasuda, Rhodes, Wang and Polk 2015; Xu, Li, Ding, Zhang, Fan, Diao and Yang 2015).

Individual differences, comprising cognitive capacity, intelligence, language skills, age, gender, and personality traits, can also influence the processing of humor. They can, for example, influence a person's efficiency in processing and updating discourse representations (cf. Prat 2011; Novick, Hussey, Teubner-Rhodes, Harbison and Bunting 2013; Kidd, Donnelly and Christiansen 2018). Thus, they can also impact incongruity processing (cf. Coulson and Kutas 2001). Additionally, sex differences impact genre preferences, activated brain areas during humor reception, executive functions, emotional reactions, and feedback mechanisms (cf. Mundorf, Bhatia, Zillmann, Lester and Robertson 1988; Johnson 1992; Derks and Arora 1993; Herzog 1999; Azim, Mobbs, Jo, Menon and Reiss 2005; Kohn, Kellermann, Gur, Schneider and Habel 2011). Further, personality traits such as extraversion and neuroticism, exhilaratability, and sense of humor influence activated brain areas and facial expressions during humor reception (cf. Mobbs, Hagan, Azim, Menon and Reiss 2005; Ruch 2005; Ruch and Proyer 2008a; Proyer 2014).

While some experiments compared humorous incongruity to other forms of incongruity, such as nonsense or revision texts, none compared it to other resolvable and emotional incongruities such as art-horror. Therefore, humor theories based on the phenomena of incongruity detection, resolution, and elaboration are not able to describe incongruities that (actually) trigger humor separately from those that cause other emotions (cf. Coulson and Kutas 1998; Coulson 2001; Coulson, Urbach and Kutas 2006; Chan, Chou, Chen and Liang 2012; Chan, Chou, Chen, Yeh, Lavallee, Liang and Chang 2013; Feng, Chan and Chen 2014; Mayerhofer and Schacht 2015; Ferstl, Israel and Putzar 2017; Canal, Bischetti, Di Paola, Bertini, Ricci and Bambini 2019). In particular, humor has not yet been compared to incongruities triggering negative emotions. This book closed this gap.

Comparing humor and art-horror experimentally: Predictions

The current book postulated a conceptual analogy between humor and art-horror and hypothesized that – if the incongruity in both genres is indeed processed by the same cognitive mechanisms – art-horror and humor show the same psycholinguistic results for the detection and resolution of incongruity and differ only in the elicited emotions. Comparing minimal quadruplets with the three conditions of coherence, humor, and horror in an SPR experiment and with a fourth condition of irresolvable incoherence in an ERP experiment, this work tested the hypotheses that art-horror elicits additional processing costs when compared to coherent stimuli. It attested whether these additional costs are due to the detection and resolution of an incongruity (semantic integration difficulties and a script-switch/discourse update) and whether recipients react emotionally after the discourse update.

Under the immediacy assumption and the eye-mind assumption (cf. Just and Carpenter 1980), reading behavior in the self-paced reading experiment provided indirect information about underlying cognitive processes (Chapter 4.2). Here, longer reading times were assumed to represent enhanced cognitive effort.

Using the Facial Action Coding System (FACS) from Ekman, Friesen and Hager (2002a; 2002b), the reading time experiment was complemented through an experiment that investigated the recipients' facial expressions measured in Action Units (AU) (Chapter 4.3). It tested whether the emotions typically correlating with humor (exhilaration: laughter, AU12 [+6]) and art-horror (fear: widened eyes and raised inner and/or outer eyebrows, AU1+2+4/5; disgust: raised upper lip, AU9 and/or 10) were visible in the participants' facial expressions.

In the ERP experiment (Chapter 4.4), enhanced neuroelectric activity, time-locked and averaged, was interpreted as additional cognitive effort to detect (predicted N400 associated with semantic prediction errors), resolve (predicted P600 associated with a reparation of the incongruent text, the switch to a coherent reading and discourse update), and emotionally react to the incongruity (predicted LPP associated with the affective reaction of exhilaration and fear/disgust). The following sections summarize the experimental findings of the current book.

Comparing humor and art-horror experimentally: Findings support a three-stage art-horror model

Expanding the results from Coulson and Kutas (1998), Mayerhofer and Schacht (2015), and Coulson, Urbach and Kutas (2006), longer reading times for the critical word and first spill-over region clearly indicated additional processing efforts for humor and art-horror, compared to the coherence condition. There was no significant difference between the reading times of humor and art-horror. This could be a hint that the underlying incongruity is processed through the same cognitive mechanisms. The result indicates, contrary to Ferstl, Israel and Putzar (2017), that humor did not induce a facilitation effect through its immediate positive feedback or that the negative feedback of art-horror generates the same reading acceleration. The correlations of questionnaires and SPR results did not reveal reliable effects, which might indicate that the attested personality features, such as exhilaratability or gelotophobia (cf. Ruch and Proyer 2008b; Proyer 2014), did not influence the experiments.

The FACS experiment only revealed (non-significant) trends. The predicted AUs were seen in the expected condition (AU 12 (+6) in humor; AU 1+2+4/5 or AU 9 or 10 in art-horror), although their numbers were small. More AUs were seen *after* than *on* the critical segment, which supported the assumption of a late emotional reaction as the third processing stage after detecting and resolving the incongruity in humor and art-horror. Nonetheless, in line with humorous facilitation effects suggested by Ferstl, Israel and Putzar (2017), some humor reactions did appear on the critical word, supporting the idea that humor's immediate, positive feedback facilitated the resolution phase so that emotional reactions appeared earlier. The FACS experiment also suggested that individual differences play a role in humor and art-horror processing: While some participants reacted frightened in the humor condition, others laughed in the art-horror condition, which offers a two-fold interpretation. On one hand, these participants might indeed have reacted exhilarated to the art-horror condition with a release of tension. On the other hand, their laughter might have been an expression of coping with a problematic situation (cf. Trouvain and Truong 2017) or a socially regulating smile in communication (cf. Ekman, Davidson and Friesen 1990). Individual differences seemed to also account for the fact that some participants only reacted in one condition or showed increased standard deviations in a given AU, within a condition. Further, the association of personality features, such as gelotophobia or cheerfulness, revealed trends that contradicted the experiment's hypotheses: High-scoring gelotophobes (predicted to react less in the humor condition) were more often present in the group of reacting participants. In addition, cheerfulness scores were higher for the non-reacting groups and bad mood was higher for the reacting participants, although the opposite was predicted. Thus, a clear pattern of how gelotophobia, cheerfulness, and bad mood influence the FACS results, was not identifiable, which might indicate that the attested personality features did not influence the experiment.

The ERP results showed effects for the three time-windows between 300–450 ms, 600–700 ms, and 950–1050 ms (see Table 22).

Table 22: Interpretation of ERP results per condition and time window.

Condition	Time window I: 300–450 ms	Time window II: 600–700 ms	Time window III: 950–1050 ms
Humor	*N400	P600	/
Art-horror	N400	P600	LPP
Incoherence	N400 (strongest)	/	/
Coherence	/	P600	/

*This negativity only approached significance.

In the first time window, enhanced negativities were observed for art-horror, incoherence, and (with results approaching significance) humor. They were interpreted as N400s, reflecting the detection of the semantic violation arising from the incongruity in humor, art-horror, and incoherence. The N400 effect was strongest for the incoherence condition, indicating that the recipients invested the highest effort in this non-resolvable condition. This result replicates humor findings from Coulson and Kutas (2001), Feng, Chan and Chen (2014), Mayerhofer and Schacht (2015), Du, Qin, Tu, Yin, Wang, Yu and Qiu (2013), and Canal, Bischetti, Di Paola, Bertini, Ricci and Bambini (2019) who associate negativities in this time window either with prediction errors, semantic integration problems, or the detection of an incongruity (reflected either in an N400 or a LAN). The N400 in the art-horror condition revealed that the same mechanism of prediction and incongruity detection is required in art-horror processing. This finding supports an art-horror model that includes a first stage of incongruity detection where the recipients compare their predictions according to a first script with the input and recognize the incongruity due to the incoming second script.

The second time window revealed enhanced positivities for humor, art-horror, and coherence in the time window of the P600, compared to incoherence. This was interpreted as the recipients' effort to integrate the input into their cognitive model, while the incoherent condition is rejected due to its non-resolvability. This result expands ERP findings on humor processing from Feng, Chan and Chen (2014), Canal, Bischetti, Di Paola, Bertini, Ricci and Bambini (2019), and Shibata, Terasawa, Osumi, Masui, Ito, Sato and Umeda (2017) who associated the P600 effect with the recipients' search for an alternative script, a reparation of a semantic violation, a reanalysis, and script-switching as a second processing stage, compared to coherent texts. Concerning art-horror, this finding supports a model with a second stage where the recipients engage in problem-solving, disambiguating strategies and resolving the incongruity. According to Rotbarth's model (2017), the arousal level (before the resolution) is supportable for the recipients (low or medium level) since they engage in the resolution and do not ignore (minimal arousal level) or avoid (high arousal level) the stimulus, so far. Compared to coherence, art-horror and humor did not require additional effort in this time-window, which suggested that the potential additional effort for resolving the incongruity is already finished at this stage. It could also be that humor and art-horror enjoy high cultural acceptance and familiarity so that the recipients might be used to resolving incongruities easily in these genres. Nevertheless, pointing to this experiment's shortcoming, this missing difference between humor, art-horror, and coherence might also be due to the brevity and strong constructiveness of the experimental items.

The enhanced positivity for art-horror in the third time window was interpreted as LPP, associated with an emotional reaction to art-horror, eliciting fear/disgust after the incongruity resolution. At this third stage of art-horror processing, the arousal level increases. Comparing this result to the model from Rothbart (2017 [1976]), it might be associated with the recipients' realization that the second script is dangerous for them or their identification figure in the text material. The emotional reaction after a resolution phase supports the aforementioned lack of Rothbart's model (2017 [1976]). In line with the conceptual findings on stimulus evaluations and their interplay with decreasing or increasing arousal (cf. Smuts 2014, Grodal 2000; Chapter 1.2.3), future experiments need to be complemented by a second verification of the context's dangerousness after the resolution and within the second script. If the recipients evaluate the second script as being dangerous (depending on their value system [cf. Tsakona 2013]), the arousal level intensifies to an art-horror reading with the emotions of fear and disgust. Implementing this stage into Rothbart's model and applying her idea of arousal levels to this second context verification, the intensified arousal can either reach a high level so that the recipients indeed show avoidance strategies (such as closing one's eyes), or if the tension is supportable, the recipients enjoy art-horror. Additionally, if the second script is not dangerous, the tension releases to an exhilarant interpretation separated into smiling or laughing depending on arousal level.

Contradicting the results of the reading time experiment, the missing difference between humor and coherence during the third time-window might also be due to humor's positive feedback, which facilitates the resolution of this condition. In analogy to humor's potential positive feedback suggested by Ferstl, Israel and Putzar (2017), this would indicate that art-horror's emotions give a negative feedback which aggravates the resolution and leads to higher processing costs. This aggravation effect might have already influenced precedent processing stages so that this positivity could also represent art-horror's delayed resolution.

The missing difference between humor and coherence might also mirror the smaller negativity/prediction error in the first time-window, suggesting that the items might not have been strong enough to make the recipients laugh. This might be due to a higher familiarity to humor stimuli and a subsequent indifference to jokes. However, multimodal stimuli with stronger punchlines, such as in comedy shows, might affect the LPP component.

Coming back to the current work's research questions, art-horror does elicit additional cognitive costs compared to coherent and incoherent texts. These costs can be associated with the detection, resolution, and emotional elaboration of incongruities. This book showed that the cognitive processing mechanisms, of incongruity detection and resolution of humorous and frightening incongruities, are the same. The main difference between humor and art-horror is the emotional response (to the second script). Incongruity and its resolution are thus important in both phenomena, but not the distinctive criterion of either. The emotions triggered by humor and art-horror make the difference in processing, which were here associated with the (non)dangerousness of the second script. While humor seems to facilitate processing and has a relaxing effect, art-horror blocks processing and increases tension. Thus, the experimental results support a three-stage model of art-horror but, in comparison with other incongruity phenomena, it is fruitful to locate art-horror within a more general incongruity processing model. This model is explained in the following section.

5.3 Incongruity processing model of humor & horror (IPM)

The incongruity model for humor and art-horror developed here represents a synthesis of conceptual and experimental humor and art-horror findings, focusing on the experiments conducted in the current work. The basis of the model is Rothbart's model (2017 [1976]), which describes different reactions to incongruity depending on arousal level and contextual dangerousness. For both humor and art-horror processing, it is supplemented by the three processing stages of humor theories, the idea of script-switching, and a second contextual verification of dangerousness. For art-horror, it is completed by a fear reaction after the resolution. This section describes the incongruity processing model for humor and art-horror (IPM) (see Figure 30) phase-by-phase and indicates which aspects of the model are supported by the experiments of the current work and which elements are added on the basis of the conceptual comparison between humor and art-horror.

Before the recipients enter into the processing of an incongruity, they interpret the incoming text according to a first mental representation/script and make predictions about future input that is compatible with this script. If there is an actual stimulus where this prediction and the incoming information match, the correct prediction pays off, the recipients can keep the selected script/mental representation and quickly achieve a coherent interpretation of the stimulus (left column of the model).

The processing of an incongruity starts if the input prediction does not come true (yellow section in the model). The SPR results of the current work have shown that, compared to coherence, additional effort is required to process art-horror and humor. The longer reading times indicated that the recipients entered into a more elaborate processing of the incongruity. The ERP results substantiated this in a finer temporal resolution. The recipients first determined that the input is incongruent to their initially established mental representation/script and that their input prediction failed. This prediction error was reflected in the ERP component of the N400 in the conditions of incoherence (with strongest N400 effect for least predictable input), art-horror and (with approximate significance) humor.

According to Rothbart's model, the recipients at this stage are aroused to varying degrees. At a minimal arousal level, they ignore the stimulus without processing it. Only at a low to high arousal level do the recipients begin cost-intensive processing. If the arousal level is weak, the recipients immediately start to examine the stimulus in more detail with regard to its violation of previously established representations.

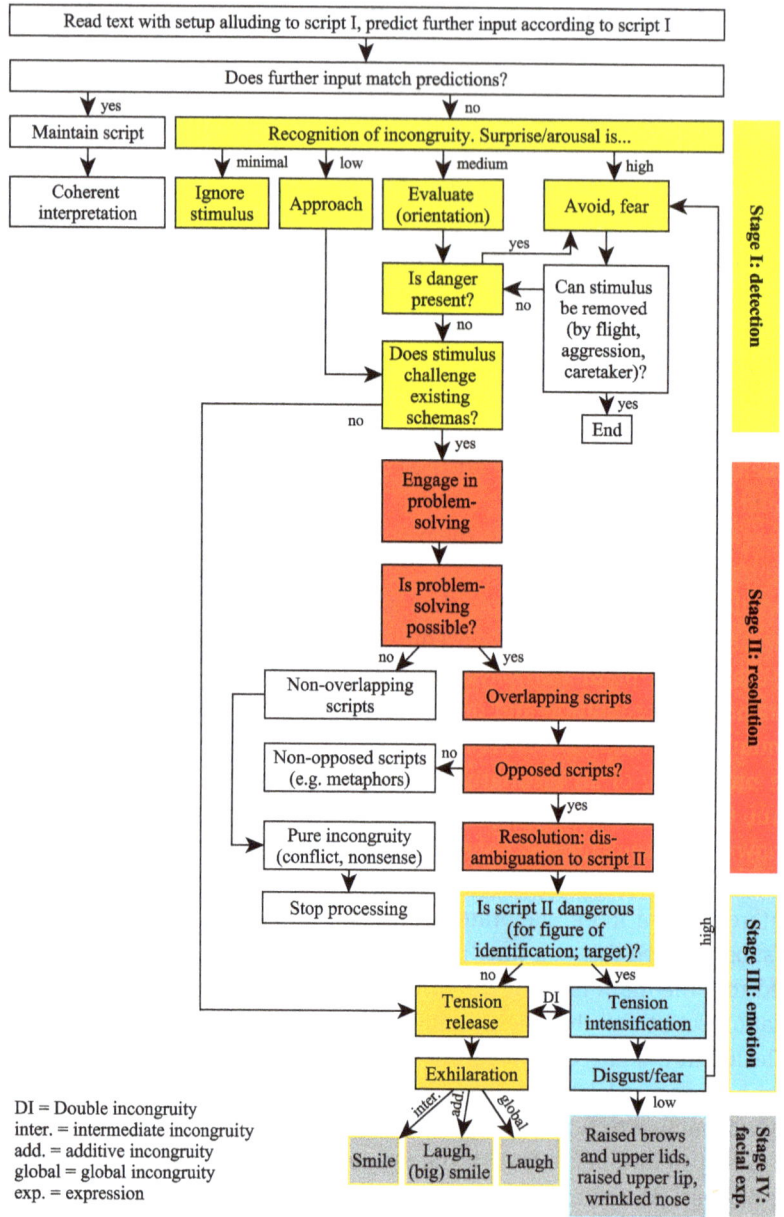

Figure 30: Incongruity processing model for humor and art-horror (IPM).

If the stimulus is of intermediate arousal level, an orientation reaction sets in and the stimulus context is checked for its dangerousness. At the highest arousal level, the recipients try to avoid the stimulus or flee from it. If avoidance is not possible, it is verified whether the context is dangerous. At both the medium and high arousal level, the stimulus is only further examined if the danger can be negated. If the danger is affirmed, further avoidance strategies are applied.

According to Rothbart's model, an art-horror stimulus with the highest arousal level would be avoided. Depending on individual differences (ID), such as extraversion, disgust sensitivity, or gelotophobia, this may be the case. However, if it is processed further, it was assumed that it only triggered low or moderate arousal.

If the stimulus does not violate the established schemes, the tension of the recipients is released, and they are exhilarated (switch to orange section in Figure 30, skipping the red section). If the stimulus violates established patterns, recipients invest in problem-solving strategies and re-analyze the stimulus in terms of the text setup (switch to red model section). In the case of non-overlapping scripts (pure incongruity, nonsense), a conflict arises (see Table 2) and no coherent reading can be developed. This is where the recipients stop the interpretation. This work's ERP results support this interpretation through the strongest N400 for incoherent texts, as the strongest violation of the established schemata and strongest prediction error, and the missing P600, indicating a missing sequence of repair and a processing stop of the incoherence condition in this time-window.

However, if the existing and incoming scripts overlap, the recipients check whether the scripts are also oppositional. If they are not (as in metaphors or metonymies [cf. Schumacher 2011; Bambini, Ghio, Moro and Schumacher 2013; Weiland 2014]), the recipients end the interpretation without amusement or fear/disgust. If the overlapping scripts are oppositional, the readers begin to disassociate the two scripts and switch to the second reading. Then, contrary to Grodal's assumption that cognitive consistency in art-horror was not possible (cf. Grodal 2000: 245), the recipients arrive at a coherent text interpretation (ERP component of the P600 for humor, art-horror, and coherence).

At the point when recipients reach the third processing stage, the model is conceptually supplemented by a second query of dangerousness. The recipients have now arrived at the second script and the context could have a different effect on stimulus interpretation and recipients' attention orienting. Recipients are only now able to finally conclude whether the context/stimulus combination is dangerous within the new interpretation. Referring back to cognitive art-horror theories, this second query of dangerousness is in line with Carroll's conceptual elaboration (1999) on differences between humor and horror. His claim that horror and humor only differ with respect to the fearsomeness of the categorical transgression (cf. Carroll 1999: 157) is represented in this model section.

If there is no danger perceived, the recipients' tension is reduced – depending on ID, such as personality traits like cheerfulness or sensation seeking – and they react in an exhilarated manner (orange section in Figure 30). According to Rothbart, the intensity of exhilaration varies depending on how strong the initial arousal of the incongruity was. If the arousal was weak, the recipients smile. With intermediate arousal, they smile or laugh. If the arousal is strong, they laugh strongly. This exhilaration intensity could be concurrently reconciled with Canestrari and Bianchi's continuum of incongruity (2013), which predicted that intermediate incongruity caused weak humor pleasure, additive incongruity caused stronger humor pleasure, and global incongruities caused the strongest chances of success for humor pleasure.

However, if the second verification of dangerousness reveals a danger for the recipients or their identification characters, the recipients react with increased, costly arousal (blue section of Figure 30). Negative feelings of fear and disgust arise, which the LPP component of the ERP results substantiated. At this point, again following Rothbart's model, a differentiation of the incongruity processing is added according to the experienced arousal. Depending on recipients' ID, this arousal is perceived as strong or weak/endurable. If it is too strong, the recipients react with avoidance strategies. However, if the recipients are able to bear this arousal (or – in line with Gaut (1993) – even evaluate the negative emotion positively), the art-horror enjoyment begins.

The FACS results – even though poor in quantity – suggest that the visible reaction to humor or art-horror only occurs with a time lag. This would indicate a fourth processing phase (grey section in Figure 30), supporting the stage of expression in the tri-component model from Chan (2016).

The IPM also explains phenomena that range between humor and art-horror, which I discussed in other publications. For example, Straßburger (2019) illuminated from a linguistic point of view why recipients are sometimes able to laugh about art-horror. Straßburger explained which (cognitive) mechanisms account for this phenomenon, extrapolating incongruity as the common denominator between humor and art-horror. She indicates that texts with more than one opposition, offer more than one switch to one further reading. In this case, readers can switch to two or more unexpected scripts. Being able to choose a preferred second, threatening or third, humorous reading, the readers participate actively in the storytelling so that they can control the situation and feel safe. Thus, readers laugh about art-horror instances, if they can switch to a dangerous but also to a secure reading. Straßburger introduces the notion of *double incongruity* (DI) for this phenomenon. For instance, the recipient's reaction to a clown brimming with oppositional traits can vary depending on whether the reading of the funny circus clown, or the creepy killer clown is chosen. The figure of the clown is therefore predestined to make recipients laugh when they would normally scream, and vice versa. In the model presented here, DI is located in the third phase of incongruity processing to indicate the change between tension release and intensification.

5.4 Desiderata & outlook

During the work on this book questions have arisen for future experiments and conceptual elaborations that were beyond the scope of this work.

Although this book deduces a rather broad concept of art-horror and thus blurs the genre boundaries to crime novel and thriller, the sentence material of the experiments and the model developed here had to be reduced to verbal garden paths and kept very short for the purpose of precise, experimental comparability of humor and art-horror. This restriction resulted in the fact that further art-horror aspects and especially more typical art-horror texts, as they were discussed in Chapter 1, could not be considered. The same is true for the study of humor, which was also limited to garden paths as a small part of numerous humor mechanisms. For example, incongruity phenomena that do not require resolution to awaken laughter (nonsense humor) could not be considered.

Nevertheless, the IPM can be extended to other linguistic phenomena:
1. Other languages: Although the text analyses and experiments conducted here were based on German material, the model claims to be applicable to all languages that dispose of the mechanism of the garden path, for example English.
2. Genre-blending: As already mentioned in 5.3, IPM is able to explain genre effects that oscillate between humor and horror, as well as the easy alternation between fright and laughter. The term *Double Incongruity* (Straßburger 2019) has already been introduced in this context. The GP mechanism and the emotion of fear are also effective in related genres such as crime novel or thriller. Thus, the IPM can be applied across genres and can also be used from psychological and literary perspectives.
3. Revision texts: In the model proposed here, resolved incongruities and script changes that do not elicit emotions (revision texts, Ferstl 2017) would be located at the end of the resolution phase without a further verification phase of dangerousness. However, the ultimately distinctive, pragmatic

mechanism that decides whether an emotion is at the end of the incongruity resolution or not remains to be further explored.

By considering humor as one of numerous semantic phenomena of incongruity, the IPM could replace previous cognitive humor models such as Sul's two-stage model, Raskin's GTVH or the NCM.

Finally, more concrete suggestions follow for further investigations of the two phenomena and refinements of the model:

Future research could investigate to what extent disgust and fear can be differentiated (cf. Xu, Li, Ding, Zhang, Fan, Diao and Yang 2015) as two different art-horror responses. As pleasure is a crucial element of art-horror (paradox of painful art), experiments could also investigate to what extent disgust and fear can be experienced positively. This differentiation could help to further investigate missing facial expressions in art-horror, which might have been lacking due the pleasurability of the art-horror items. Additionally, different degrees of valence (positive/negative) and arousal (intensity) within a condition could be investigated (cf. Citron, Weekes and Ferstl 2014a; Citron, Weekes and Ferstl 2014b). This investigation would also include analyzing the affective content of the punchlines in more detail, for example using the *Affektives Lexikon München* (cf. Tsiknaki 2005; Schwarz-Friesel 2013).

It has already been recognized that the experiment stimuli were kept short due to the experimental design. This might have hindered the participants to immerse into the context's situation and enjoy it entirely. Future research could therefore work with more intense and longer items (such as minimal pairs of movies).

Further, using the same material from Questionnaire II, art-horror could be compared to coherent texts as minimal pairs in a single experiment. Even though there were many more items with high(er) art-horror scores, the experiments of this book only included items that worked well in all three/four conditions. Comparing only art-horror and coherence would also allow to use the highly frightening art-horror items that did not work after the punchline changes to a humorous reading. Additionally, art-horror could be systematically compared with revision texts. In this context, a more systematic correlation of personality traits and art-horror or humor reaction would be useful.

Further experimental investigation of the presented model could directly attest the second verification for dangerousness and the association of the incongruity continuum from Canestrari and Bianchi (2013) with the arousal level from Rothbart (2017 [1976]).

Changing the punch line of the sentence material, the current book did not investigate how the same stimulus is actually processed in different contexts. This could be investigated by changing the setup of the sentence material.

Overall, it was shown in the current book that, despite different emotional effects, there are structural parallels between humor and art-horror that lead to a similar processing. Extrapolating the phenomenon of incongruity and its resolution, this work was highly successful in investigating art-horror for the first time from a linguistic, cognitive angle and comparing it to humor with a conceptual and experimental foundation. In garden paths of both humor and art-horror, the incongruity between an initial script and the punchline is resolved through switching to a second script and a discourse update. While this mechanism leads to the positive emotion of exhilaration in humorous instances, it elicits negative emotions of fear and disgust in art-horror. The experiments showed that art-horror causes the same cognitive costs as humor, which can be associated with detecting, resolving, and emotionally reacting to incongruities. The model of incongruity processing for humor and art-horror (IPM) juxtaposes art-horror and humor due to their common denominator of incongruity. Thus, despite their opposing emotional effects, humor and art-horror are not understood as contradictory phenomena, but as two sides of the same coin.

References

Dictionaries, technical manuals, and statistics handbooks

American Encephalographic Society. 1994. Guideline thirteen: Guidelines for standard electrode position nomenclature. *Journal of Clinical Neurophysiology* 11(1). 111–113.

Bates, Douglas, Martin Maechler, Ben Bolker, Steven Walker, Rune H. B. Christensen, Henrik Singmann, Bin Dai, Fabian Scheipl, Gabor Grothendieck, Peter Green & John Fox. 2019. lme4: linear mixed-effects models using 'eigen' and S4. https://cran.r-project.org/web/packages/lme4/index.html (accessed 23 July 2019).

Collins Dictionary. 2021. Exhilarate. https://www.collinsdictionary.com/dictionary/english/exhilarate.

Jaeger, Florian. 2008a. Categorical data analysis: Away from ANOVAs (transformation or not) and towards logit mixed models. *Journal of memory and language* 59(4). 434–446.

Jaeger, Florian. 2008b. Modeling self-paced reading data: Effects of word length, word position, spill-over, etc. https://hlplab.wordpress.com/2008/01/23/modeling-self-paced-reading-data-effects-of-word-length-word-position-spill-over-etc/ (accessed 21 October 2019).

Kuznetsova, Alexandra, Per B. Brockhoff & Rune H. B. Christensen. 2017. lmerTest package: Tests in linear mixed effects models. *Journal of Statistical Software* 82(13). 1–26. https://doi.org/10.18637/jss.v082.i13 (accessed 24 July 2019).

Mathôt, Sebastiaan, Daniel Schreij & Jan Theeuwes. 2012. OpenSesame: An open-source, graphical experiment builder for the social sciences. *Behavior Research Methods* 44(2). 314–324.

Preisendanz, Wolfgang. 2010a. Humor. In Joachim Ritter (ed.), *Historisches Wörterbuch der Philosophie*, 11143–11149. Basel: Schwabe.

Preisendanz, Wolfgang. 2010b. Humor. In Klaus Weimar, Georg Braungart, Klaus Grubmüller, Friedrich Vollhardt, Harald Fricke & Jan-Dirk Müller (eds.), *Reallexikon der deutschen Literaturwissenschaft*, 3rd edn., 100–103. Berlin, Boston: de Gruyter.

Prolific. 2014. *Prolific*. Oxford, England. https://www.prolific.co (accessed 5 March 2020).

Qualtrics. 2005. *Qualtrics*. Provo, Utah, USA. https://www.qualtrics.com (accessed 5 March 2020).

Singmann, Henrik, Ben Bolker, Jake Westfall, Frederik Aust & Mattan S. Ben-Shachar. 2019. afex: Analysis of Factorial Experiments: R Package Version 0.24-1. https://CRAN.R-project.org/package=afex (accessed 21 October 2019).

Stowasser, Josef M., Michael Petschenig & Franz Skutsch. 2009. *Stowasser: Lateinisch-Deutsches Schulwörterbuch*. München: Oldenbourg.

The Language Archive. 2018. *ELAN*. Nijmegen: Max Planck Institute for Psycholinguistics. https://tla.mpi.nl/tools/tla-tools/elan/ (accessed 5 March 2020).

Universität Leipzig. 2021. Wortschatzportal. http://wortschatz.informatik.uni-leipzig.de (accessed 12 October 2021).

Primary sources: Literature

Aristotle, Stephen Halliwell, W. H. Fyfe, Donald A. Russell, Doreen C. Innes & W. Rhys Roberts. 1995 [ca. 335 BC]. *Digital Loeb classical library*. Cambridge, MA: Harvard University Press. https://www.loebclassics.com/view/aristotle-poetics/1995/pb_LCL199.45.xml (accessed 22 June 2020).
Asquith, Cynthia. 1947 [1929]. The playfellow. In Cynthia Asquith (ed.), *This mortal coil*, 138–168. Sauk City: Arkham House.
Barker, Clive. 1998 [1984]. *Books of blood (1–3)*. New York: Berkley Books.
Blatty, William P. 1971. *The exorcist*. New York: Harper & Row.
Blaylock, James P. 1988. *The last coin* (The Christian Trilogy 1). New York: Ace Books.
Bloch, Robert. 2000. *Psycho*. Stuttgart: Reclam.
Brite, Poppy Z. 1992. *Lost souls*. New York: Delacorte Press.
Brite, Poppy Z. 1993. *Drawing blood*. New York: Delacorte Press.
Carter, Angela. 1967. *The magic toyshop*. London: Heinemann.
Collier, John. 2016. *Green thoughts & other stories*. Leyburn, North Yorkshire: Tartarus Press.
Cooper, Alice & Michael Bruce. 1971. Desperado. In Alice Cooper & Michael Bruce (eds.), *Killer*, 4: Warner Bros.
Du Maurier, Daphne. 1952. *The apple tree: A short novel and some stories*. London: Gollancz.
Ewers, Hanns H. 1910. *Der Zauberlehrling [The sorcerer's apprentice]*. München: Müller.
Gomez, Jewelle. 1991. *The Gilda stories: A novel*. Ithaca, NY: Firebrand Books.
Hall, Richard. 2013. 10 awesome scary stories told in only two sentences. https://oklahoman.com/article/3888332/10-awesome-scary-stories-told-in-only-two-sentences (accessed 22 June 2020).
Harris, Thomas. 1981. *Red dragon*. New York: Putnam.
Harris, Thomas. 1988. *The silence of the lambs*. New York: St. Martin's Press.
Harris, Thomas. 1999. *Hannibal*. New York: Delacorte Press.
Harris, Thomas. 2006. *Hannibal rising*. New York: Delacorte Press.
Heine, Heinrich. 2013 [1853]. The gods in exile. *Arion: A Journal of Humanities and the Classics* 21(1). 193.
Hoffmann, Ernst T. A. 1816. *Die Elixiere des Teufels: Nachgelassene Papiere des Bruders Medardus eines Capuziners [The devil's elixirs]*. Berlin: Duncker und Humblot.
Hoffmann, Ernst T. A. 2015 [1816]. *Der Sandmann [The sandman]*, Berliner Ausgabe, 5. ed. Berlin: Holzinger.
Jeter, Kevin W. 1984. *Dr. Adder*. New York: Bluejay Books.
King, Stephen. 1974. *Carrie*. New York: Anchor Books.
King, Stephen. 1977. *The shining*. Garden City: Doubleday.
King, Stephen. 1983. *Christine*. New York: Viking Press.
King, Stephen. 1986. *It*. New York: New American Library.
King, Stephen. 1997. *The green mile: A novel in six parts*. New York: Plume.
Le Fanu, Sheridan. 1872. *In a glass darkly*. London: R. Bentley & Son.
Levin, Ira. 2011 [1967]. *Rosemary's baby* (Easy Readers). London: Corsair.
Lewis, M. G. 1796. *The monk: A romance*. Auckland: The Floating Press.
Maupassant, Guy d. 1908. Le Horla [The Horla]. In Guy de Maupassant (ed.), *Oeuvres complètes illustrées*. Paris: Société d'édition littéraires et artistiques.

Meimberg, Florian. 2011. *Auf die Länge kommt es an*: *Tiny Tales. Sehr kurze Geschichten* (Fischer-Taschenbücher). Frankfurt am Main: Fischer Taschenbuch Verlag.
Meyrink, Gustav. 1908. *Das Wachsfigurenkabinett: Sonderbare Geschichten [Waxworks]*. München: Albert Langen Verlag.
Plato, Dorothea Frede & Ernst Heitsch. 1997. *Philebos* (Werke 3.2). Göttingen: Vandenhoeck & Ruprecht.
Poe, Edgar A. 1809–1849. *The raven, the fall of the house of Usher, and other poems and tales*. Boston, New York, Chicago: Houghton Mifflin Company. https://babel.hathitrust.org/cgi/pt?id=uva.x000178804&view=1up&seq=5 (accessed 22 June 2020).
Rogers, Katie. 2016. Creepy clown sightings in South Carolina cause a frenzy. https://www.nytimes.com/2016/08/31/us/creepy-clown-sightings-in-south-carolina-cause-a-frenzy.html?action=click&module=RelatedCoverage&pgtype=Article&region=Footer (accessed 22 June 2020).
Shelley, Mary W. 2008 [1818]. *Frankenstein, or, the modern prometheus*. Waiheke Island: Floating Press.
Stevenson, Robert L. 2008. *The strange case of Dr. Jekyll and Mr. Hyde*. Waiheke Island: Floating Press.
Stoker, Bram. 2011 [1897]. *Dracula*. Oxford: OUP Oxford (Oxford World's Classics).
Weldon, Fay. 1983. *The life and loves of a she-devil*. London: Hodder and Stoughton.
Wells, Herbert G. 1898. *The time machine and the island of Doctor Moreau*. Leipzig: Tauchnitz.

Primary sources: Movies and series

Barker, Clive. 1987. *Hellraiser*. UK: Entertainment Film Distributors.
Browning, Tod. 1931. *Dracula*. USA: Universal Pictures.
Carpenter, John & Debra Hill. 1978. *Halloween*. USA: Compass International Pictures.
Craig, Eli. 2010. *Tucker & Dale vs. evil*. Canada, USA: Magnet Releasing.
Crichton, Michael. 1978. *Coma*. USA: United Artists; Cinema International Corporation.
Cuesta, Michael, Robert Lieberman, Tony Goldwyn, Steve Shill, Adam Davidson & Keith Gordon. 2006. *Dexter*. Second season. USA: Showtime.
Friedkin, William. 1973. *The exorcist*. USA: Warner Bros.
Fulci, Lucio. 1982. *Lo squartatore di New York*. Italy: Fulvia Film.
Henenlotter, Frank. 1990. *Basket case 2*. USA: Shapiro Glickenhaus Entertainment.
Hitchcock, Alfred. 1960. *Psycho*. USA: Paramount Pictures.
Kubrick, Stanley. 1980. *The shining*. UK, USA: Warner Bros.
Landers, Lew. 1943. *The return of the vampire*. USA: Columbia Pictures Corporation.
Lucas, George. 1977. *Star Wars: episode IV – A new hope*. USA: 20th Century Fox.
Murnau, Friedrich W. 1922. *Nosferatu, eine Symphonie des Grauens [Nosferatu: a symphony of horror]*. Germany: Film Arts Guild.
Muschietti, Andy. 2017. *It*. USA: Warner Bros. Pictures.
Muschietti, Andy. 2019. *It chapter two*. USA: Warner Bros. Pictures.
Nolan, Christopher. 2008. *The dark knight*. USA: Warner Bros.
Philipps, Todd. 2019. *Joker*. USA: Warner Bros. Pictures; Wealth Media Finance.
Polanski, Roman. 1965. *Repulsion*. UK: Compton Films.

Reeves, Michael. 1968. *Witchfinder general*. UK, USA: Tigon British Film Productions (UK); American International Pictures (USA).
Robertson, John S. 1920. *Dr. Jekyll and Mr. Hyde*. USA: Paramount Pictures.
Roth, Eli. 2005. *Hostel*. USA, Czech Republic: Lionsgate; Screen Gems.
Serling, Rod. 1959–1964. *The twilight zone*. USA: CBS.
Shyamalan, Manoj N. 1999. *The sixth sense*. USA: Buena Vista Pictures Distribution.
Spielberg, Stephen. 1975. *Jaws*. USA: Universal Pictures.
Wan, James. 2004. *Saw*. USA: Lionsgate Films.

Secondary sources: Research articles, edited books, and monographies

Aldana Reyes, Xavier. 2016. *Horror film and affect: Towards a corporeal model of viewership* (Routledge Advances in Film Studies). New York: Taylor and Francis.
Allen, Mark, William Badecker & Lee Osterhout. 2003. Morphological analysis in sentence processing: An ERP study. *Language and Cognitive Processes* 18(4). 405–430.
Alpers, Hans J., Werner Fuchs & Ronald M. Hahn. 1999. *Lexikon der Horrorliteratur*. Erkrath: Fantasy Productions.
Antoniou, Kyriakos, Chris Cummins & Napoleon Katsos. 2016. Why only some adults reject under-informative utterances. *Journal of Pragmatics* 99. 78–95.
Aristotle. 1984. *The complete works of Aristotle* (Bollingen series 71.2). Princeton, New Jersey: Princeton University Press.
Aristotle & Lane Cooper. 1922. *An Aristotelian theory of comedy with an adaptation of the poetics and a translation of the 'Tractatus Coislinianus'*. New York: Harcourt, Brace and Company.
Attardo, Salvatore. 1994. *Linguistic theories of humor* (Humor Research 1). Berlin, New York: Mouton de Gruyter.
Attardo, Salvatore. 1997. The semantic foundations of cognitive theories of humor. *HUMOR – International Journal of Humor Research* 10(4). 395–420.
Attardo, Salvatore. 2017a. Humor and pragmatics. In Salvatore Attardo (ed.), *The Routledge handbook of language and humor*, 174–188. Florence: Taylor and Francis.
Attardo, Salvatore. 2017b. The General Theory of Verbal Humor. In Salvatore Attardo (ed.), *The Routledge handbook of language and humor*, 126–142. Florence: Taylor and Francis.
Attardo, Salvatore. 2020. Scripts, frames, and other semantic objects. In Salvatore Attardo (ed.), *Script-based semantics: Foundations and applications. Essays in honor of Victor Raskin*, 11–42. Boston, Berlin: de Gruyter Mouton.
Attardo, Salvatore, Christian F. Hempelmann & Sara Di Maio. 2002. Script oppositions and logical mechanisms: Modeling incongruities and their resolutions. *HUMOR – International Journal of Humor Research* 15(1). 3–46.
Attardo, Salvatore & Victor Raskin. 2017. Linguistics and humor theory. In Salvatore Attardo (ed.), *The Routledge handbook of language and humor*, 49–63. Florence: Taylor and Francis.
Azim, Eiman, Dean Mobbs, Booil Jo, Vinod Menon & Allan L. Reiss. 2005. Sex differences in brain activation elicited by humor. *Proceedings of the National Academy of Sciences of the United States of America* 102(45). 16496–16501.

Baayen, Harald, Davidson, Doug, J. & Douglas M. Bates. 2008. Mixed-effects modeling with crossed random effects for subjects and items. *Journal of memory and language* 59(4). 390–412.

Bain, Alexander. 1876. *The Emotions and the will*, 3. ed. New York: D. Appleton & Company.

Balint, Michael. 2018 [1959]. *Thrills and regressions* (Rororo-Studium). London: Routledge.

Bambini, Valentina, Chiara Bertini, Walter Schaeken, Alessandra Stella & Francesco Di Russo. 2016. Disentangling metaphor from context: an ERP study. *Frontiers in Psychology* 7. 559.

Bambini, Valentina, Marta Ghio, Andrea Moro & Petra B. Schumacher. 2013. Differentiating among pragmatic uses of words through timed sensicality judgments. *Frontiers in Psychology* 4. 1–16.

Barr, Dale J., Roger Levy, Christoph Scheepers & Harry J. Tily. 2013. Random effects structure for confirmatory hypothesis testing: keep it maximal. *Journal of memory and language* 68(3). 255–278.

Barsalou, Lawrence W. 1992. Frames, concepts, and conceptual fields. In Adrienne Lehrer & Eva F. Kittay (eds.), *Frames, Fields, and Contrasts: New Essays in Semantic and Lexical Organization*, 21–74. Hillsdale, NJ: Lawrence Erlbaum Associates.

Baumann, Hans D. 1989. *Horror: Die Lust am Grauen* (Psychologie heute Sachbuch). Weinheim: Beltz.

Bekinschtein, Tristan A., Matthew H. Davis, Jennifer M. Rodd & Adrian M. Owen. 2011. Why clowns taste funny: the relationship between humor and semantic ambiguity. *The Journal of Neuroscience: The Official Journal of the Society for Neuroscience* 31(26). 9665–9671.

Berger, Hans. 1929. Über das Elektrenkephalogramm des Menschen. *Archiv für Psychiatrie und Nervenkrankheiten* 87. 527–570.

Bergson, Henri L. 1988. *Das Lachen: Ein Essay über die Bedeutung des Komischen [Laughter: an essay of the meaning of the comic]*. Darmstadt: Luchterhand.

Billings, Andrew G. & Rudolf H. Moos. 1984. Coping, stress, and social resources among adults with unipolar depression. *Journal of Personality and Social Psychology* 46(4). 877–891.

Binder, Jeffrey R., Einat Liebenthal, Edward T. Possing, David A. Medler & B. D. Ward. 2004. Neural correlates of sensory and decision processes in auditory object identification. *Nature Neuroscience* 7(3). 295–301.

Blanchette, Isabelle & Serge Caparos. 2013. When emotions improve reasoning: the possible roles of relevance and utility. *Thinking & Reasoning* 19(3–4). 399–413.

Blanchette, Isabelle & Anne Richards. 2010. The influence of affect on higher level cognition: a review of research on interpretation, judgement, decision making and reasoning. *Cognition & Emotion* 24(4). 561–595.

Boisgueheneuc, F. d., R. Levy, E. Volle, M. Seassau, H. Duffau, S. Kinkingnehun, Y. Samson, S. Zhang & B. Dubois. 2006. Functions of the left superior frontal gyrus in humans: A lesion study. *Brain: A Journal of Neurology* 129(12). 3315–3328.

Bordwell, David. 1989. *Making meaning: inference and rhetoric in the interpretation of cinema*. Cambridge, Mass: Harvard University Press.

Bornkessel-Schlesewsky, Ina, Markus Philipp, Phillip M. Alday, Franziska Kretzschmar, Tanja Grewe, Maike Gumpert, Petra B. Schumacher & Matthias Schlesewsky. 2015. Age-related changes in predictive capacity versus internal model adaptability: electrophysiological evidence that individual differences outweigh effects of age. *Frontiers in Aging Neuroscience* 7. 1–13.

Bornkessel-Schlesewsky, Ina & Matthias Schlesewsky. 2016. The argument dependency model. In Gregory Hickok & Steven L. Small (eds.), *Neurobiology of language*, 357–369. Amsterdam: Academic Press.
Bornkessel-Schlesewsky, Ina & Petra B. Schumacher. 2016. Towards a neurobiology of information structure. In Caroline Féry & Shinichiro Ishihara (eds.), *The Oxford Handbook of Information Structure*, First edition (Oxford Handbooks in Linguistics), 581–598. Oxford, New York, NY: Oxford University Press.
Botting, Fred. 2014. *Gothic*, 2. ed. London: Routledge.
Brandstätter, Veronika, Julia Schüler, Rosa M. Puca & Ljubica Lozo. 2018. *Motivation und Emotion*: *Allgemeine Psychologie für Bachelor*. Berlin, Heidelberg: Springer Berlin Heidelberg.
Brittnacher, Hans R. 1994. *Ästhetik des Horros*: *Gespenster, Vampire, Monster, Teufel und Künstliche Menschen in der Phantastischen Literatur*. Frankfurt am Main: Suhrkamp.
Brocher, Andreas, Sofiana I. Chiriacescu & Klaus von Heusinger. 2018. Effects of information status and uniqueness status on referent management in discourse comprehension and planning. *Discourse Processes* 55(4). 346–370.
Brône, Geert. 2017. Cognitive linguistics and humor research. In Salvatore Attardo (ed.), *The Routledge handbook of language and humor*, 250–266. Florence: Taylor and Francis.
Bruhm, Steven. 2002. The contemporary gothic: why we need it. In Jerrold Hogle (ed.), *Gothic fiction*, 259–276. Cambridge: Cambridge University Press.
Burke, Edmund. 2014 [1757]. *A philosophical enquiry into the origin of our ideas of the sublime and beautiful*. Cambridge: Cambridge University Press.
Burkhardt, Petra. 2006. Inferential bridging relations reveal distinct neural mechanisms: evidence from event-related brain potentials. *Brain and Language* 98(2). 159–168.
Burkhardt, Petra. 2007. The P600 reflects cst of nw iformation in dscourse mmory. *Neuroreport* 18(17). 1851–1854.
Buxbaum, Laurel J. & Eleanor M. Saffran. 2002. Knowledge of object manipulation and object function: Dissociations in apraxic and nonapraxic subjects. *Brain and Language* 82. 179–199.
Calvo, Manuel G. & Manuel Carreiras. 1993. Selective influence of test anxiety on reading processes. *British Journal of Psychology* 84. 375–388.
Canal, Paolo, Luca Bischetti, Simona Di Paola, Chiara Bertini, Irene Ricci & Valentina Bambini. 2019. 'Honey, shall I change the baby? – Well done, choose another one': ERP and time-frequency correlates of humor processing. *Brain and Cognition* 132. 41–55.
Canestrari, Carla. 2010. Meta-communicative signals and humorous verbal interchanges: a case study. *HUMOR – International Journal of Humor Research* 23(3). 327–349.
Canestrari, Carla. 2012. A model of humor syntony: from failed to successful humor in interaction. In Paola Gremigni (ed.), *Humor and Health Promotion* (Health psychology research focus), 59–77. New York: Nova Science Publication; Nova Science Publishers.
Canestrari, Carla & Ivana Bianchi. 2013. From perception of contraries to humorous incongruities. In Marta Dynel (ed.), *Developments in linguistic humour theory* (Topics in Humor Research 1), 3–24. Amsterdam, Philadelphia: John Benjamins Publishing Company.
Cantor, Joanne R. 2004. "I'll never have a clown in my house" – why movie horror lives on. *Poetics Today* 25(2). 283–304.
Caplan, D. & G. S. Waters. 1999. Verbal working memory and sentence comprehension. *The Behavioral and Brain Sciences* 22(1). 77–126.

Carroll, Noël. 1990. *The philosophy of horror or paradoxes of the heart* (Communications Philosophy). New York, NY: Routledge.
Carroll, Noël. 1995. Enjoying horror fictions: A reply to Gaut. *British Journal of Aesthetics* 35(1). 67–72.
Carroll, Noël. 1999. Horror and humor. *The Journal of Aesthetics and Art Criticism* 57(2). 145–160.
Carroll, Noël. 2003. The general theory of horrific appeal. In Steven J. Schneider & Daniel Shaw (eds.), *Dark thoughts*: *Philosophic reflections on cinematic horror*, 1–9. Lanham, Md: Scarecrow Press.
Carroll, Noël. 2004. Afterword: psychoanalysis and the horror film. In Steven J. Schneider (ed.), *Horror Film and Psychoanalysis*: *Freud's Worst Nightmare* (Cambridge studies in film), 257–270. Cambridge: Cambridge University Press.
Chan, Yu-Chen. 2016. Neural correlates of sex/gender differences in humor Processing for different joke types. *Frontiers in Psychology* 7. 1–18.
Chan, Yu-Chen, Tai-Li Chou, Hsueh-Chih Chen & Keng-Chen Liang. 2012. Segregating the comprehension and elaboration processing of verbal jokes: an fMRI study. *NeuroImage* 61(4). 899–906.
Chan, Yu-Chen, Tai-Li Chou, Hsueh-Chih Chen, Yu-Chu Yeh, Joseph P. Lavallee, Keng-Chen Liang & Kuo-En Chang. 2013. Towards a neural circuit model of verbal humor processing: an fMRI study of the neural substrates of incongruity detection and resolution. *NeuroImage* 66. 169–176.
Chan, Yu-Chen & Joseph P. Lavallee. 2015. Temporo-parietal and fronto-parietal lobe contributions to theory of mind and executive control: an fMRI study of verbal jokes. *Frontiers in Psychology* 6. 1–13.
Chang, Yi-Tzu, Li-Chuan Ku & Hsueh-Chih Chen. 2018. Sex differences in humor processing: an event-related potential study. *Brain and Cognition* 120. 34–42.
Channon, Shelley & Jane Baker. 1994. Reasoning strategies in depression: effects of depressed mood on a syllogism task. *Personality and individual differences* 17(5). 707–711.
Chen, Hsueh-Chih, Yu-Chen Chan, Ru-Huei Dai, Yi-Jun Liao & Cheng-Hao Tu. 2017. Neurolinguistics of humor. In Salvatore Attardo (ed.), *The Routledge handbook of language and humor*, 282–294. Florence: Taylor and Francis.
Chovanec, Jan & Villy Tsakona. 2018. Investigating the dynamics of humor: towards a theory of interactional humor. In Villy Tsakona & Jan Chovanec (eds.), *The Dynamics of Interactional Humor* (7), 1–26. Amsterdam: John Benjamins Publishing Company.
Cicero, Marcus T., Edward W. Sutton & Harris Rackham. 1942. *De oratore* (Digital Loeb Classical Library). Cambridge, MA: Harvard University Press.
Citron, Francesca M. M., Brendan S. Weekes & Evelyn C. Ferstl. 2014a. Arousal and emotional valence interact in written word recognition. *Language, cognition and neuroscience* 29(10). 1257–1267.
Citron, Francesca M. M., Brendan S. Weekes & Evelyn C. Ferstl. 2014b. How are affective word ratings related to lexicosemantic properties? evidence from the Sussex affective word list (SAWL). *Applied Psycholinguistics* 35(2). 313–331.
Clore, Gerald L. & Janet E. Palmer. 2009. Affective guidance of intelligent agents: how emotion controls cognition. *Cognitive Systems Research* 10(1). 21–30.
Corbetta, Maurizio & Gordon L. Shulman. 2002. Control of goal-directed and stimulus-driven attention in the brain. *Nature Reviews Neuroscience* 3(3). 201–215.

Coulson, Seana. 2001. *Semantic leaps:* Cambridge University Press.
Coulson, Seana & Marta Kutas. 1998. Frame-shifting and sentential integration. *Technical Report CogSci* 3. 1–32.
Coulson, Seana & Marta Kutas. 2001. Getting it: human event-related brain response to jokes in good and poor comprehenders. *Neuroscience Letters* 316(2). 71–74.
Coulson, Seana, Thomas P. Urbach & Marta Kutas. 2006. Looking back: joke comprehension and the space structuring model. *HUMOR* 19(3). 229–250.
Cuthbert, Bruce N., Harald T. Schupp, Margaret M. Bradley, Niels Birbaumer & Peter J. Lang. 2000. Brain potentials in affective picture processing: Covariation with autonomic arousal and affective report. *Biological Psychology* 52(2). 95–111.
Daneman, Meredyth. 1980. Individual differences in working memory and reading. *Journal of Verbal Learning and Verbal Behavior* 19. 450–466.
Darke, Shane. 1988. Anxiety and working memory capacity. *Cognition & Emotion* 2(2). 145–154.
Davis, Hallowell, Pauline Davis, Alfred L. Loomis, E. N. Harvey & Garret Hobart. 1939. Electrical reactions of the human brain to auditory stimulation during sleep. *Journal of Neurophysiology* 2(6). 500–514.
Davis, Pauline. 1939. Effects of acoustic stimuli on the waking human brain. *Journal of Neurophysiology* 2(6). 494–499.
Decety, Jean & François Michel. 1989. Comparative analysis of actual and mental movement times in two graphic tasks. *Brain and Cognition* 11. 87–97.
Der Polizeipräsident in Berlin. 2016. Versuchter Raubüberfall – Maskierte Täter Geflüchtet. http://www.berlin.de/polizei/polizeimeldungen/pressemitteilung.526617.php (accessed 23 June 2020).
Derks, Peter & Sanjay Arora. 1993. Sex and salience in the appreciation of cartoon humor. *HUMOR* 6(1). 57–69.
Douglas, Margaret M. 1970 [1966]. *Purity and danger: An analysis of concepts of pollution and taboo.* Harmondsworth: Penguin.
Du, Xue, Yigui Qin, Shen Tu, Huazhan Yin, Ting Wang, Caiyun Yu & Jiang Qiu. 2013. Differentiation of stages in joke comprehension: Evidence from an ERP study. *International Journal of Psychology* 48(2). 149–157.
Ekman, Paul. 2005 [1999]. Basic emotions. In Tim Dalgleish & Michael J. Power (eds.), *Handbook of Cognition and Emotion*, 45–60. Hoboken, NJ: Wiley-Interscience.
Ekman, Paul. 2010 [2003]. *Gefühle lesen: Wie Sie Emotionen erkennen und richtig interpretieren*, 2nd edn. (Spektrum Taschenbuch).
Ekman, Paul, Richard J. Davidson & Wallace V. Friesen. 1990. The Duchenne smile: Emotional expression and brain physiology II. *Journal of Personality and Social Psychology* 58(2). 342–353.
Ekman, Paul & Wallace V. Friesen. 2003. *Unmasking the face: A guide to recognizing emotions from facial clues.* Cambridge, MA: Malor Books.
Ekman, Paul, Wallace V. Friesen & Sonia Ancoli. 1980. Facial signs of emotional experience. *Journal of Personality and Social Psychology* 39(6). 1125–1134.
Ekman, Paul, Wallace V. Friesen & Joseph C. Hager. 2002a. *Facial action coding system: Investigator's guide.* Salt Lake City, Utah: Research Nexus.
Ekman, Paul, Wallace V. Friesen & Joseph C. Hager. 2002b. *Facial Action Coding System: The Manual* (A research Nexus eBook). Salt Lake City, Utah: Research Nexus.

El Refaie, Elisabeth. 2011. The pragmatics of humor reception: Young people's responses to a newspaper cartoon. *HUMOR – International Journal of Humor Research* 24(1). 87–108.

Eysenck, Hans-Jürgen & Michael W. Eysenck. 1987. *Persönlichkeit und Individualität: Ein naturwissenschaftliches Paradigma*. München: Psychologie Verlags Union.

Eysenck, Michael W., Nazanin Derakshan, Rita Santos & Manuel G. Calvo. 2007. Anxiety and cognitive performance: Attentional control theory. *Emotion* 7(2). 336–353.

Feagin, Susan L. 1991. Monsters, disgust and fascination. *Philosophical Studies: An International Journal for Philosophy in the Analytic Tradition* 65(1/2). 75–84.

Federmeier, Kara D. 2007. Thinking ahead: The role and roots of prediction in language comprehension. *Psychophysiology* 44(4). 491–505.

Federmeier, Kara D. & Marta Kutas. 1999. A rose by any other name: Long-term memory structure and sentence processing. *Journal of memory and language* 41. 469–495.

Feng, Yen-Ju, Yu-Chen Chan & Hsueh-Chih Chen. 2014. Specialization of neural mechanisms underlying the three-stage model in humor processing: An ERP study. *Journal of Neurolinguistics* 32. 59–70.

Ferreira, Fernanda & Charles Clifton. 1986. The independence of syntactic processing. *Journal of memory and language* 25. 348–368.

Ferstl, Evelyn C. 2007. Making sense of nonsense: An fMRI study of task induced inference processes during discourse comprehension. *Brain research* 1166. 77–91.

Ferstl, Evelyn C., Laura Israel & Lisa Putzar. 2017. Humor facilitates text comprehension: Evidence from eye movements. *Discourse Processes* 54(4). 259–284.

Foolen, Ad. 2012. The relevance of emotion for language and linguistics. In Ad Foolen, Ulrike Lüdtke, Timothy P. Racine & Jordan Zlatev (eds.), *Moving ourselves, moving others: Motion and emotion in intersubjectivity, consciousness and language* (Consciousness & Emotion Book Series 6), 349–368. Amsterdam, Philadelphia, Berlin: John Benjamins Publishing Company.

Foolen, Ad, Ulrike Lüdtke, Timothy P. Racine & Jordan Zlatev (eds.). 2012. *Moving ourselves, moving others: Motion and emotion in intersubjectivity, consciousness and language* (Consciousness & Emotion Book Series 6). Amsterdam, Philadelphia, Berlin: John Benjamins Publishing Company.

Forabosco, Giovannantonio & Willibald Ruch. 1994. Sensation seeking, social attitudes and humor appreciation in Italy. *Personality and individual differences* 16(4). 515–528.

Frazier, Lyn & Keith Rayner. 1982. Making and correcting errors during sentence comprehension: Eye movements in the analysis of structurally ambiguous sentences. *Cognitive Psychology* 14(2). 178–210.

Freeland, Cynthia. 2004. Horror and art-dread. In Stephen Prince (ed.), *The Horror film*, 189–205.

Freud, Sigmund. 2012 [1919]. Das Unheimliche [The uncanny]. In Alexander Mitscherlich, Angela Richards & James Strachey (eds.), *Psychologische Schriften: Studienausgabe*, 11th edn. (Freud-Studienausgabe 4), 241–274. Frankfurt am Main: S. Fischer.

Freud, Sigmund. 2012 [1927]. Der Humor. In Alexander Mitscherlich, Angela Richards & James Strachey (eds.), *Psychologische Schriften: Studienausgabe*, 11th edn. (Freud-Studienausgabe 4), 275–282. Frankfurt am Main: S. Fischer.

Freud, Sigmund. 2012 [1905]. Der Witz und seine Beziehung zum Unbewussten [Jokes and their relation to the unconscious]. In Alexander Mitscherlich, Angela Richards & James Strachey (eds.), *Psychologische Schriften: Studienausgabe*, 11th edn. (Freud-Studienausgabe 4), 9–219. Frankfurt am Main: S. Fischer.

Freud, Sigmund. 2012. *Psychologische Schriften*: *Studienausgabe*, 11th edn. (Freud-Studienausgabe 4). Frankfurt am Main: S. Fischer.
Friederici, Angela D., Erdmut Pfeifer & Anja Hahne. 1993. Event-related brain potentials during natural speech processing: Effects of semantic, morphological and syntactic violations. *Cognitive Brain Research* 1. 183–192.
Friston, Karl. 2010. The free-energy principle: A unified brain theory? *Nature Reviews. Neuroscience* 11(2). 127–138.
Galambos, Robert & Guy C. Sheatz. 1962. An electroencephalograph study of classical conditioning. *The American Journal of Physiology* 203. 173–184.
Gaut, Berys. 1993. The paradox of horror. *British Journal of Aesthetics* 33(4). 333–345.
Gaut, Berys. 1995. The enjoyment theory of horror: A response to Carroll. *British Journal of Aesthetics* 35(3).
Gernsbacher, Morton A. 1990. *Language comprehension as structure building*. Hillsdale, NJ: Lawrence Erlbaum Associates.
Giora, Rachel. 1991. On the cognitive aspects of the joke. *Journal of Pragmatics* 16(5). 465–485.
Giora, Rachel. 2004. On the graded salience hypothesis. *Intercultural Pragmatics* 1(1). 93–103.
Giora, Rachel, Ofer Fein, Ann Kronrod, Idit Elnatan, Noa Shuval & Adi Zur. 2004. Weapons of mass distraction: Optimal innovation and pleasure ratings. *Metaphor and Symbol* 9(2). 115–141.
Girard, Jeffrey M., Gayatri Shandar, Zhun Liu, Jeffrey F. Cohn, Lijun Yin & Louis-Philippe Morency. 2019. Reconsidering the Duchenne smile: Indicator of positive emotion or artifact of smile intensity? *International Conference on Affective Computing and Intelligent Interaction and workshops: [proceedings]. ACII (Conference)* 2019. 594–599.
Golder, Werner. 2007. *Hippokrates und das Corpus Hippocraticum*: *Eine Einführung für Philologen und Mediziner*. Würzburg: Königshausen & Neumann.
Gray, Heather M., Nalini Ambady, William T. Lowenthal & Patricia Deldin. 2004. P300 as an index of attention to self-relevant stimuli. *Journal of Experimental Social Psychology* 40 (2). 216–224.
Grodal, Torben K. 2000. *Moving pictures*: *A new theory of film genres, feelings and cognition*. Oxford: Clarendon.
Groom, Nick. 2014. Introduction. In Nick Groom & Horace Walpole (eds.), *The Castle of Otranto*: *A gothic story*, New edition (Oxford World's Classics), ix–xxxviii. Oxford: Oxford University Press.
Gross, James J. & Robert W. Levenson. 1995. Emotion elicitation using films. *Cognition & Emotion* 9(1). 87–108.
Gruner, Charles R. 1997. *The game of humor*: *A comprehensive theory of why we laugh*. New York: Taylor and Francis.
Hagenaars, Muriel A., Karin Roelofs & John F. Stins. 2013. Human freezing in response to affective films. *Anxiety Stress Coping* 27(1). 27–37.
Hagoort, Peter, Colin Brown & Jolanda Groothusen. 1993. The syntactic positive shift (SPS) as an ERP measure of syntactic processing. *Language and Cognitive Processes* 8(4). 439–483.
Hagoort, Peter, Lea Hald, Marcel Bastiaansen & Karl M. Petersson. 2004. Integration of word meaning and world knowledge in language comprehension. *Science* 304(5669). 438–441.

Hahn, Ronald M. & Rolf Giesen. 2002. *Das neue Lexikon des Horrorfilms*: *Alles über die dunkle Seite des Kinos: Mehr als 1800 Horrorfilme mit Inhaltsangaben, Filmografien und Kritiken*. Berlin: Lexikon.

Haidt, Jonathan. 2012. The disgust scale home page. http://people.stern.nyu.edu/jhaidt/disgustscale.html (accessed 22 June 2020).

Hajcak, Greg, Jonathan P. Dunning & Dan Foti. 2009. Motivated and controlled attention to emotion: Time-course of the late positive potential. *Clinical Neurophysiology: Official Journal of the International Federation of Clinical Neurophysiology* 120(3). 505–510.

Hajcak, Greg & Sander Nieuwenhuis. 2006. Reappraisal modulates the electrocortical response to unpleasant pictures. *Cognitive, Affective & Behavioral Neuroscience* 6(4). 291–297.

Hajcak, Greg & Doreen M. Olvet. 2008. The persistence of attention to emotion: Brain potentials during and after picture presentation. *Emotion (Washington, D.C.)* 8(2). 250–255.

Hajcak, Greg, Anna Weinberg, Annmarie MacNamara & Dan Foti. 2012. ERPs and the study of emotion. In Steven J. Luck & Emily S. Kappenman (eds.), *The Oxford handbook of event-related potential components*, 441–472. New York, Oxford: Oxford University Press.

Hale, Terry. 2002. French and german gothic: The beginnings. In Jerrold Hogle (ed.), *Gothic fiction*, 63–84. Cambridge: Cambridge University Press.

Hanich, Julian. 2010. *Cinematic Emotion in Horror Films and Thrillers: The Aesthetic Paradox of Pleasurable Fear:* Routledge.

Hanich, Julian. 2011. Towards a poetics of cinematic disgust. *Film-Philosophy* 15(2). 11–35.

Hartikainen, Kaisa M., Anna R. Siiskonen & Keith H. Ogawa. 2012. Threat interferes with response inhibition. *Neuroreport* 23(7). 447–450.

Hatfield, Elaine, Megan Carpenter & Richard L. Rapson. 2014. Emotional contagion as a precursor to collective emotions. In Christian von Scheve & Mikko Salmela (eds.), *Collective Emotions: Perspectives from Psychology, Philosophy, and Sociology*, First edition (Series in affective science), 108–122. Oxford: Oxford University Press.

Hay, Jennifer. 2001. The pragmatics of humor support. *HUMOR – International Journal of Humor Research* 14(1). 55–82.

Heintz, Sonja, Willibald Ruch, Tracey Platt, Dandan Pang, Hugo Carretero-Dios, Alberto Dionigi, Catalina Argüello Gutiérrez, Ingrid Brdar, Dorota Brzozowska, Hsueh-Chih Chen, Władysław Chłopicki, Matthew Collins, Róbert Ďurka, Najwa Y. E. Yahfoufi, Angélica Quiroga-Garza, Robert B. Isler, Andrés Mendiburo-Seguel, Tamil S. Ramis, Betül Saglam, Olga V. Shcherbakova, Kamlesh Singh, Ieva Stokenberga, Peter S. O. Wong & Jorge Torres-Marín. 2018. Psychometric comparisons of benevolent and corrective humor across 22 countries: The virtue gap in humor goes international. *Frontiers in Psychology* 9. 464.

Hempelmann, Christian F. & Salvatore Attardo. 2011. Resolutions and Their Incongruities: Further Thoughts on Logical Mechanisms. *HUMOR – International Journal of Humor Research* 24(2). 125–149.

Hendricks, Michelle A. & Tony W. Buchanan. 2016. Individual Differences in Cognitive Control Processes and Their Relationship to Emotion Regulation. *Cognition & Emotion* 30(5). 912–924.

Hennig, Jürgen & Petra Netter. 2000. Ekel und Verachtung. In Jürgen H. Otto, Harald A. Euler & Heinz Mandl (eds.), *Emotionspsychologie: Ein Handbuch*, 284–296. Weinheim: Beltz Psychologie Verlags Union.

Herzog, Thomas. 1999. Gender differences in humor appreciation revisited. *HUMOR* 12(4). 411–423.
Heusinger, Klaus von & Petra B. Schumacher. 2019. Discourse prominence: Definition and application. *Journal of Pragmatics* (154). 117–127.
Hills, Matt. 2003. An event-based definition of art-horror. In Steven J. Schneider & Daniel Shaw (eds.), *Dark thoughts: Philosophic reflections on cinematic horror*, 138–157. Lanham, Md: Scarecrow Press.
Hills, Matt. 2005. *The pleasures of horror*. New York, NY: Continuum.
Hippocrates, Heraclitus of Ephesus, William H. S. Jones & Paul Potter. 1931. *Hippocrates* (Loeb classical library IV). London: William Heinemann Ltd.
Hobbes, Thomas. 1812 [1739]. *The treatise on human nature and that on liberty and necessity with a supplement to which is prefixed an account of his life and writings by the editor*. London: Johnson; M'Creery.
Hofmann, Jennifer, Tracey Platt & Willibald Ruch. 2017. Laughter and smiling in 16 positive emotions. *IEEE TRANSACTIONS ON AFFECTIVE COMPUTING* 8(4). 495–507.
Hofmeister, Philip. 2011. Representational Complexity and Memory Retrieval in Language Comprehension. *Language and Cognitive Processes* 26(3). 376–405.
Hofmeister, Philip, T. F. Jaeger, Inbal Arnon, Ivan A. Sag & Neal Snider. 2013. The source ambiguity problem: Distinguishing the effects of grammar and processing on acceptability judgments. *Language and Cognitive Processes* 28 (1–2).48–87.
Hogle, Jerrold. 2002. Introduction: The gothic in western culture. In Jerrold Hogle (ed.), *Gothic fiction*, 1–20. Cambridge: Cambridge University Press.
Hsu, Nobuaki & Zacharias Schütt (eds.). 2012. *Psychology of priming* (Psychology research progress). Hauppauge, N.Y: Nova Science Publishers.
Hume, David. 1996 [1985]. *Of tragedy*. Boulder, Colo, Raleigh, N.C: NetLibrary; Alex Catalogue.
Humphries, Colin, Jeffrey R. Binder, David A. Medler & Einat Liebenthal. 2006. Syntactic and semantic modulation of neural activity during auditory sentence comprehension. *Journal of cognitive neuroscience* 18(4). 665–679.
Humphries, Colin, Jeffrey R. Binder, David A. Medler & Einat Liebenthal. 2007. Time Course of Semantic Processes During Sentence Comprehension: An fMRI Study. *NeuroImage* 36 (3924–932).
Hung, Yu-Chen. 2011. *Topic Matters – Impact of information structure on referential processing: electrophysiological evidence from Chinese and German: Inauguraldissertation zur Erlangung des Akademischen Grades eines Dr. phil*. Mainz: Johannes Gutenberg-Universität Dissertation.
Hung, Yu-Chen & Petra B. Schumacher. 2012. Topicality matters: position-specific demands on chinese discourse processing. *Neuroscience Letters* 511(2). 59–64.
Huntsinger, Jeffrey R. 2013. Does emotion directly tune the scope of attention? *Current Directions in Psychological Science* 22(4). 265–270.
Huntsinger, Jeffrey R. & Simone Schnall. 2014. Emotion–cognition interactions. In Daniel Reisberg (ed.), *The Oxford Handbook of Cognitive Psychology* (Oxford Library of Psychology), 571–584. Oxford: Oxford Univ. Press.
Huynh, Huynh & Leonard S. Feldt. 1970. Conditions under which mean square ratios in repeated measurements designs have exact F-distributions. *Journal of the American Statistical Association* 65(332). 1582–1589.
Jancovich, Mark. 1992. *Horror* (Batsford cultural studies). London: Batsford.

Jasinska, Agnes J., Marie Yasuda, Rebecca E. Rhodes, Cheng Wang & Thad A. Polk. 2015. Task difficulty modulates the impact of emotional stimuli on neural response in cognitive-control regions. In Florin Dolcos, Lihong Wang & Mara Mather (eds.), *Current Research and Emerging Directions in Emotion-cognition Interactions*, 345: Frontiers in NeuroScience; Frontiers in Psychology.

Jasper, Herbert H. 1958. The ten twenty electrode system of the international federation. *Electroencephalography and Clinical Neurophysiology* 10(2). 371–375.

Jeannerod, M. 2001. Neural simulation of action: A unifying mechanism for motor cognition. *NeuroImage* 14. 103–109.

Jegerski, Jill. 2014. Self-paced reading. In Jill Jegerski & B. VanPatten (eds.), *Research Methods in Second Language Psycholinguistics*, 20–49. New York: Routledge.

Jentsch, Ernst. 1906. Zur Psychologie des Unheimlichen. *Psychiatrisch-Neurologische Wochenschrift* 22. 195–198.

Johnson, A. M. 1992. Language ability and sex affect humor appreciation. *Perceptual and Motor Skills* 75(2). 571–581.

Johnson, Jeffrey, Patricia Cohen, Smailes, Elizabeth M., Kasen, Stephanie & Judith S. Brook. 2002. Television viewing and aggressive behavior during adolescence and adulthood. *Science* 295 (5564).2468–2471.

Johnson-Laird, Philip N. 2010. Mental models and human reasoning. *Proceedings of the National Academy of Sciences of the United States of America* 107(43). 18243–18250.

Just, Marcel A. & Patricia A. Carpenter. 1980. A theory of reading: From eye fixations to comprehension. *Psychological Review* 87(4). 329–354.

Just, Marcel A. & Patricia A. Carpenter. 1992. A capacity theory of comprehension: Individual differences in working memory. *Psychological Review* 99(1). 122–149.

Just, Marcel A., Patricia A. Carpenter & Jacqueline Woolley. 1982. Paradigms and processes in reading comprehension. *Journal of Experimental Psychology* 111(2). 228–238.

Kablitz, Andreas. 2010. Komik. In Joachim Ritter (ed.), *Historisches Wörterbuch der Philosophie*, 289–293. Basel: Schwabe.

Kagan, Jerome. 1994. *Galen's prophecy: Temperament in human nature*. New York: Westview Press.

Kanske. 2015. On the influence of emotion on conflict processing. In Florin Dolcos, Lihong Wang & Mara Mather (eds.), *Current Research and Emerging Directions in Emotion-cognition Interactions*: Frontiers in NeuroScience; Frontiers in Psychology.

Kanske, Philipp & Sonja A. Kotz. 2011. Emotion speeds up conflict resolution: A new role for the ventral anterior cingulate cortex? *Cerebral Cortex* 21(4). 911–919.

Kant, Immanuel. 1912 [1798]. *Anthropologie in pragmatischer Hinsicht [anthropology from a pragmatic point of view]*. Leipzig: Meiner.

Kant, Immanuel. 2010 [1790]. *Kritik der Urteilskraft [Critique of the power of judgement]* (Reclams Universal-Bibliothek 1026). Stuttgart: Reclam.

Kaufman, James C., Scott B. Kaufman & Jonathan A. Plucker. 2014. Contemporary theories of intelligence. In Daniel Reisberg (ed.), *The Oxford Handbook of Cognitive Psychology* (Oxford Library of Psychology), 811–835. Oxford: Oxford Univ. Press.

Keith-Spiegel, Patricia. 1972. Early conceptions of humor: Varieties and issues. In Jeffrey H. Goldstein & Paul E. McGhee (eds.), *The psychology of humor: Theoretical perspectives and empirical issues*, 3–39. New York: Academic Press.

Keppel, Geoffrey & Thomas D. Wickens. 2004. *Design and analysis: A researcher's handbook*. Upper Saddle River, N.J: Pearson Prentice Hall.

Kidd, Evan, Seamus Donnelly & Morten H. Christiansen. 2018. Individual differences in language acquisition and processing. *Trends in Cognitive Sciences* 22(2). 154–169.

King, Jonathan W. & Marta Kutas. 1995. Who did what and when? Using word- and clause-level ERPs to monitor working memory usage in reading. *Journal of cognitive neuroscience* 7(3). 376–395.

King, Stephen. 1981. *Stephen King's danse macabre*. New York: Everest House.

Kleinginna, Paul R. & Anne M. Kleinginna. 1981. A categorized list of emotion definitions, with suggestions for a consensual definition. *Motivation and Emotion* 5(4). 345–379.

Kluge, Friedrich & Alfred Schirmer. 1957. *Etymologisches Wörterbuch der Deutschen Sprache*. Berlin, Boston: de Gruyter.

Koestler, Arthur. 1966. *Der Göttliche Funke: Der Schöpferische Akt in Kunst und Wissenschaft*. Bern, München: Scherz Verlag.

Kohn, N., T. Kellermann, R. C. Gur, F. Schneider & U. Habel. 2011. Gender differences in the neural correlates of humor processing: Implications for different processing modes. *Neuropsychologia* 49(5). 888–897.

Kozhevnikov, Maria. 2014. Cognitive style. In Daniel Reisberg (ed.), *The Oxford Handbook of Cognitive Psychology* (Oxford Library of Psychology), 842–856. Oxford: Oxford Univ. Press.

Kristeva, Julia. 1982. *Powers of horror: An essay on abjection*. New York: Columbia University Press.

Krohne, Heinz W. 1996. *Angst und Angstbewältigung*. Stuttgart: Kohlhammer.

Kropotov, Juri D. 2016. Functional magnetic resonance imaging. In Juri D. Kropotov (ed.), *Functional Neuromarkers for Psychiatry: Applications for Diagnosis and Treatment*, 17–25. Amsterdam: Academic Press.

Ku, Li-Chuan, Yen-Ju Feng, Yu-Chen Chan, Ching-Lin Wu & Hsueh-Chih Chen. 2017. A re-visit of three-stage humor processing with readers' surprise, comprehension, and funniness ratings: An ERP study. *Journal of Neurolinguistics* 42. 49–62.

Kuperberg, Gina R., David Caplan, Tatiana Sitnikova, Marianna Eddy & Phillip J. Holcomb. 2006. Neural correlates of processing syntactic, semantic, and thematic relationships in sentences. *Language and Cognitive Processes* 21(5). 489–530.

Kuperberg, Gina R., Philip K. McGuire, Ed T. Bullmore, Michael J. Brammer, Sophia Rabe-Hesketh, Ian C. Wright, David J. Lythgoe, Steven C. R. Williams & Anthony S. David. 2000. Common and distinct neural substrates for pragmatic, semantic, and syntactic Processing of spoken sentences: An fMRI study. *Journal of cognitive neuroscience* 12(2). 321–341.

Kuperberg, Gina R., Tatiana Sitnikova, David Caplan & Phillip J. Holcomb. 2003. Electrophysiological distinctions in processing conceptual relationships within simple sentences. *Cognitive Brain Research* 17(1). 117–129.

Kurby, Christopher A. & Jeffrey M. Zacks. 2012. Starting from scratch and building brick by brick in comprehension. *Memory & Cognition* 40(5). 812–826.

Kutas, M. & S. A. Hillyard. 1984. Brain potentials during reading reflect word expectancy and semantic association. *Nature* 307(5947). 161–163.

Kutas, Marta & Kara D. Federmeier. 2011. Thirty years and counting: Finding meaning in the N400 component of the event-related brain potential (ERP). *Annual Review of Psychology* 62. 621–647.

Kutas, Marta & Kara D. Federmeier. 2018. Event-related brain potential (ERP) studies of sentence processing. In Shirley-Ann Rueschemeyer & M. G. Gaskell (eds.), *The Oxford*

Handbook of Psycholinguistics, 2nd edn. (Oxford Handbooks Online), 385–406. Oxford: Oxford University Press.

Kutas, Marta & Steven A. Hillyard. 1980. Reading senseless sentences: Brain potentials reflect semantic incongruity. *Science* 207(4427). 203–205.

LaBar, Kevin S. 2016. Fear and anxiety. In Lisa Feldmann Barrett, Michael Lewis & Jeannette M. Haviland-Jones (eds.), *Handbook of emotions*, 4th edn., 751–773. New York, London: The Guilford Press.

Lee, Shu-Hui, James R. Booth, Shiou-Yuan Chen & Tai-Li Chou. 2011. Developmental changes in the inferior frontal cortex for selecting semantic representations. *Developmental Cognitive Neuroscience* 1(3). 338–350.

Leeder, Murray. 2018. *Horror film: A critical introduction* (Bloomsbury Film Genres Series). New York, London: Bloomsbury Academic.

Levy, Roger. 2008. Expectation-based syntactic comprehension. *Cognition* 106(3). 1126–1177.

Levy, Roger. 2011. Integrating surprisal and uncertain-input models in online sentence comprehension: Formal techniques and empirical results. In Association for Computational Linguistics (ed.), *49th Annual Meeting of the Association for Computational Linguistics*, 1055–1065.

Lin, Jih-Hsuan T. 2017. Fear in virtual reality (VR): Fear elements, coping reactions, immediate and next-day fright responses toward a survival horror zombie virtual reality game. *Computers in Human Behavior* 72. 350–361.

Löbner, Sebastian. 2015. Functional concepts and frames. In Thomas Gamerschlag, Doris Gerland, Rainer Osswald & Wiebke Petersen (eds.), *Meaning, frames, and conceptual representations*, 15–42. Düsseldorf: dup.

López-Benítez, Raúl, Alberto Acosta, Juan Lupiáñez & Hugo Carretero-Dios. 2018. High trait cheerfulness individuals are more sensitive to the emotional environment. *Journal of Happiness Studies* 19(6). 1589–1612.

Lovecraft, Howard P. 1973. *Supernatural horror in literature*. New York: Dover Publications, Inc.

Luck, Steven J. 2014. *An introduction to the event-related potential technique*, 2nd ed. Cambridge: The MIT Press.

Luo, Yu, Weilin Shen, Yu Zhang, Ting-yong Feng, Hao Huang & Hong Li. 2013. Core disgust and moral disgust are related to distinct spatiotemporal patterns of neural processing: An event-related potential study. *Biological Psychology* 94(2). 242–248.

Maggi, Vincenzo. 1970 [1550]. De ridiculis. In Bernard Weinberg (ed.), *Trattati poetica e retorica del cinquecento*, 91–125. Bari: Gius. Laterza & Figli.

Magistrale, Tony. 2008. Introduction. In Tony Magistrale (ed.), *The films of Stephen King: From Carrie to Secret Window*, 1–10. New York: Palgrave Macmillan.

Marszalek, Agnes. 2013. "It's not funny out of context!": A cognitive stylistic approach to humorous narratives. In Marta Dynel (ed.), *Developments in linguistic humour theory* (Topics in Humor Research 1), 393–421. Amsterdam, Philadelphia: John Benjamins Publishing Company.

Martin, G. N. 2019. (Why) do you like scary movies? A review of the empirical research on psychological responses to horror films. *Frontiers in Psychology* 10. 1–22.

Martin, Rod A. 2007. *The psychology of humor: An integrative approach*. Amsterdam: Elsevier.

Mayerhofer, Bastian & Annekathrin Schacht. 2015. From incoherence to mirth: Neuro-cognitive processing of garden-path jokes. *Frontiers in Psychology* 6. 1–19.

McGhee, Paul E. 2010. *Humor as survival training for a stressed-out world*: The 7 humor habits program. Bloomington, Indiana: AuthorHouse.
Meteling, Arno. 2006. *Monster*: Zu Körperlichkeit und Medialität im Modernen Horrorfilm: transcript Film.
Meyer, Wulf-Uwe, Rainer Reisenzein & Michael Niepel. 2000. Überraschung. In Jürgen H. Otto, Harald A. Euler & Heinz Mandl (eds.), *Emotionspsychologie*: Ein Handbuch, 253–263. Weinheim: Beltz Psychologie Verlags Union.
Miles, Tobert. 2002. The 1790s: The effulgence of gothic. In Jerrold Hogle (ed.), *Gothic fiction*, 41–62. Cambridge: Cambridge University Press.
Minsky, Marvin. 1974. A framework for representing knowledge. *Artificial Intelligence* 306. 1–79.
Mobbs, Dean, Cindy C. Hagan, Eiman Azim, Vinod Menon & Allan L. Reiss. 2005. Personality predicts activity in reward and emotional regions associated with humor. *Proceedings of the National Academy of Sciences of the United States of America* 102(45). 16502–16506.
Molinaro, Nicola, Horacio A. Barber & Manuel Carreiras. 2011. Grammatical agreement processing in reading: ERP findings and future directions. *Cortex* 47(8). 908–930.
Molinaro, Nicola & Manuel Carreiras. 2010. Electrophysiological evidence of interaction between contextual expectation and semantic integration during the processing of collocations. *Biological Psychology* 83(3). 176–190.
Moratti, Stephan, Cristina Saugar & Bryan A. Strange. 2011. Prefrontal-occipitoparietal coupling underlies late latency human neuronal responses to emotion. *The Journal of Neuroscience: The Official Journal of the Society for Neuroscience* 31(47). 17278–17286.
Mori, Masahiro. 2012 [1970]. The uncanny valley. Translated by Karl F. MacDorman and Norri Kageki. *IEEE Robotics & Automation Magazine* 19(2). 98–100.
Morreall, John. 1983. *Taking laughter seriously*, 5th edn. Albany, NY: State Univ. of New York Press.
Morreall, John. 1985. Enjoying negative emotions in fictions. *Philosophy and Literature* 9(1). 95–103.
Morreall, John. 2004. Verbal humor without switching scripts and without non-bona fide communication. *HUMOR – International Journal of Humor Research* 17(4).
Müller, Horst M. 2009. *Arbeitsbuch Linguistik*: Eine Einführung in die Sprachwissenschaft, 2., überarbeitete und aktualisierte Auflage (UTB Sprachwissenschaft 2169). Paderborn, München, Wien, Zürich: Ferdinand Schöningh.
Mundorf, Norbert, Azra Bhatia, Dolf Zillmann, Paul Lester & Susan Robertson. 1988. Gender differences in humor appreciation. *HUMOR* 1(3). 231–243.
Newman, Aaron J., Roumyana Pancheva, Kaori Ozawa, Helen J. Neville & Michael T. Ullman. 2011. An event-related fMRI study of syntactic and semantic violations. *Journal of Psycholinguistic Research* 30(3). 339–364.
Ni, Weiguo., Robert T. Constable, W. E. Mencl, Kenneth R. Pugh, Robert K. Fulbright, Sally E. Shaywitz, Benneth A. Shaywitz, John C. Gore & Donald Shankweiler. 2000. An event-related neuroimaging study distinguishing form and content in sentence processing. *Journal of cognitive neuroscience* 12(1). 120–133.
Novick, Jared M., Erika Hussey, Susan Teubner-Rhodes, J. I. Harbison & Michael F. Bunting. 2013. Clearing the garden-path: Improving sentence processing through cognitive control training. *Language and Cognitive Processes* 29(2). 186–217.
Nozari, Nazbanou, John C. Trueswell & Sharon L. Thompson-Schill. 2016. The interplay of local attraction, context and domain-general cognitive control in activation and suppression of

semantic distractors during sentence comprehension. *Psychonomic Bulletin & Review* 23(6). 1942–1953.

Oatley, Keith & P. N. Johnson-Laird. 2014. Cognitive approaches to emotions. *Trends in Cognitive Sciences* 18(3). 134–140.

Oring, Elliott. 2011. Parsing the joke: The General Theory of Verbal Humor and appropriate incongruity. *HUMOR – International Journal of Humor Research* 24(2). 203–222.

Osterhout, Lee & Phillip J. Holcomb. 1992. Event-related brain potentials elicited by syntactic anomaly. *Journal of memory and language* 31(6). 785–806.

Owen, Adrian M. 2000. The role of the lateral frontal cortex in mnemonic processing: The contribution of functional neuroimaging. *Experimental Brain Research* 133. 33–43.

Paik, Haejung & George Comstock. 1994. The effects of television violence on antisocial behavior: A Meta-Analysis. *Communication Research* 21(4). 516–546.

Papenberg, Goran, Lars Bäckman, Christian Chicherio, Irene E. Nagel, Hauke R. Heekeren, Ulman Lindenberger & Shu-Chen Li. 2011. Higher intraindividual variability is associated with more forgetting and dedifferentiated memory functions in old age. *Neuropsychologia* 49(7). 1879–1888.

Paul, William. 1994. *Laughing, screaming*: Modern Hollywood horror and comedy (Film and Culture). New York: Columbia University Press.

Pendery, David R. 2017. Biochemical responses to horror, or, 'Why do we like this stuff?'. *Horror Studies* 8(1). 147–163.

Petrides, Michael. 2005. Lateral prefrontal cortex: Architectonic and functional organization. *Philosophical transactions of the royal society of London. Series B, biological sciences* 360(1456). 781–795.

Plato, Harold N. Fowler & W. R. M. Lamb. 1925. *Philebus*. Cambridge, MA: Harvard University Press.

Platt, Tracey, Jennifer Hofmann, Willibald Ruch & René Proyer. 2020. Duchenne Display responses towards sixteen enjoyable emotions: Individual differences between no and high fear of being laughed at. In Erika L. Rosenberg & Paul Ekman (eds.), *What the face reveals*: Basic and applied studies of spontaneous expression using the Facial Action Coding System (FACS), 490–505. Oxford: Oxford University Press.

Plebe, Armando. 1952. *La teoria del comico da Aristotele a Plutarco*: Pubblicazioni della facoltà di lettere e filosofia, 4th edn. Turino: Univ. di Torino.

Poldrack, Russell A., Jeanette A. Mumford & Thomas E. Nichols (eds.). 2011. *Handbook of functional MRI data analysis*. Cambridge: Cambridge University Press.

Polich, John. 2012. Neuropsychology of P300. In Steven J. Luck & Emily S. Kappenman (eds.), *The Oxford Handbook of Event-Related Potential Components* (Oxford Library of Psychology), 159–188. Oxford: Oxford Univ. Press.

Prat, Chantel S. 2011. The brain basis of individual differences in language comprehension abilities. *Language and Linguistics Compass* 5(9). 635–649.

Price, Cathy J., Cath J. Mummery, C. J. Moore, Richard S. J. Frackowiak & Karl Friston. 1999. Delineating necessary and sufficient neural systems with functional imaging studies of neuropsychological patients. *Journal of cognitive neuroscience* 11(4). 371–382.

Proyer, René. 2014. Gelotophobia. In Salvatore I. Attardo (ed.), *Encyclopedia of humor studies*, 256–259. Thousand Oaks: SAGE Publications.

Punter, David. 1980. *The literature of terror: A history of gothic fictions from 1765 to the present day* (A Longman paperback). London: Longman.

Quintilian & Donald A. Russell. 2002 [1 AC – 100 AC]. *The orator's education* (Loeb classical library II). Cambridge, MA: Harvard University Press. https://www.loebclassics.com/view/quintilian-orators_education/2002/pb_LCL126.75.xml?mainRsKey=BXDMbm&result=4&rskey=Jr8x8R.

R Core Team. 2019. *R: A language and environment for statistical computing*. Vienne, Austria. https://www.R-project.org/.

Raskin, Victor. 1985. *Semantic mechanisms of humor* (Synthese language library 24). Dordrecht: Reidel. https://books.google.de/books?id=KKCnecQtYcIC&printsec=frontcover&hl=de&source=gbs_ViewAPI&redir_esc=y#v=onepage&q&f=false (accessed 23 June 2020).

Raskin, Victor & Salvatore Attardo. 1991. Script theory revis(it)ed: Joke similarity and joke representation model. *HUMOR* 4(3/4). 293–347.

Rayner, Keith, Gretchen Kambe & Susan A. Duffy. 2000. The effect of clause wrap-up on eye movements during reading. *The Quarterly Journal of Experimental Psychology A* 53(4). 1061–1080.

Rehbock, Helmut. 2016. Holzwegeffekt. In Helmut Glück & Michael Rödel (eds.), *Metzler Lexikon Sprache*, 220, 273. Stuttgart: J.B. Metzler.

Reynaud, Emmanuelle, Myriam El Khoury-Malhame, Jérôme Rossier, Olivier Blin, Stéphanie Khalfa & Antonio V. García. 2012. Neuroticism modifies psychophysiological responses to fearful films. *PloS one* 7 (3).e32413.

Ritchie, Graeme. 2014. Logic and reasoning in jokes. *European Journal of Humor Research* 2(1). 50–60.

Rodd, Jennifer, Gareth Gaskell & William Marslen-Wilson. 2002. Making sense of semantic ambiguity: Semantic competition in lexical access. *Journal of memory and language* 46 (2). 245–266.

Roehm, Dietmar, Ina Bornkessel-Schlesewsky, Frank Rösler & Erik Schleef. 2007. To predict or not to predict: Influences of task and strategy on the processing of semantic relations. *Journal of cognitive neuroscience* 19(8). 1259–1274.

Rommer, Joost & Kara D. Federmeier. 2018. Electrophysiological methods. In de Groot, Anette M. B. de & Peter Hagoort (eds.), *Research methods in psycholinguistics and the neurobiology of language*: *A practical guide* (Guides to research methods in language and linguistics 9), 247–265. Hoboken, NJ, Chichester, W. Sussex: John Wiley & Sons, Inc.

Rosch, Eleanor H. 1973. Natural categories. *Cognitive Psychology* 4(3). 328–350.

Rosenberg, Erika L. & Paul Ekman. 2020. Coherence between expressive and experiential systems in emotion. In Erika L. Rosenberg & Paul Ekman (eds.), *What the face reveals*: *Basic and applied studies of spontaneous expression using the Facial Action Coding System (FACS)*, 200–221. Oxford: Oxford University Press.

Rothbart, Mary K. 2017 [1976]. Incongruity, problem-solving and laughter. In Antony J. Chapman & Hugh C. Foot (eds.), *Humor and Laughter*: *Theory, Research, and Applications*, 37–54. New York, Abingdon: Routledge.

Roye, Anja, Thomas Jacobsen & Erich Schröger. 2007. Personal significance is encoded automatically by the human brain: An event-related potential study with ringtones. *The European Journal of Neuroscience* 26(3). 784–790.

Rozin, Paul & April E. Fallon. 1987. A perspective on disgust. *Psychological Review* 94(1). 23–41.

Rozin, Paul, Jonathan Haidt & Clark McCauley. 2016. Disgust. In Lisa Feldmann Barrett, Michael Lewis & Jeannette M. Haviland-Jones (eds.), *Handbook of emotions*, 4th edn., 815–834. New York, London: The Guilford Press.

Rozin, Paul, Jonathan Haidt, Clark McCauley, Lance Dunlop & Michelle Ashmore. 1999. Individual differences in disgust sensitivity: Comparisons and evaluations of paper-and-pencil versus behavioral measures. *Journal of Research in Personality* 33. 330–351.

Rozin, Paul, Laura Lowery & Rhonda Ebert. 1994. Varieties of disgust faces and the structure of disgust. *Journal of Personality and Social Psychology* 66(5). 870–881.

Ruch, Willibald. 1993. Exhilaration and humor. In Michael Lewis & Jeannette M. Haviland-Jones (eds.), *Handbook of emotions*, 605–616. New York, London: The Guilford Press.

Ruch, Willibald. 1997. State and trait cheerfulness and the induction of exhilaration. *European Psychologist* 2(4). 328–341.

Ruch, Willibald. 1998. Foreword and overview: The sense of humor: A new look at an old concept. In Willibald Ruch (ed.), *The sense of humor*: Explorations of a personality characteristic (Humor Research 3), 3–14. Berlin: Mouton de Gruyter.

Ruch, Willibald. 2000. Erheiterung. In Jürgen H. Otto, Harald A. Euler & Heinz Mandl (eds.), *Emotionspsychologie*: Ein Handbuch, 231–238. Weinheim: Beltz Psychologie Verlags Union.

Ruch, Willibald. 2005. Will the real relationship between facial expression and affective experience please stand up?: The case of exhilaration. In Paul Ekman & Erika L. Rosenberg (eds.), *What the face Reveals*: Basic and applied studies of spontaneous expression using the Facial Action Coding System (FACS), 89–109: Oxford University Press.

Ruch, Willibald. 2017. State-trait-cheerfulness-inventory (STCI). https://www.psychologie.uzh.ch/de/bereiche/sob/perspsy/forschung/stci.html#versions (accessed 17 January 2019; 29 June 2020; ongoing development of STCI-T30).

Ruch, Willibald, Salvatore Attardo & Victor Raskin. 1993. Toward an empirical verification of the general theory of verbal humor. *HUMOR – International Journal of Humor Research* 6(2). 123–136.

Ruch, Willibald, Jennifer Hofmann, Tracey Platt & René Proyer. 2014. The state-of-the art in gelotophobia research: A review and some theoretical extensions. *HUMOR* 27(1).

Ruch, Willibald, Gabriele Köhler & Christoph van Thriel. 1996. Assessing the "humorous temperament": construction of the facet and standard trait forms of the state-trait-cheerfulness inventory – STCI. *HUMOR* 9(3/4). 303–339.

Ruch, Willibald, Gabriele Köhler & Christoph van Thriel. 1997. To be in good or bad humor: Construction of the state form of the state-trait-cheerfulness-inventory – STCI. *Personality and individual differences* 22. 447–491.

Ruch, Willibald, Paul E. McGhee & Franz-Josef Hehl. 1990. Age differences in the enjoyment of incongruity-resolution and nonsense humor during adulthood. *Psychology and Aging* 5(3). 348–355.

Ruch, Willibald & René T. Proyer. 2008a. The fear of being laughed at: Individual and group differences in gelotophobia. *HUMOR* 21(1). 15.

Ruch, Willibald & René T. Proyer. 2008b. Who is gelotophobic?: Assessment criteria for the fear of being laughed at. *Swiss Journal of Psychology* 67(1). 19–27.

Rumelhart, David E. & Donald A. Norman. 1976. Accretion, tuning and restructuring: Three modes of learning. *DTIC AND NTIS*. 1–26 (accessed 13 December 2019).

Rymarczyk, Krystyna, Łukasz Żurawski, Kamila Jankowiak-Siuda & Iwona Szatkowska. 2016. Emotional empathy and facial mimicry for static and dynamic facial expressions of fear and disgust. *Frontiers in Psychology* 7. 1853.
Samson, Andrea C., Christian F. Hempelmann, Oswald Huber & Stefan Zysset. 2009. Neural substrates of incongruity-resolution and nonsense humor. *Neuropsychologia* 47(4). 1023–1033.
Savaki, Helen E. & Vassilis Raos. 2019. Action perception and motor imagery: Mental practice of action. *Progress in Neurobiology* 175. 107–125.
Scarantino, Andrea. 2016. The philosophy of emotions and its impact on affective science. In Lisa Feldmann Barrett, Michael Lewis & Jeannette M. Haviland-Jones (eds.), *Handbook of emotions*, 4th edn., 3–48. New York, London: The Guilford Press.
Schank, Roger C. & Robert P. Abelson. 1977. *Scripts, plans, goals and understanding*: An inquiry into human knowledge structures (The Artificial Intelligence Series). Hillsdale, NJ: Erlbaum.
Scherer, Klaus R. 2005. What are emotions?: And how can they be measured? *Social Science Information* 44(4). 695–729.
Schienle, Anne, Gabriele Dietmaier, Rottraut Ille & Verena Leutgeb. 2010. Eine Skala zur Erfassung der Ekelsensitivität (SEE). *Zeitschrift für Klinische Psychologie und Psychotherapie* 39(2). 80–86.
Schienle, Anne, Bertram Walter, Rudolf Stark & Dieter Vaitl. 2002. Ein Fragebogen zur Erfassung der Ekelempfindlichkeit (FEE). *Zeitschrift für Klinische Psychologie und Psychotherapie* 31(2). 110–120.
Schiller, Friedrich. 1793. Vom Erhabenen: Zur weitern Ausführung einiger Kantischen Ideen. *Neue Thalia* 3. 320–394. https://de.wikisource.org/wiki/Vom_Erhabenen (accessed 25 June 2020).
Schneider, Steven J. 2003. Murder as art/ The art of murder: Aestheticizing violence in modern cinematic horror. In Steven J. Schneider & Daniel Shaw (eds.), *Dark thoughts*: *Philosophic reflections on cinematic horror*, 174–197. Lanham, Md: Scarecrow Press.
Schopenhauer, Arthur. 2010 [1819]. *The world as will and representation* (The Cambridge Edition of the Works of Schopenhauer). Cambridge: Cambridge University Press.
Schumacher, Petra B. 2009. The given-new distinction: Insights from inferables. In Linguistic Society of Korea (ed.), *Current issues in unity and diversity of languages*, 359–379. Korea: Dongnam Publishing Company.
Schumacher, Petra B. 2011. The hepatitis called . . . Electrophysiological evidence for enriched composition. In Jörg Meibauer & Markus Steinbach (eds.), *Experimental Pragmatics/Semantics* (Linguistik Aktuell / Linguistics Today v. 175), 199–219. Amsterdam, Philadelphia Pa.: John Benjamins Pub. Co.
Schumacher, Petra B. 2019. Metonymy. In Chris Cummins & Napoleon Katsos (eds.), *The Oxford handbook of experimental semantics and pragmatics*, 315–330: Oxford University Press.
Schumacher, Petra B. & Jörg Meibauer. 2013. Pragmatic inferencing and expert knowledge. In Frank Liedtke & Cornelia Schulze (eds.), *Beyond words*: *Content, context, and inference* (Mouton series in pragmatics 15), 231–246. Berlin: de Gruyter.
Schupp, Harald T., Bruce N. Cuthbert, Margaret M. Bradley, John T. Cacioppo, Tiffany Ito & Peter J. Lang. 2000. Affective picture processing: The late positive potential is modulated by motivational relevance. *Psychophysiology* 37. 257–261.
Schupp, Harald T., Markus Junghöfer, Almut I. Weike & Alfons O. Hamm. 2004. The selective processing of briefly presented affective pictures: An ERP analysis. *Psychophysiology* 41(3). 441–449.

Schupp, Harald T., Arne Ohman, Markus Junghöfer, Almut I. Weike, Jessica Stockburger & Alfons O. Hamm. 2004. The facilitated processing of threatening faces: An ERP analysis. *Emotion (Washington, D.C.)* 4(2). 189–200.
Schwarz-Friesel, Monika. 2013. *Sprache und Emotion*, 2., aktualisierte und erw. Aufl. (utb-studi-e-book 2939). Stuttgart, Tübingen: UTB GmbH; Francke.
Schwarz-Friesel, Monika. 2015. Emotion and language: The cognitive linguistic perspective. In Ulrike M. Lüdtke (ed.), *Emotion in language. theory – research – application*, 157–173. Philadelphia: John Benjamins Publishing Company.
Seeßlen, Georg. 1995. *Thriller: Kino der Angst*. Marburg: Schüren.
Seeßlen, Georg & Fernand Jung. 2006. *Horror: Grundlagen des populären Films*. Marburg: Schüren.
Shammi, Prathiba & Donald T. Stuss. 2003. The effects of normal aging on humor appreciation. *Journal of the International Neuropsychological Society* 9(6). 855–863.
Shaw, Daniel. 2003. The mastery of Hannibal Lecter. In Steven J. Schneider & Daniel Shaw (eds.), *Dark thoughts: Philosophic reflections on cinematic horror*, 10–24. Lanham, Md: Scarecrow Press.
Sherzer, Joel. 1985. Puns and jokes. In Teun van Dijk (ed.), *Handbook of discourse analysis* (Discourse and Dialog), 213–221. London: Academic Press.
Shibata, Midori, Yuri Terasawa, Takahiro Osumi, Keita Masui, Yuichi Ito, Arisa Sato & Satoshi Umeda. 2017. Time course and localization of brain activity in humor comprehension: An ERP/sLORETA study. *Brain research* 1657. 215–222.
Sirigu, Angela, Jean-René Duhamel, Lauren Cohen, Bernard Pillon, Bruno Dubois & Yves Agid. 1996. The mental representation of hand movement after parietal cortex damage. *Science* 273. 1564–1568.
Smuts, Aaron. 2003. Haunting the house from within: Disbelief mitigation and spatial experience. In Steven J. Schneider & Daniel Shaw (eds.), *Dark thoughts: Philosophic reflections on cinematic horror*, 158–173. Lanham, Md: Scarecrow Press.
Smuts, Aaron. 2009. Horror. In Paisley Livingston (ed.), *The Routledge Companion to Philosophy and Film* (Routledge Philosophy Companions), 505–514. London: Routledge.
Smuts, Aaron. 2014. Cognitive and philosophical approaches to horror. In Harry M. Benshoff (ed.), *A companion to the horror film*, 3–20. Chichester, West Sussex, Malden, MA: John Wiley and Sons Inc.
Spielberger, Charles D. (ed.). 1972. *Anxiety: Current trends in theory and research*. New York: Academic Press.
Steinbach, Markus, Ruth Albert, Heiko Girnth, Annette Hohenberger, Bettina Kümmerling-Meibauer, Jörg Meibauer, Monika Rothweiler & Monika Schwarz-Friesel. 2007. *Schnittstellen der germanistischen Linguistik*. Stuttgart, Weimar: Verlag J.B. Metzler.
Stelmack, Robert M. & Anastasios Stalikas. 1991. Galen and the humour theory of temperament. *Personality and individual differences* 12(3). 255–263.
Stiglegger, Marcus. 2006. *Ritual & Verführung: Schaulust, Spektakel & Sinnlichkeit im Film* (Deep focus 3). Berlin: Bertz + Fischer.
Stiglegger, Marcus. 2007. Horrorfilm. In Thomas Koebner (ed.), *Reclams Sachlexikon des Films*, 2nd edn., 311–315. Stuttgart: Reclam.
Stiglegger, Marcus. 2010. *Terrorkino: Angst/Lust und Körperhorror*, 3rd edn. (Kultur & Kritik 1). Berlin: Bertz + Fischer.

Stöber, Joachim & Ralf Schwarzer. 2000. Angst. In Jürgen H. Otto, Harald A. Euler & Heinz Mandl (eds.), *Emotionspsychologie: Ein Handbuch*, 189–198. Weinheim: Beltz Psychologie Verlags Union.
Straßburger, Lena. 2015. *Inkongruenz in Humor und Horror am Beispiel der US-Serie DEXTER*. Cologne: University of Cologne Staatsexamen.
Straßburger, Lena. 2019. How to kill with a smile – how to smile about a kill: Violent clowns as double incongruity. *Comedy Studies*. 1–11.
Strohminger, Nina. 2014. Disgust talked about. *Philosophy Compass* 9(7). 478–493.
Suls, Jerry M. 1972. A two-stage model for the appreciation of jokes and cartoons: An information-processing analysis. In Jeffrey H. Goldstein & Paul E. McGhee (eds.), *The psychology of humor: Theoretical perspectives and empirical issues*, 81–100. New York: Academic Press.
Sutton, Samuel, Patricia Tueting, Joseph Zubin & E. R. John. 1967. Information delivery and the sensory evoked potential. *Science* 155(3768). 1436–1439.
Swaab, Tamara Y., Kerry Ledoux, C. C. Camblin & Megan A. Boudewyn. 2012. Language-related ERP components. In Steven J. Luck & Emily S. Kappenman (eds.), *The Oxford handbook of event-related potential components*. New York, Oxford: Oxford University Press.
Taylor, Wilson L. 1953. "Cloze procedure": A new tool for measuring readability. *Journalism Quarterly* 30. 415–433.
Triezenberg, Katrina. 2008. Humor in literature. In Victor Raskin (ed.), *The primer of humor research* (Humor Research), 523–542. Berlin, New York: Mouton de Gruyter.
Trissino, Giovan G. 1970 [1549]. Quinta e la sesta divisione della poetice. In Bernard Weinberg (ed.), *Trattati poetica e retorica del cinquecento*, 5–90. Bari: Gius. Laterza & Figli.
Trouvain, Jürgen & Khiet P. Truong. 2017. Laughter. In Salvatore Attardo (ed.), *The Routledge handbook of language and humor*, 340–355. Florence: Taylor and Francis.
Trueswell, John C. & Michael K. Tanenhaus. 1994. Semantic influences on parsing: Use of thematic role information in syntactic ambiguity resolution. *Journal of memory and language* 33. 285–318.
Tsakona, Villy. 2013. Okras and the metapragmatic stereotypes of humour. In Marta Dynel (ed.), *Developments in linguistic humour theory* (Topics in Humor Research 1), 25–48. Amsterdam, Philadelphia: John Benjamins Publishing Company.
Tsiknaki, Ourania. 2005. *Emotionsprognose: Das affektive Lexikon München. Entwurf eines Modells zur Vorhersage der Affektivität eines Textes* (Forum Sprachwissenschaften 3). München: Meidenbauer.
Tu, Shen, Xiaojun Cao, Xuyan Yun, Kangcheng Wang, Guang Zhao & Jiang Qiu. 2014. A new association evaluation stage in cartoon apprehension: Evidence from an ERP study. *Journal of Behavioral and Brain Science* 04(02). 75–83.
Uekermann, Jennifer, Shelley Channon & Irene Daum. 2006. Humor processing, mentalizing, and executive function in normal aging. *Journal of the International Neuropsychological Society* 12(2). 184–191.
van Berkum, Jos J. A., Peter Hagoort & Colin Brown. 1999. Semantic integration in sentences and discourse: evidence from the N400. *Journal of cognitive neuroscience* 11(6). 657–671.
van Berkum, Jos J. A., Bregje Holleman, Mante S. Nieuwland, Marte Otten & Jaap Murre. 2009. Right or wrong? The brain's fast response to morally objectionable statements. *Psychological Science* 20(9). 1092–1099.
van Dijk, Teun A. & Walter Kintsch. 1983. *Strategies of discourse comprehension*. San Diego: Academic Press.

van Dyke, Julie A., Clinton L. Johns & Anuenue Kukona. 2014. Low working memory capacity is only spuriously related to poor reading comprehension. *Cognition* 131(3). 373–403.

van Petten, Cyma K., Marta Kutas, Mike Mitchinger & Heather McIsaac. 1991. Fractioning the word repetition effect with event-related potentials. *Journal of cognitive neuroscience* 3(2). 131–150.

Vespignani, Francesco, Paolo Canal, Nicola Molinaro, Sergio Fonda & Cristina Cacciari. 2009. Predictive mechanisms in idiom comprehension. *Journal of cognitive neuroscience* 22(8). 1682–1700.

Viering, Jürgen. 2010. Schauerroman. In Klaus Weimar, Georg Braungart, Klaus Grubmüller, Friedrich Vollhardt, Harald Fricke & Jan-Dirk Müller (eds.), *Reallexikon der deutschen Literaturwissenschaft*, 3rd edn., 365–368. Berlin, Boston: de Gruyter.

Vuong, Loan C. & Randi C. Martin. 2014. Domain-specific executive control and the revision of misinterpretations in sentence comprehension. *Language, cognition and neuroscience* 29. 312–325.

Walter, Grey, R. Cooper, V. J. Aldridge, W. C. McCallum & A. L. Winter. 1964. Contingent negative variation: An electric sign of sensori-motor association and expectancy in the human brain. *Nature* 203. 380–384.

Warren, Paul. 1995. Prosody, phonology, and parsing in closure ambiguities. *Language and Cognitive Processes* 10(5). 457–486.

Weiland, Hanna. 2014. *Experimental research into non-literal language. ERP studies on metaphors and metonymies*. Mainz: Johannes Gutenberg-Universität Dissertation.

Weiland-Breckle, Hanna & Petra B. Schumacher. 2018. A direct comparison of metonymic and metaphoric relations in adjective–noun pairs. *Acta Linguistica Academica* 65(2–3). 443–472.

Whitney, Carin, Walter Huber, Juliane Klann, Susanne Weis, Sören Krach & Tilo Kircher. 2009. Neural correlates of narrative shifts during auditory story comprehension. *NeuroImage* 47(1). 360–366.

Wiggs, Cheri L., Jill Weisberg & Alex Martin. 1999. Neural correlates of semantic and episodic memory retrieval. *Neuropsychologia* 37. 103–118.

Williams, Leanne M., Donna Palmer, Belinda J. Liddell, Le Song & Evian Gordon. 2006. The 'when' and 'where' of perceiving signals of threat versus non-threat. *NeuroImage* 31(1). 458–467.

Wilson, Deirdre & Dan Sperber. 2004. Relevance Theory. In Laurence R. Horn & Gregory Ward (eds.), *The Handbook of pragmatics*, 606–632: Blackwell.

Wisker, Gina. 2005. *Horror fiction: An introduction* (Continuum Studies in Literary Genre). New York, NY: Continuum.

Wood, Robin. 1986. *Hollywood from Vietnam to Reagan*. New York, NY: Columbia Univ. Press.

Wood, Robin. 2012. *Hollywood from Vietnam to Reagan . . . and beyond: A revised and expanded edition of the classic text*. New York: Columbia University Press.

Wróbel, Monika & Kamil K. Imbir. 2019. Broadening the perspective on emotional contagion and emotional mimicry: The correction hypothesis. *Perspectives on psychological science: A journal of the association for psychological science* 14(3). 437–451.

Xu, Mengsi, Zhiai Li, Cody Ding, Junhua Zhang, Lingxia Fan, Liuting Diao & Dong Yang. 2015. The divergent effects of fear and disgust on inhibitory control: An ERP study. *PloS one* 10(6). 1–15.

Yus, Francisco. 2016. *Humour and relevance* (Topics in Humor Research 4). Amsterdam, Philadelphia: John Benjamins Publishing Company.

Zacks, Jeffrey M. & Evelyn C. Ferstl. 2016. Discourse comprehension. In Gregory Hickok & Steven L. Small (eds.), *Neurobiology of language*, 661–673. Amsterdam: Academic Press.
Zacks, Jeffrey M., Nicole K. Speer & Jeremy R. Reynolds. 2009. Segmentation in Reading and Film Comprehension. *Journal of Experimental Psychology. General* 138(2). 307–327.
Zuckerman, Marvin. 1994. *Behavioral expressions and biosocial bases of sensation seeking.* Cambridge: Cambridge University Press.
Zuckerman, Marvin. 2015 [1979]. *Sensation Seeking*: Beyond the Optimal Level of Arousal (Psychology Revivals). Hove, England: Psychology Press.

Sources of experimental items

Hall, Richard. 2013. 10 awesome scary stories told in only two sentences. https://oklahoman.com/article/3888332/10-awesome-scary-stories-told-in-only-two-sentences (accessed 22 June 2020).
140signs.2015. 140 sehr kurze Geschichten. https://www.facebook.com/140signs (accessed 12 October 2021).
Betzold, Arnulf. 2021. Sportlehrer. https://i.pinimg.com/originals/c3/01/f1/c301f1841d186eac9540a4882680a037.jpg (accessed 12 October 2021).
Componeo. 2016a. Spruch 1324. https://www.istdaslustig.de/spruch/1324 (accessed 12 October 2021).
Componeo. 2016b. Spruch 274. https://www.istdaslustig.de/spruch/274.
Componeo. 2016c. Spruch 906. https://www.istdaslustig.de/spruch/906 (accessed 12 October 2021).
Componeo. 2021. Spruch 1599. https://www.istdaslustig.de/spruch/1599 (accessed 12 October 2021).
Dewi, Torsten. 2014. Zur Spannung noch die Gänsehaut: 3 Zeilen Horror. https://wortvogel.de/2014/03/zur-spannung-noch-die-gaensehaut-3-zeilen-horror/ (accessed 12 October 2021).
Garcia Rosas, René. 2010. Blondinenwitze. https://www.r-ene.de/witze/blondinenwitze/ (accessed 12 October 2021).
Hormann, Martin. 2018. Witze über das Thema Schule. http://www.bigbear.de/witz/witze_schule.php (accessed 12 October 2021).
Made My Day GmbH. 2021. Zitat 21260. https://mademyday.com/21260 (accessed 12 October 2021).
Pohl, Andreas. 2010. Arztwitze. https://www.witze-platz.de/der-arzt-zum-patienten-tut-mir-leid-aber-ich-kann-416.html.
Quadrasophics. 2015. Weihnachten. https://quadrasophics.tumblr.com/image/135767709214 (accessed 12 October 2021).
Ullrich, Patrick R. 2018. Tweet vom 24.01.2018. https://twitter.com/PatrickRUllrich/status/956076976472813571 (accessed 12 October 2021).
Webfail Entertainment GmbH. 2012. Text 999. http://de.webfail.at/text/999 (accessed 12 October 2021).
Webfail Entertainment GmbH. 2020. 15 kurze Horrorgeschichten. https://de.webfail.com/1e68122beb2 (accessed 12 October 2021).

Index

Abject 23
Abnormal 13
Additive contrariety 66
Affect 17
Ambiguity 40, 42
Appraisal Theory 96
Art-horror 4

Bad mood 146
Bisociation 51

Cheerfulness 146
Coherence 87
Compensation Theory 27
Complex Discovery Plot 14
Complex script 56
Continuum of incongruity 66
Contrariety 66
Control Theory 26
Conversion Theory 26

Detection 89
Discourse representation 50, 88, 104
Disgust 19, 147
Dissonance 32

Electroencephalogram (EEG) 158
Electroencephalography 158
Emotion 16, 101
Event-related brain potentials (ERP) 92, 158
Exhilaration 37, 146
Eye-mind assumption 130

Facial Action Coding System (FACS) 139
Failure of humorous interaction 65
Fear 18
Feeling 17
Frame 53
Frame-shifting 68, 90, 92

Garden path effect 15
General Theory of Verbal Humor (GTVH) 54, 58

Gothic 6
Graded Informativeness 70
Gross out 38

Horror 4–5
Horror clown 11
Humor 37, 44–45
Humorism 41

Immediacy assumption 130
Impurity 28
Incoherence 87
Incongruity 50, 67, 77, 84, 88
Incongruity processing model for humor and art-horror (IPM) 187
Individual differences 103
Inference 59
Interstitialty 28, 38
Intrigue 13

Language 61
Late Left Anterior Negativity (LLAN) 93
Late Positive Complex (LPC) 98, 101
Late Positive Potential (LPP) 97, 163
Laughter 37
Left-Anterior Negativity (LAN) 92–93, 95, 161
Logical mechanism 58

Macroscript 56
Metapragmatic stereotype 63
Monster 8, 30, 38
Mystified geography 13

N400 92–94, 160
Narrative structure 61
Natural horror 4
New Horror 10
Non-bona-fide mode 55
Norming 114

Opposition 12, 28, 56
Optimal innovation 70

Overlap 56
Overreacher Plot 14

P300 92
P600 95, 161
Paradox of horror 20
Pleasure of horror 24
Power Theory 26
Prediction error 85
Priming 29
Problem-solving 77
Processing costs 85–86
Prototype Theory 70
Psychoanalysis 7, 48

Reading time 90–91
Referential humor 42
Relevance Theory 71
Resolution 89
Revision text 88

Schema 53
Script 54

Script opposition 57–58
Script switch trigger 58
Self-paced 131
Self-paced reading (SPR) 130, 163
Semantic Script Theory of Humor (SSTH) 54
Situation 60
Social humor theories 47
Sociocultural presupposition 63
Space Structuring Model 68
Splatstick 38
Sublime 21
Superiority 44
Surprise 19, 40
Syntagmatic 58

Target 60
Temperament 41
Thought Theory 29
Two-Stage Model 51

Uncanny 22

Verbal humor 42, 60

www.ingramcontent.com/pod-product-compliance
Lightning Source LLC
Chambersburg PA
CBHW071739150426
43191CB00010B/1634